What Your Colleagues Are

"A few years back, after visiting Barry Hoonan's classroom and experiencing his teaching and his students' learning, I looked squarely into his reflective eyes and said, 'Please write a book about what I just saw.' Educators, welcome to Barry and Julie's classrooms. Their most important thinking and learning has been poured into this book for us, the virtual visitors to their rooms. They invite us into their joy-filled classrooms, engaging us as their colleagues. We learn alongside them by listening in to their conversations with their students, and kidwatch by joining in their thinking and discovering students' next steps. We lean into their questions and inquiry as the authors share their reverence for teaching, respect of all students, and above all, how we are doing this together because 'exquisite things that happen when we are inquisitive together.'"

—**Gail Boushey,** Co-Author of *The Daily 5: Fostering Literacy Independence in the Elementary Grades* and Co-Founder of The Daily Café

"This book is a fresh reminder that the best teaching is responsive—that kids are much more likely to flourish when they have a teacher whose primary focus is on teaching students rather than on teaching stuff. Julie Wright and Barry Hoonan effectively argue that the one of the best ways to be responsive to your students is through small-group learning experiences, and the five teacher moves they outline in this book—kidwatching, pivoting, assessing, curating, and planning—are moves that should be woven through all K–12 classrooms. I highly recommend this book."

—**Kelly Gallagher,** Teacher and Author of *Readicide: How Schools Are Killing Reading and What You Can Do About It* and *Write Like This*

"In this nimble and invigorating profile of small group settings, Julie Wright and Barry Hoonan offer practical tools and actionable steps that lift small group instruction from a static focus on reading levels to one of setting learning in motion. They outline five critical teacher moves—kidwatching, pivoting, assessing, curating, and planning—that work together to help teachers take a flexible stance while elevating learner responsibility."

—**Linda Hoyt,** Author of *Revisit, Reflect, Retell: Time-Tested Strategies for Teaching Reading Comprehension*

"The authors reframe, redefine, and refresh the notion of small group reading instruction. In doing so, they remind us that small group instruction is not only for our 'struggling' students, but rather that it's about leaning in and meeting all students where they are so that we can move them forward. This gem of a book includes strategies for engaging students as readers, encouraging voluminous reading, and finding joy in our reading instruction. It's a must-read for any elementary teacher of reading."

—**Diane Sweeney,** Author of *Student-Centered Coaching: The Moves*

"Wherever I go, teachers ask me about small group instruction and how to do it. At last, there is book with systems and structures that make small group instruction manageable and meaningful. Julie Wright and Barry Hoonan provide lots of examples to show how to honor and meet the individual needs of students."

—**Cris Tovani,** Teacher, Author of *I Read It, But I Don't Get It* and *Do I Really Have to Teach Reading?*, and Instructional Coach

"These teaching moves are just what I needed to refine my flexibility and problem-solving sophistication in small group instruction. The strategies and examples read as the encouraging voices of the authors over my shoulder, grounded in powerful beliefs, inspiring me to open up my classroom practices in the quest for empowering and joyful student-centered learning. With specific, easily implementable steps to bridge the gap between the formula of best practices in differentiation and the heart and soul of giving each student what they need today for powerful learning, this book is an essential handbook for new and experienced teachers."

—**Shelley Hays,** Elementary Teacher, Upper Arlington City Schools

"For anyone who is looking to *lift* small group instruction to make it more meaningful, efficient, and joyful, this book is for you. Whether you are someone who is just embarking on utilizing small groups or are looking to breathe new life into this structure, the authors hold your hand and walk you through innovative, practical, and student-centered approaches to reading instruction. Because of this book, there is no longer just one way to hold a guided reading group or a coach book club. The roles a teacher can assume are now dynamic and flexible within small groups and the authors show us how to customize instruction with confidence and insight, adjusting for the readers in front of us. This book is the next generation of small group instruction."

—**Patty McGee,** Author of *Feedback That Moves Writers Forward*

"Julie Wright and Barry Hoonan's insistence on JOY at the heart of every instructional decision ensures that a teacher's focus is not on the structure, but on each child—what they know, what they can do, and what they need next to grow—which is as it should be. One of my favorite lines is, 'Students' curiosity and interests are more trustworthy and energizing drivers of grouping decisions than anything else.' *What Are You Grouping For?* will energize YOU as you plan worthy work for your students and focus on compelling reasons for them to read, write, and talk. Trust Julie and Barry when they say in the first pages, 'Together, we'll figure it out.' Thanks, Julie and Barry, for being our wing-people. Kids need us to work together and model courageous risk taking in our classrooms. Together is the best way forward."

—**Samantha Bennett,** Author of *That Workshop Book*, Instructional Coach, and Education Consultant

"It's pretty rare these days to find a book that fills both our minds and our pockets. But Julie Wright and Barry Hoonan's *What Are You Grouping For?* does just that. It meets us exactly where we are as teachers, with all our questions and concerns, about time and organization and materials and strategies, and helps us not only understand what's possible, but how to enact it too. This is the book to keep in our laps as we teach. Thank you, Barry and Julie!"

—**Donna Santman,** Author of *Shades of Meaning* and Middle School English Teacher, New York City

"Barry and Julie have produced a must-read book for teachers of reading. This work is a practical guide to the use of small group instruction as a means of improving reading skills. These two master teachers provide clear, focused techniques from their own practice while making a case for 'less is more' relative to taking on too many initiatives in schools. This is thoughtful and provocative."

—**Allan Bredy,** Head of School, American School of Brasilia, Brazil

"Julie Wright and Barry Hoonan have hit the 'sweet spot' of helping each student become exquisite readers. Through authentic classroom examples, they demonstrate how small groups are the fulcrum between one-to-one instruction and whole group instruction. This book is a gift to educators desiring to create voluminous readers!"

—**Michael Nelson,** Superintendent, Enumclaw School District, Enumclaw, WA

"Julie Wright and Barry Hoonan take us on an adventure, redefining small group instruction and broadening our vision of what it can look like when we carefully plan and then step aside and take note of student interactions. With 'five teacher moves,' Julie and Barry talk us through meaningful strategies for employing a variety of fluid and flexible small group instruction and work where students 'think about and appreciate texts.' Julie and Barry share ideas for getting started, as well as specific examples of small groups that will inspire students all year. This book is for every teacher who strives to create meaningful small group instruction and work in their classrooms."

—**Megan Sloan,** Literacy Specialist and Author of *Into Writing: The Primary Teacher's Guide to Writing Workshop*

"*What Are You Grouping For?* is a must-have resource. Julie Wright and Barry Hoonan give practical strategies followed with examples from the classroom for supporting students' reading independence through small groups. This book incorporates the importance of building relationships and knowing your students to gain maximum impact in the classroom. The book leaves the reader motivated and inspired to get started tomorrow!"

—**Amber Reed,** Instructional Coach, Albia Community School District

To all of my Chickadees for showing me how to teach with curiosity and compassion.

—JW

For my mom who taught me the importance of being present in the here and now, especially during our many treasured car ride conversations.

—BH

WHAT ARE YOU GROUPING FOR?

How to Guide Small Groups Based on Readers—Not the Book

GRADES 3–8

JULIE WRIGHT | BARRY HOONAN
Foreword by Mary Howard

FOR INFORMATION:

Corwin

A SAGE Company

2455 Teller Road

Thousand Oaks, California 91320

(800) 233-9936

www.corwin.com

SAGE Publications Ltd.

1 Oliver's Yard

55 City Road

London EC1Y 1SP

United Kingdom

SAGE Publications India Pvt. Ltd.

B 1/I 1 Mohan Cooperative Industrial Area

Mathura Road, New Delhi 110 044

India

SAGE Publications Asia-Pacific Pte. Ltd.

3 Church Street

#10-04 Samsung Hub

Singapore 049483

Director and Publisher, Corwin Classroom: Lisa Luedeke

Acquisitions Editors: Wendy Murray and Tori Bachman

Editorial Development Manager: Julie Nemer

Editorial Assistant: Sharon Wu

Production Editor: Melanie Birdsall

Copy Editor: Melinda Masson

Typesetter: C&M Digitals (P) Ltd.

Proofreader: Wendy Jo Dymond

Indexer: Mary Mortensen

Cover Designer: Gail Buschman

Marketing Manager: Brian Grimm

Copyright © 2019 by Corwin

All rights reserved. When forms and sample documents are included, their use is authorized only by educators, local school sites, and/or noncommercial or nonprofit entities that have purchased the book. Except for that usage, no part of this book may be reproduced or utilized in any form or by any means, electronic or mechanical, including photocopying, recording, or by any information storage and retrieval system, without permission in writing from the publisher.

All trademarks depicted within this book, including trademarks appearing as part of a screenshot, figure, or other image, are included solely for the purpose of illustration and are the property of their respective holders. The use of the trademarks in no way indicates any relationship with, or endorsement by, the holders of said trademarks.

Printed in the United States of America

Library of Congress Cataloging-in-Publication Data

Names: Wright, Julie, author. | Hoonan, Barry, author.

Title: What are you grouping for? grades 3-8 : how to guide small groups based on readers—not the book / Julie Wright, Barry Hoonan ; foreword by Mary Howard.

Description: Thousand Oaks, California : Corwin, [2018] | Includes bibliographical references and index.

Identifiers: LCCN 2018013115 | ISBN 9781544324128 (pbk. : alk. paper)

Subjects: LCSH: Group reading. | Reading (Elementary) | Reading (Middle school)

Classification: LCC LC6631 .W75 2018 | DDC 372.41/62—dc23

LC record available at https://lccn.loc.gov/2018013115

This book is printed on acid-free paper.

18 19 20 21 22 10 9 8 7 6 5 4 3 2 1

DISCLAIMER: This book may direct you to access third-party content via web links, QR codes, or other scannable technologies, which are provided for your reference by the author(s). Corwin makes no guarantee that such third-party content will be available for your use and encourages you to review the terms and conditions of such third-party content. Corwin takes no responsibility and assumes no liability for your use of any third-party content, nor does Corwin approve, sponsor, endorse, verify, or certify such third-party content.

Contents

Photo by Christian Ford

Photo by Christian Ford

Photo by Christian Ford

Photo by Rachel Langosch

CHAPTER FIVE

Pivoting Into Flexible Groups   **119**

*(because it's the teacher moves that
keep readers moving forward)*

Photo by Rachel Langosch

Photo by Christian Ford

CHAPTER SIX

Assessing Student Work   149

*(because looking at our readers' work
lifts their strategies, skills, and thinking)*

Photo by Rachel Langosch

CHAPTER SEVEN

Curating 177

*(because selecting the right texts
inspires readers to be connoisseurs)*

Photo by Christian Ford

Photo by Christian Ford

For downloadable versions
of the resources in the Appendix and
a sample unit planning calendar,
visit the companion website at
resources.corwin.com/wrighthoonan

Types of Groups

Foreword

When I first settled in to peruse the manuscript of the book you are now holding, well, the authors had me at

> *Hello, Trusted Colleagues! . . .*
>
> *We hope you see* joy. *The joy in looking across pages. The joy in reading something you find interesting. The joy in sharing texts with friends. The joy in finding a comfy spot to read.*

Mission accomplished: Lifelong professional joy advocate hooked!

Julie Wright and Barry Hoonan may have captivated me early with their commitment to the pedagogy of joy (yes, joy *is* pedagogy), but it is their abundant hard work in the classroom, pushing back against all sorts of norms, that sustained my respect from cover to cover. To explain how they accomplished this, I need to pause for a moment to paint a blurry, uncertain picture of a small group framework known as guided reading. Across the years, guided reading has gradually morphed into an inflexible lesson-centered, level-driven, teacher-controlled approach that is too often devoid of the joy Julie and Barry describe in their opening.

I still believe in the potential of guided reading, but as Julie and Barry point out, it was never intended as a sole reading instructional approach. In recent months, I have been on a professional quest to develop clear new thinking about small group instruction based on these two premises:

1. Guided reading can be a powerful temporary instructional support experience when it is done in the spirit of flexible, engaging, and, yes, joyful reading.

2. A broader perspective can offer a small group design to invite student choice and interest beyond levels and put students back in the reader driver's seat.

Julie and Barry tackle both of these premises, and I believe this wisdom-filled book can correct existing missteps we see in small group instruction. They address the unfortunate oversights of guided reading while broadening our vision for what small groups *could be* if choice and interest were at the heart of those experiences. Using specific guidelines and examples from diverse classrooms, they show us what this small group transformation looks and sounds like. We learn how to explicitly teach and support students in flexible ways that allow learners to gradually assume the reins of responsibility as we fade into a facilitative role.

While this book is written for Grades 3 to 8, it can easily be adapted in the earlier grades—not for the purpose of replacing guided reading but to add another small group layer that would widen our lens of purpose.

Through step-by-step descriptions with a *from now to next* mindset, Julie and Barry help us to redefine small groups from an "inquiry stance." With this renewed vision, they show us how to alter our role from teacher-centered leader to teacher as supportive kidwatcher ready to notice and use on-the-spot opportunities to gently nudge readers to new understandings while maintaining our sights on student independence and problem solving. Julie and Barry offer detailed descriptions of powerful small group options to help us make this gradual transition from modeling, to supporting, to listening in—and ultimately stepping back as students become small group thought negotiators.

Through their wisdom, we learn how to plant those seeds of independence as we fill students with conversational curiosity with support so that they can then pose and respond to their own queries. Julie and Barry encourage us to trust students as they gain control of this process in small groups that celebrate a discovery approach. Over time, they ask us to assume a renewed role as "consummate concierge" ready to observe, notice, and seize teachable opportunities in small groups where needs and wants overlap. And as we view from the sidelines, stepping in as needed, we envision student collaborations that grow our learners collectively within the peer conversations that are designed to lift their understandings exponentially even when we are no longer in view.

What Are You Grouping For? clearly elevates the need to create small group experiences grounded in "voluminous reading, choice, and access to texts" so that we can use small groups as a force of readerly good. Julie and Barry ask us to embrace small groups designed to motivate, teach, and support learning. They show us how to inspire students to assume ownership of deeper reading and reflection through thoughtful conversations with peers. By providing ongoing opportunities for students to engage in reader-centered dialogue and decision making, we afford them the experiences that help them gain increasing control over their own reading process. Students do this in the company of peers as the teacher assumes a less supportive role. Through Julie's and Barry's eyes, we begin to imagine the immense possibilities of flexible, engaging, student-centered small groups.

So I'd like to bring this foreword full-circle from my opening words to the closing words Julie and Barry write in their conclusion. Their book's beginning and ending, and all points in between, remind us that our students deserve small groups with a renewed intent. Their last words are

It's About Joy. Period.

And it is, and this is the reason I wholeheartedly endorse this exquisite book.

—Mary Howard
Literacy Consultant and Author
www.drmaryhoward.com

Acknowledgments

So where do two educators, who met by happenstance in a New York City middle school four years ago, begin to acknowledge all of the people who have mattered to us? Before we get to the oodles of people, we begin by thanking each other.

Dear Barry,

Thank you for the hours of noodling around with unit and lesson planning. Our Sunday morning planning jams have been a highlight. Working alongside you and your students has ignited new ideas and evolved my thinking about what matters most for kids today. For a long time I've worked to live by a motto, "What matters is what counts and what counts is what matters!" I'm proud that our book captures what matters to us and that we are making it count by putting small group learning into action each day.

With gratitude,
Julie

To our loving families…
David, Sydney, Noah, Max, Jing, Isabelle, and Keats,

Thank you for being our biggest fans! We appreciate your patience during our frequent and long, bicoastal phone calls. Your love, kindness, smiles, words of encouragement, cups of coffee, text messages, extra errands, takeout dinners, and picking up more than your fair share at home has made our work possible.

Much love,
Julie and Barry

Dear Julie,

Life happens between deadlines. Whether it is the passing away of a close friend or a daughter's escape from a near fatal car accident, writing partners lean on each other in brave and unselfish ways. You were a captain of certainty and optimism through rough seas of writings and deadlines. I am extremely grateful for your vision, your care, and your heavy lifting to get this book across the finish line. It will come as no surprise when I echo the sentiments of teachers across the country—you are one great coach.

Thanks a million,
Barry

To our editor…
Dear Wendy,

Where to begin? It seemed fitting to put this information in a list. (Hopefully that made you smile!)

- Thank you for nudging lightly and then letting us live in our own messy process.
- Thank you for offering up structures and then letting us make them our own.
- Thank you for believing in us, believing in our ideas, and believing in this book.

You have made a difference in our lives, and we are blessed to know you.

Julie and Barry

To all of our colleagues,
both near and far...
Dear Colleagues
We Also Call Friends,

Thank you for everything you've taught us and pushed us to think about across the years and across the miles. It has impacted our growth as teachers and human beings.

To Julie's crew in Upper Arlington, Ohio, colleagues in New York, and across the country . . . our learning labs, book clubs, writing retreats, workshops, and coffee talks have filled my bucket beyond measure. To Sam and Missy, thanks for being my biggest cheerleaders, always! And, to Diane Sweeney and my Student-Centered Coaching colleagues . . . our collective think tank and work with schools makes me smarter every step of the way.

To Barry's Odyssey school community for our day-to-day learning adventures and stories, chronicled in this book. Thank you for your enthusiasm to be "better, smarter, and brighter." And to Jan Donaldson, Kathy Egawa, and Peggy Koivu for helping me be the teacher I am today.

With warm regards,
Julie and Barry

To the village...
Dear Crew,

Judy Wallis, Megan Sloan, Kristen Bright, and Shelley Hays took this book from stormy gray to clear blue skies with margin comments worth their weight in gold. Photographers Christian Ford, Rachel Langosch, and Natalie Guerrero used their talent for capturing the joy on students' faces, which is the state of being that matters most to us.

Julie and Barry

To the Corwin team...
Dear Colleagues,

Who knew? We have been reading professional books for years and rubbing elbows with many authors over the course of our careers, but it's not until you go through the process yourself that you appreciate the diverse talent that goes into putting a book together.

Hats off to Lisa Luedeke for bringing Corwin Literacy into the world. To Brian Grimm and Rebecca Eaton, we admire how you get the word out. Designer Gail Buschman proves you *can* judge a book by its cover (not to mention her gorgeous interior design). Tori Bachman, Julie Nemer, Sharon Wu, Melanie Birdsall—all part of the excellence factor Corwin has going for them.

Julie and Barry

To the educators we
haven't met, yet...
Dear Readers,

Thank you for your fortitude illustrated by getting out of bed every day to serve our children. They need you, and we are pretty sure, like us, you need them too. That's the power of this amazing profession. We are just a connection away and hope you will call upon us if you need our support.

In service of students,

Julie and Barry
@juliewright4444
@BarryHoonan

Publisher's Acknowledgments

Corwin gratefully acknowledges the contributions of the following reviewers:

Kristen Bright
Middle School Teacher
Baltimore, MD

Carmen Gordillo
Middle School Teacher and Adjunct Processor, Rutgers University
Union City, NJ

Patty McGee
Literacy Consultant
Harrington Park, NJ

Melanie Spence
K–12 Curriculum Coordinator/Assistant Principal, Educational Consultant
Sloan-Hendrix School District
Imboden, AR

Judy M. Wallis, EdD
Educational Consultant
Sugar Land, TX

Five Teacher Moves for
Small Group Reading Success

1 **Kidwatching** helps us figure out students' interests, curiosities, passions, and needs. If you can't figure it out, ask them!

2 **Pivoting** into flexible, responsive groups versus static ones will motivate, engage, and lift students toward growth.

3 **Assessing** and mining all sources of data is key in helping you figure out what students know and are able to do. Data go beyond students' reading level—observations, conferring notes, interest surveys, discussions, and student work give us the insight we need to help students grow.

4 **Curating** delicious, engaging mentor texts makes students crave more! Invite students to curate for themselves and others, and you'll increase students' reading volume and independence.

5 **Planning** small group learning experiences has the biggest takeaways if we strategically plan for small groups and we leave some open time for in-the-moment small groups. The key is to plan with students' needs and interests in mind.

Preface

Hello, Trusted Colleagues!

Maybe you're picking up this book for the first time. Maybe you're revisiting it after switching grade levels or schools or just to refuel your energy for meeting students' collective and individual needs. Maybe it's summer and you finally have time to sit back, breathe, and read a professional text that has been in your pile. Regardless, we want you to know you are in good company.

Before we dig in . . . look at the photos and think about what you see.

Photo by Rachel Langosch

Photo by Rachel Langosch

We hope you see *joy*. The joy in looking across pages. The joy in reading something you find interesting. The joy in sharing texts with friends. The joy in finding a comfy spot to read.

Imagine a classroom where students slide into Monday mornings, greeted by friendly hellos and short exchanges. Spotlighted on the board is a reminder to students to prepare for small groups to update their reading calendars and to have their latest book in hand and ready to talk about. There is a quiet hustle among the students. This routine is revisited every Monday, when the chiming of the bells signals to students that it's time to saddle up to their small group meeting areas.

Our actions match our words: "Let's get started so there is time for every student to talk." The small group captain records the titles of books being read and number of pages turned. The class goal is for each student to turn at least 120 pages a week. Some students are working their way up to this goal, and others are doubling and tripling it. The role of this small group is to motivate and support. We want to create reading habits that effectively lead students to read and read and read. When members of the group are struggling to find time to read or are uninspired by their book choice, group members turn to recommend possible solutions to help the students get back on track. At the heart of the work is supporting one another's reading habits . . . when, where, what, how, and how often. And the result is that every Monday for 10 minutes, kids *lift* each other up. They know that reading counts. You can see and feel it across the room.

Speaking of *lift* . . . that's what this book is all about. It's the ways we (teachers and students) can *lift* one another toward greater reading success. We call this *lift* because it's a savvy way of saying that if we believe learning is continuous, then giving ourselves and others a *lift* by making meaning together, talking things out, modeling for one another, wrestling with content, uncovering new words, taking hold of big ideas in books, and thinking about how those ideas show up in our own lives . . . well, that's the work of reading every day. So, needing a lift is a good thing. It means we rely on one another, and that collaboration makes us better learners. We'll talk about reading muscles (that's the idea of bulking up our skills and strategies so that we are more proficient readers), and we'll talk about growing stronger and smarter together (that's the idea that we are all in this work together because learning is cyclical and process-oriented and we are never really done learning).

SO WHO IS THIS BOOK WRITTEN FOR?

The reading process is a process. There isn't one experience that will make readers progress. It's a progression of learning opportunities, texts, and interactions that compound across time that make the difference. Educators have been told for decades to differentiate. They've been told to meet students where they are and help them grow their reading skills and strategies. Each year, new programs and approaches are put into the world in an attempt to make things a little easier on literacy teachers. So, why are we offering up another one? Many things that teachers do, ourselves included, come and go. Priorities and initiatives change. But only a few things have stood the test of time. They remain because they are founded in decades of research and they work. For us, small group learning experiences have held educational value because it's instruction focused on differentiation. So, this book is written for you. More specifically, this book is for

- Classroom teachers in Grades 3 through 8, plus high school teachers who are curious about supporting readers using small groups
- Tier 1 and 2 response-to-intervention support
- Special educators differentiating reading instruction, across grade levels and through inclusion
- ENL (English as a new language) teachers who want kids to bolster their reading and speaking skills at the same time through language-rich, collaborative, small group experiences
- Instructional coaches, curriculum directors, and building administrators

OUR BELIEFS

Experience indicates that we are like many other educators. We work alongside colleagues and students, enhancing our knowledge about what makes the most difference in growing students' muscles. We create a set of beliefs—sometimes informally through conversation and sometimes more formally by placing a stake in the ground proclaiming what we believe and why. Like most, we aspire to put our beliefs into action. In doing so, there is sometimes a gap between what we believe and how those beliefs show up in our daily practice. Like you, we hold ourselves accountable for taking a stand in what we believe. This isn't about defending our stance . . . it's about articulating what we believe and why it makes a difference for those whom we are serving. In *The Teacher You Want to Be*, Heidi Mills and Tim O'Keefe (2015) remind us that "if we are deliberately growing and changing as professionals, our cutting-edge beliefs are often ahead of our practices. We grow new beliefs and then strive to live into them" (p. 33).

As we articulate what we believe, we need to ensure our beliefs are demonstrated in our work moving them from hypothetical (or theory) to practical, in-the-moment, across-time practices lifting the learning of those around us. In doing so, we can more easily articulate what we believe and why it matters as our work becomes the testimonial . . . our work becomes the place where others can see and hear what we mean and determine for themselves if the same matters for them. Small group learning experiences matter to the growth and development of the students we serve. Here are four beliefs that keep us grounded and focused on that goal.

We believe small group learning experiences increase opportunities and purpose for voluminous reading, choice, and access to texts.

Richard Allington's (2014) research on voluminous reading and access to high-level texts takes the guesswork away. Students become better readers when spending time, lots of time, "simply expanding not only the volume of reading but also expanding the numbers of texts [they] read" (p. 15). We dedicate our reading workshop time to "pumping up the reading volume." This begins during whole group instruction where we book talk, share texts, and teach into them. We outline what kids need to know and be able to do, then model and show them through minilessons and shared experiences. This learning leads us to small group learning where students' individual needs are addressed. Sometimes small group is directly tied to whole group experiences, while other times it's indirectly related and focused more specifically on the skills and strategies that are unique to individuals or small groups of students.

Small group instruction is a fundamental means to this end. It's where we can introduce texts and help students access the ideas at the small group table. The power of student conversation with peers improves comprehension and engagement and fosters the handing off of books and texts for further reading.

Allington's charge is simple and direct. Let's get books and texts in the hands of readers. Let's give them time to read appropriate books for their level and hold them accountable for voluminous reading. In Allington's exemplary school practice, students would spend upwards of 90 minutes a day engaged in reading. We help ensure kids are reading tons by creating a noninterruptive reading environment.

To increase the amount kids read, we need to make available a vast variety of texts that they can read. Access not only means placing books in close proximity through bountiful classroom libraries; it also means curating texts and text sets with kids' interests and curiosities at the forefront of our planning. In addition, we provide opportunities for kids to curate collections for themselves and others, and hold book talks to show and model where good books can be found.

Whoever is talking is probably doing the most thinking. So if you want to boost engagement, comprehension, and brand reading as one of the most popular activities of your school day, place talk front and center in your reading classroom. Purposeful talk solves problems, illuminates new ideas and insights, and shows kids ways to create powerful reading habits.

We believe small group learning experiences increase opportunities for exploring rich, engaging texts that feed students' curiosities, passions, habits, and needs.

When kids are excited and interested in what they are reading, they are more engaged and motivated to read. Curating texts for small group learning opportunities focused on students' curiosities, passions, habits, and needs is key to both independent and instructional reading. As we will explain more in Chapter One, this student-centered approach has been sidelined by overfocusing on teaching into the skills and strategies of comprehension and fretting about book levels. Small grouping becomes easier when used flexibly, frequently, and in response to what we see readers need.

Readers improve reading by reading. Odds are in our favor for students internalizing and transferring the strategic thinking of effective reading far more easily when they are engaged because texts have a feel and purpose of being hand-picked for them. Yes, it can be that simple.

We believe small group learning experiences increase opportunities for students to know and care about themselves, others, and the world around them in different and sophisticated ways.

Knowing and caring about each other is vital to a learning community. Leaning into different texts and all of the learning they offer up—the characters, the decisions, the lessons, the information—builds our knowledge of self, others, and the world. This knowledge provides the boost to go into the world and do better. Over and over in this book we will set the compass on due north . . . getting to know the students in front of us; learning their interests, passions, and curiosities; and letting the students get to know one another and the world around them, which builds compassion and empathy. Our knowledge of our students gives us direction, and show us when to slow down, when to stay temporarily idle, when to speed up, and when to change things up.

We believe small group learning experiences increase opportunities for teachers and students to reflect regularly in service of growth and development.

Teachers ought to constantly weigh options and determine high-leverage moves that will move students forward. Affording kids opportunities to constantly weigh in and provide powerful feedback adds to our knowledge and confidence in making good decisions to move forward. Taking time to pause and reflect helps us situate our decisions in something more than a well-intentioned unit plan. It keeps our students front and center.

It's All About Curiosity, Joy, and Gratitude

Kids make us curious. Our interactions with them help answer some of the questions we have about serving their needs and, inevitably, creating more wonderings. If we listen to them, really listen, they have a way of teaching us what we need to know in order to teach them better.

Kids make us curious!

Photo by Christian Ford

Teaching brings us joy. Surrounding ourselves with the work of kids each day fills us up, makes us smarter, and gives us professional purpose. Teaching, with small group learning at the forefront, is our North Star. Small groups provide the landscape for us to use proximity—getting up close to students' reading, writing, conversation, and work—so that we know what they can do and what they need next.

Teaching brings us joy!

Photos by Christian Ford

Gratitude keeps us humble. We haven't figured everything out yet, and our guess is you haven't either. That's the amazing part of the work we do! Being curious, teaching into kids' wants and needs, and working together toward a common goal while leaning on one another . . . this keeps us humble.

Key Terms We Use in This Book

Education is filled with language, or jargon. Whether it's the way we talk with our colleagues or our students, language matters. Our goal was to write this book in a conversational way—sophisticated in action, but easy to understand. So that we are all on the same page, the following is a list of key terms that we use in this book and what we mean by them.

Anchor chart: typically a piece of chart paper, a place where the teacher and students can co-construct meaning, hold their thinking, or take notes that can be used by the whole class and hung up so that everyone has easy access to the information at any time

Asset-based evidence: a focus on what students can do versus what they can't do

Bends: when instruction or focus needs to change direction in order to meet students' wants and needs

Book talk: talking up a book to inspire others to read it too

Co-constructing: building, creating, and doing together with students or colleagues

Debrief/share-out: how we wrap up a workshop time

End demonstration of learning: something students produce at the end of a learning progression or unit of study to make their learning or thinking visible

Feed/fuel: when we say something feeds or fuels us, it means it gives us what we need to know, as facilitators of learning, so that we know what to do next; the same can be true for students in relation to their own learning

Gist: main idea

Holding thinking: making thinking visible by taking note, doodling, marking, or annotating text or writing ideas on a chart, on a piece of paper, or in a notebook

Kickoff: quick snippet or sharing of an idea at the beginning of the workshop to orient everyone in the work ahead

Kiddo: a term of endearment for the students we teach

Kids as consumers: anything kids read, watch, or listen to

Kids as producers: anything kids write, make, create, design, or do

Knee partners: students who sit facing one another, knee to knee, and share

Knowledge check: a way to check students' knowledge, skills, or understanding about something they've recently learned

Learning progressions: a series of connected lessons

Learning targets: describe to students what they should know, understand, and be able to do in a unit or lesson

Lift: giving students the support they need to move forward (developing students' assets and areas of challenge)

Menu of Opportunities: in order to build independence, we give students a menu of work time opportunities, a list written on the whiteboard or projected on the screen (teachers determine whether the work time opportunities are "must dos"—they must be completed—or "can dos"—they can be completed if students have time or interest)

Minilesson: what teachers will show, model, and talk about with students to lift the work at the table during the workshop

Noodle: brainstorm, write to think, or write down drafty ideas

Nudge: giving students a small amount of support to move forward

Organizing feature: something that creates "glue" or a commonality for the group (e.g., small groups reading about dolphins, animal heroes, or influential women scientists)

Performance task: any learning activity or assessment that asks students to demonstrate their knowledge, skills, or understandings

Reader's Notebook: a place for students to write down their thinking about their reading across time (in a composition notebook, binder with loose-leaf paper, spiral notebook, etc.)

Shared agreements: creating agreements in the ways we work together

Shoulder partners: students who sit right next to each other, shoulder to shoulder, and share

Sketch to stretch: making meaning of text by doodling images you see, big ideas that come from the text, and icons or symbols that capture the emotion you feel while reading, hearing, or viewing a text

Skinny work/thinking: work that is lacking depth, complexity, and rigor

Small group catch: when you know that a student or small group of students could benefit from an invitational, on-the-spot, in-the-moment small group to lift their learning (this happens during independent work time and is not typically preplanned; it occurs when a teacher notices that something is in students' way and a "catch" could get them back on track)

Success criteria: the standards by which student work products will be judged; agreements with what counts as success in meeting or exceeding the learning targets

Text: anything that can be read with eyes or ears

Text set: multiple texts that are connected by some type of organizing feature

Thick work/thinking: work that has depth, complexity, and rigor

Tripped up: a place in the text where something in the text confuses or is difficult for students

Turn and Talk: sharing out with the person next to you

Work time: time during the workshop when students will read, write, talk about, create, design, or do during the workshop

CHAPTER ONE

A New Way of Thinking About Small Group Learning Experiences

(because being up close to students is what drives discovery)

It is early October. The rain pours outside. Inside, the students have just watched a short video about a teenage boy who sneaks out of his apartment and spray-paints "be brave" on the building across from his ailing sister's bedroom window. A large group discussion follows, and then students settle into independent reading. Four restless and inquisitive students ask if they can carry on a conversation about this powerful story.

Meeting at a round table designated for small groups, reading notebooks in hand, Maggie gets things under way by asking, "Wow. What was that boy doing?" Sian leans forward and says, "Yeah. At first I thought he was just causing trouble. Then at the end, well, I figured it out. I mean, I get the 'be brave' part, but the painted rose . . . that's symbolic . . . the rose is so beautiful and frail, and the thorns show the pain of love."

The students pause, like they all need air and room to think about what Sian is saying. Barry, their teacher, is standing outside the small group taking notes and watching intently as his students take the lead.

Photo by Christian Ford

Kate then interrupts the silence by adding, "Yes, it's about pain. For the little sister. But how is it for the mom? And what about the money? That little girl is barely surviving on the life machine." Maggie nods. Siaya leans forward on the table and says, "I have an older brother. That would mean a lot to me if my brother did that."

And Kate interjects, "But he broke the law."

Barry jots down these kids' keen insights. Sometimes our first best steps are to linger in what we see and hear kids say. Sometimes we *listen in*, observing and listening for ways kids are making connections and processing what they are reading. We can study interactions and conversations—the back-and-forth as thinking unfolds. We look for evidence of the inner workings of readers' thoughts, interpretations, feelings, wonderings, and conclusions. Other times we *join in*, asking the right questions, nudging students to make different connections or think deeply about something they may have missed. We are closing the gap of missed opportunities for meaning making and working to inspire further reading or inquiry about ideas the text surfaces. In either case, proximity—being up close to students and their work—gives us a perch from which to inquire about their knowledge, skills, and understandings. It gives us a way to understand what students know and are able to do, which helps guide us on what to do next. For us, the sweet spot—the place where you can lean in—is during small group learning experiences.

Small group instruction is a household name to elementary teachers, particularly those in K–2 classrooms. Small group learning in the primary grades has a specific shape and feel. In these classrooms, small group reading instruction is typically focused on guided reading structures. Here, students gather to read a common text through both shared and independent experiences, usually relative to the students' reading level. You may ask, "Why are K–2 teachers so good at small group learning?" It's because when you lean in and gather information about your readers and then join in in response to what they know and understand, you can coach the *need to know* on the spot, addressing students' real needs in real time. That little lift, sometimes just 15 minutes in duration, can give students the nudge they need to move forward on their own. It's magical. It's not too much and not too little. It's just the right instruction at just the right time. Many primary teachers have mastered the guided reading structure, making the most out of small group learning by being effective and efficient. It's a good thing.

Ah, but here's the curious thing, and the spark for writing this book: Along our travels, we have observed that small group learning is sparse in classrooms beyond second grade. It appears small group learning is reserved for the few—the students who struggle or are deemed behind the curve. When we ask intermediate- and middle-grade teachers how often small group instruction happens in their classrooms, some say they meet with students who are struggling or reading below the grade-level benchmark expectation. Kids are grouped by reading levels, and teachers meet with students one-on-one if time permits. Other teachers say they organize book clubs and float between them, joining every so often to weigh in, clear up confusion, or ask questions to monitor understanding. And some teachers tell us that they try to get to a group of students if there is time, but because of increasing curricular demands, they rarely preplan small group reading instruction because of the slim chances of being able to make it happen.

We understand the challenges, so this book conceptualizes appropriate small group structures for older readers. However, we believe this book puts Bob Sullo's research into action. In *The Motivated Student: Unlocking the Enthusiasm for Learning* (2009), Sullo suggests a different approach where teachers cultivate students' inner drive to learn by building positive relationships with students, creating realistic expectations, and developing lesson plans that are relevant to students' lives. Our approach to small group learning captures Sullo's ideas of giving up control and replacing it with a desire to engage, inspire, and foster collaboration with students. We want to shift the mindset about teaching so that we are prioritizing individualization—going from thinking about many to thinking about one—through small group learning experiences. We want to foster student engagement, and inspire teachers and students to read widely and deeply about things that they find interesting and are curious about. We'd also like to harness collaboration because we get stronger and smarter when we work together.

Small Group Instruction Redefined

Small group instruction is best thought of as small group *learning experiences*. This is because so often the readers in a group grow as a result of peer insight and response. Teachers lift up and teach, but when we reconceptualize small groups as meeting places for thinking about and appreciating texts, we no longer have to shoulder the heavy weight of high teacher-led differentiated instruction. Sometimes teachers need to lead small group learning experiences. Sometimes they need to be nearby. And sometimes they need to get out of their students' way. In each instance, the teacher is supporting students to just the right extent. Teachers know how to position themselves at any given time to move kids forward.

In the Preface, we reference four foundational beliefs about small group learning. We talk about the importance of voluminous reading, student choice, and access to texts. We also talk about opportunities for exploring engaging texts, building empathy, and the power of reflection as a tool for growth. See the Preface for more about our foundational beliefs. If we had to distill our stance, it would be this: *Students' curiosity and interests are more trustworthy and energizing drivers of grouping decisions than anything else. When we harness the power of the social and personal, it becomes far easier for us to teach into their academic needs as readers.*

One of the best ways to understand our approach to small group instruction beyond Grade 2 is to contrast it with the structures inherent in guided reading, because guided reading is the most commonly known type of small group. Guided reading has an important place in primary classrooms and for striving readers beyond second grade (those who may not yet have met grade-level expectations). These readers might also benefit from small group learning opportunities that are a good fit for both striving and thriving readers (and everyone in between).

We grew our teaching and thinking by applying and interpreting the work of educators such as Marie Clay, Richard Allington, Mary Howard, and Laura Robb. We are reminded of Robb's (2008) stance: "Differentiation is a way of teaching; it's not a program or a package of worksheets. It asks teachers to know their students well so they can provide each one with experiences and tasks that will improve learning" (p. 13). There's a lot that gets in the way of intentional small group instruction. Together, we'll figure it out and find solutions to ensure that students get the differentiated instruction they deserve. This book will be your proverbial toolbox because it's designed to be leveraged on the fly when you need to find a particular tool to lift small group instruction. Use the table of contents like an index.

> *[You] wanna fly, you got to give up the [stuff] that weighs you down.*
>
> —Toni Morrison

The following graphic offers a model of small group work nestled inside a workshop model that lifts small group instruction through five teacher moves. The workshop model is recommended, but you can implement the five moves without it. The five moves are founded on knowing students, and providing opportunities for them to regularly meet in small groups to read, discuss, and make meaning of texts and companion texts that are matched to their interests, inquiries, passions, and needs (see Chapter Seven on curating texts for more details). Like the gears of a machine, the five moves operate in tandem to put teaching and learning in motion. And, in the same way gears change rotational speed, the five moves of small groups rev up readers' engagement and growth because they are powered by students' interests and readiness.

The Five Teacher Moves

This graphic depicts how the five teacher moves work together to support students' reading independence through small group learning.

1. Kidwatching 2.0
2. Pivoting
3. Assessing
4. Curating
5. Planning

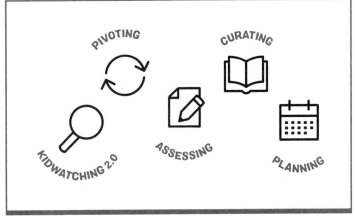

iStock.com/artvea

MOVE 1: KIDWATCHING 2.0 (BECAUSE IT'S ALL ABOUT *ORIENT*, *NOTICE*, *TAKE STOCK*, AND *INQUIRE*)

For starters, we encourage you to begin by studying students in your room. The beginning of the school year is an ideal time to do this; observing throughout the year is equally important. When we know our readers, the reasons for grouping arise naturally from students' curiosities, passions, habits, and needs. The more we know about our kids, the more likely we will strike a decision that will have value for them. Instead of being first and foremost guided by a reading curriculum, we invest in knowing as much as we can about the lives of our students. If we don't do this, we may as well cling to whole class mode. Once we can name what is going on in our students' lives—or what is not going on—we can begin matching kids' knowledge, experiences, interests, and needs to meaningful small group instruction. (See Chapter Four.)

MOVE 2: PIVOTING INTO FLEXIBLE GROUPS (BECAUSE IT'S THE TEACHER MOVES THAT KEEP READERS MOVING FORWARD)

Flexible small groups require leaning into students' interests as people, their habits as readers, and their needs as learners. When we are pivoting—moving to the side as we move forward—we live out the promise of dynamic, versus static, groups. Our purpose is to move students in and out of working groups as needed or desired. They often originate from a teacher's careful, intentional planning for differentiated instruction, as well as from the "on-the-spot" decision making teachers do in the midst of daily instruction and in response to kids' evolving interests. (See Chapter Five.)

> *Flexible, small groups require leaning into students' interests as people, their habits as readers, and their needs as learners.*

MOVE 3: ASSESSING STUDENT WORK (BECAUSE LOOKING AT OUR READERS' WORK *LIFTS* THEIR STRATEGIES, SKILLS, AND THINKING)

How do you know what to do each day with and for your students? We spent years playing guessing games—shooting to hit the middle—all in hopes that it would be something that our students needed. Then, we began worrying less about benchmark assessments and holistic district-anchored assessments (although they can be powerful when coupled with other assessments along the way), and we started looking across student work. That's when something wonderful happened. When we looked at students' work, we turned into brilliant planners. Why? Because students' work tells us a story of what they know and are able to do. Or, what they almost know and are almost able to do. Or, what they don't quite know and aren't quite able to do—yet. Assessing students' work gives us, the instructional architects, daily opportunities to dig into each student's literacy narrative. In doing so, we get smarter about what will make a difference for them. We can then figure out the next nudge or lift they need to move forward. (See Chapter Six.)

MOVE 4: CURATING (BECAUSE SELECTING THE RIGHT TEXTS INSPIRES READERS TO BE CONNOISSEURS)

The hardest and most glorious part of designing small group learning is its dynamic and nimbleness. Here's how it goes: You preplan a unit of study, using a backward design approach so that you outline your intent for student learning at the onset. We love that part. Next, you think through what resources you need: what mentor texts, models, and examples you plan to show learners. This is related to the what, when, how, and why of the content they are taking on. In this chapter, we show you how to curate your mentors so that they can support students as they clear up confusion, uncover new learning, and apply what they've learned in their work. Get ready—this part is messy! (See Chapter Seven.)

MOVE 5: PLANNING (BECAUSE WHEN WE USE WEEKLY AND DAILY PLANS TO CHART THE COURSE, OUR BIG IDEAS SAIL FORTH)

Planning for small group learning experiences springs from kidwatching and all the other moves. Planning that prioritizes students' curiosities, reading habits, and needs is a multistep process focused on developing the big picture—unit planning—as well as weekly and day-to-day lesson planning. Kids grow. Readers evolve, and they change at different rates. That's why planning, with an emphasis on flexible, small group opportunities, keeps us focused on what the whole class needs *and* pushes us to design small group learning experiences that are responsive to individual students. (See Chapters Eight and Nine.)

TAKING TIME TO REFLECT

As you use these five moves, remember that grouping is a cyclical process and that ongoing reflection is what keeps its wheels turning. Traditionally, small group instruction has a "lifer" feel to it. You are reading a level *N* book. When you are secure, you'll move to an *O* book, and then meet with other *O*-level readers for small group instruction until you are ready to move on. To break free of that, get in the habit of thinking about what's working and what's not. In the words of Margaret Wheatley (2002), "without reflection, we go blindly on our way, creating more unintended consequences, and failing to achieve anything useful." We agree. Our students are the most valuable of human capital, and if we don't pause and reflect, we could move forward *blindly* and jeopardize opportunities for growth.

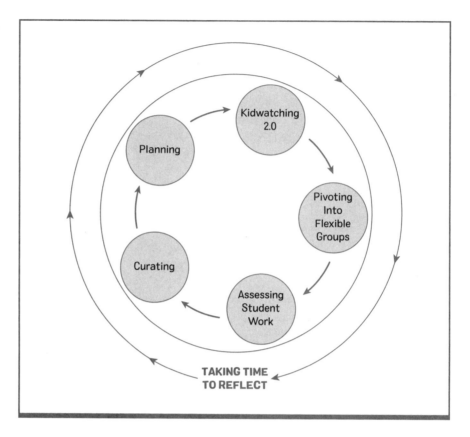

Reflection will help you figure out what students need next:

- Whom do they need to learn with and from?
- What do they need to learn next?
- When/how often should this learning take place?
- Where should they experience the learning?
- Why is this learning going to nudge or lift them?
- How will we know this learning is what they needed?

Asking and answering these questions requires a reflective stance most of the time. If learning opportunities are provided each day, then students will be growing and changing each day. Small group instruction must meet students' individual and collective needs, and the best way to figure out the answers to the questions posed above is to reflect—often.

Combating the Challenges
So You Can Do the Five Moves

Whether you are wrestling with time demands or managing aspects of small groups, we have answers for your understandable "yes, buts." We share solutions to obstacles that virtually every teacher and school faces. It's not that we want to wallow in the mud of the challenges; it's that we have cleared up a lot of the messiness for you and want to share our shortcuts!

CHALLENGE: THE PERCEPTION THAT THERE ISN'T ENOUGH TIME

There just isn't enough time. We know the increased demands on schools from society and government are unprecedented. Schools respond with the best of intentions, but they take on too many initiatives at once. You can name them—mindfulness, character education, STEM, STEAM, scripted curriculum with pacing guides, MAP testing, Habits of Mind assemblies, STAR assessments, PALS, Town Meeting, and Crew—all compete for time in your teaching schedule. We call these competing opportunities, and we aren't saying that some aren't important. In fact, we argue that building in initiatives that support students' development of self-regulation and stress reduction, inquiry, citizenship, and community should be a priority. What we are, saying, however, is that it's time to take a hard look at our schedules and ask: What's working? What's getting in the way? What's *nice-to-have* but not *need-to-have*? Do we see an erosion of effective structures and practices happening, and why?

Take a look at an excerpt from a study that Julie compiled for a school district in New York. District administrators were working to figure out why there was a significant increase in the number of students receiving extra reading intervention. To help illustrate some of the issues, Julie took stock of classroom schedules and use of time. A generalization follows.

Content/Use of Time	Time
Building Community and Transition Times (beginning of the day, throughout the day, end of the day)	10 minutes
Literacy • Reading Workshop • Writing Workshop • Word Study	90 minutes (not necessarily a blocked period of time)
Math	60 minutes
Science/Social Studies	45 minutes
Lunch and Recess	60 minutes
Related Arts • Music • Art • PE • Library • Technology	40 minutes
Intervention/Enrichment Period (aka differentiated instruction period, small group instruction, enrichment block, "no new teaching" time, etc.) • Students are either working on long-term projects, meeting in small groups, or pulled out for specialized services • Students in Grades 3–5 have extra music options during this time (choir, band, orchestra)	60 minutes
Total = 6 hours, 5 min	

In general, the chart above is what an elementary classroom teacher's schedule looks like on paper. In the chart that follows, we look at where these daily actions and mindsets come from at the district/building level. In the right-hand column, there are comments on how good intentions get distorted and knocked out of alignment when put into practice across classrooms.

District/Building Belief	Misalignment of District Priorities as Operationalized Across Classrooms
Building classroom and school community is a shared value	10 minutes per day is not enough time to build classroom/school community
There are three components in balanced literacy, and all are important. Reading, writing, and word study are essential for students to thrive.	90 minutes is not enough time allocated for all three components of balanced literacy, especially if the district believes in voluminous reading and writing for the sake of building a love of literacy.

District/Building Belief	Misalignment of District Priorities as Operationalized Across Classrooms
Differentiated instruction time was created so that students could participate in optional enrichment opportunities (choir, band, orchestra) during the school day and *not* miss any new teaching.	There are competing priorities/opportunities for students during this time. Those who could be lifted from small group instruction are often choosing to expand their musical lives (which is a good thing!). Since these two experiences coincide and music teachers travel between and among schools, the music schedule is the priority.
The math block is allotted 60 minutes each day, although it takes 75 minutes to get through each component of one lesson. As teachers get used to the new instructional materials associated with the scripted program, it will take less time.	Since this program is scripted, the pacing guide doesn't allow for much wiggle room, and no components of the program are being eliminated, it will always take 75 minutes (if not more!) to complete one lesson.

There are more competing opportunities for learning than the school day has minutes on the clock. The examples above highlight that students are involved in academic learning opportunities for six hours five minutes. Let's play around with this fact. The school day, in this example, is only six hours in total. We are already five minutes over the allotted time. We haven't even taken into account the simple, but real, eater-uppers of time, such as

- Transition time students need to get from one place to another
- Unpacking and repacking their belongings
- Locker visits
- Assemblies, town halls, fire drills, celebrations, school closures, and late starts/early releases

We are easily 30 to 40 minutes in the red when we consider the eater-uppers of time, plus the extra time needed for math. So what should we do? We can't have kids run down the hall to decrease the amount of transition time. We can't borrow from the "no new teaching" intervention/enrichment time because we have no way to give it back. We can't opt out of schoolwide assemblies if we want to grow our school learning culture. So, what do teachers do? What have we done for years? We steal time from some academic part of the day because something has to give. More times than not, we shorten academic blocks and decrease or eliminate the time we would—or could—use for small group learning. If we want to prioritize small group instruction, we have to give up the stuff that weighs us down.

Middle school schedules present the same challenges with time. English teachers are often given an inadequate chunk of time to accomplish a large number of standards and content. In both suburban and urban middle schools where Julie and Barry have worked, instructional time looks like the following chart.

Instructional Block	Content	Intervention Block
50 minutes 5 days per week	Reading Writing Speaking and Listening Language	50 minutes in one or more of the following configurations: • Focused on remediation, not enrichment • One semester per year • In place of related arts course • For intervention or remediation, content not often a double dip of content taught during instructional block

It's not difficult to sum up all of the unintended consequences that this type of schedule creates. Some include

- Insufficient time is allocated for four important areas of content
- Intervention is focused on students' deficits versus harnessing students' assets
- Students miss opportunities to participate in related arts programs (such as choir, band, orchestra, or art) so that they can receive intervention
- No room is built in for enrichment

It's time to be brave and cut out what takes away from essential learning time. Our solution includes small group learning experiences during independent work time.

CHALLENGE: SCHOOLS LEAN ON THE WHOLE GROUP BECAUSE SMALL GROUPS SEEM UNMANAGEABLE

Research shows that the lowest rates of on-task behavior occur when children are engaged in whole group instructional formats (Godwin et al., 2016). Nevertheless, schools sometimes have a tough time recognizing that students are sitting in whole group teacher-directed lessons for far too many minutes of the school day, and that this needs fixing. Misimplementation of the workshop model falls into the same trap. The two most common reasons workshops go awry are (1) not enough time being devoted to it and (2) a veneer of student choice but, in actuality, too high a degree of teacher talking and control. Workshop is about the reading and writing process. Students need and deserve big chunks of uninterrupted work time to read, to write, to talk, to create, and to figure things out. When this time is lacking, it ultimately creates competition between whole group instruction and opportunities for small groups to meet. When there isn't sufficient time, whole group instruction gets favored.

A workshop model is important. It's necessary because it gives ownership of learning time over to students where they use the time to grow their own muscles. A workshop model provides time for a whole group *minilesson* (time we teach something, model something, or do something together to plant a new idea or reteach something that was tricky for the majority of the class), *work time* (time for students to work independently, or with peers in small groups), and a *debrief* (time to wrap up learning, share out, or make decisions about next steps). We can see quickly that a workshop is student-centered if two-thirds of the learning time is devoted to students reading, writing, thinking, talking, and creating. Workshop is the structure that gives us room to make small group learning opportunities happen. Calling something Reading Workshop on your daily schedule or in your plan book doesn't make it a workshop. What makes a workshop a workshop is the fact that students have time to wrestle with and do the work. They can't wrestle if they don't have the time. Workshop can stray from the course for a number of reasons, including

> Schools sometimes have a tough time recognizing that students are sitting in whole group teacher-directed lessons for far too many minutes of the school day.

- Minilessons become lectures
- Work at the table is too skinny (there's too much focus on skills and not enough on process work), and there's not enough for kids to wrestle with
- Teachers walk the room and manage instead of working with students in small groups to lift understanding, which can lead to interrupting independent work time with more whole group instruction, instead of giving students time to work

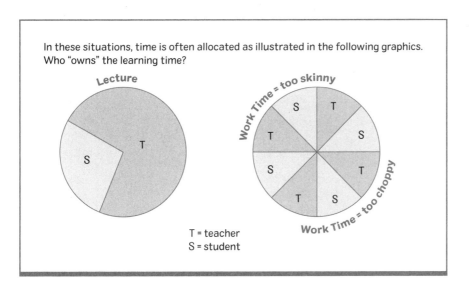

In these situations, time is often allocated as illustrated in the following graphics. Who "owns" the learning time?

Lecture

Work Time = too skinny

Work Time = too choppy

T = teacher
S = student

When workshops go off course, it makes pulling off small group instruction regularly and consistently nearly impossible.

SOLUTION: GIVE KIDS TIME TO WORK DURING WORK TIME

Naming the solution is easy. Putting it into action can be tricky, but not impossible. Start by assessing authenticity and time dedicated to the workshop model that's in action. Does it provide the appropriate time and space, with a focus on students owning two-thirds of the work time to do the work? During work time, do teachers have a well-planned and well-intentioned schedule to meet with students in a small group or one-on-one?

We learned the importance of building independence during student work time and giving students time needed and deserved to read and write from Donald Graves. Graves (1985), the "father" of the process approach to writing, reminds us to prioritize giving more time and choice to students so they may own their learning. His teachings about writing apply to a student's overall literacy journey and directly relate to small group learning experiences by prioritizing time, student choice, opportunities to respond, and a community with which to learn. Today, we still are reminded of that importance by Samantha Bennett (2007), who nudges us to take action by making student work time a priority and by giving students the time they need to do the work at the table. The following illustration outlines how you can design workshop time where students have time to do the work.

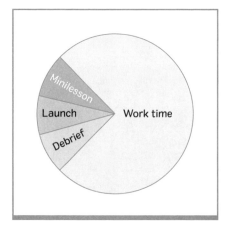

Source: Adapted from Bennett (2007).

See page 266 in the Appendix for a template to analyze the percentage of time teachers are teaching and students are working.

All around the small group, ideas we share are the research-hewn architecture of our reading workshop. At the center, always, is independent reading. It's not only a time but also a goal. The other four components in the graphic shown below support the goal of developing learners who independently read across their lives. Purposefully connecting the work of large groups, small groups, and individual conferences is the focus of our work. (For more details on workshop components, see page 70 of Chapter Three.)

Big Advice

If you are looking for ideas of how students can do more of the work during read-alouds, shared reading, guided reading, and independent reading, see *Who's Doing the Work* by Jan Burkins and Kim Yaris (2016).

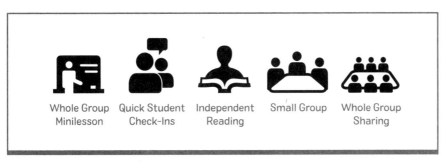

Whole Group Minilesson   Quick Student Check-Ins   Independent Reading   Small Group   Whole Group Sharing

iStock.com/-VICTOR-; iStock.com/Tiyas

In this next graphic, we depict how proximity to learners operates. Small group is the fulcrum between whole group and one-on-one instruction.

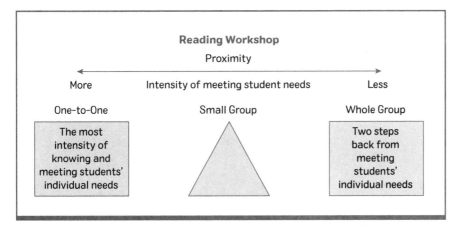

CHALLENGE: CONCEIVING OF SMALL GROUPS ONLY AS A TIME TO PRACTICE A MINILESSON SKILL/STRATEGY

Teaching a minilesson to the whole class, and then pulling a small group of four students to practice the skill or strategy five minutes later, is like ordering spaghetti and meatballs at an Italian restaurant. Nothing wrong with it, but there is so much more to choose from with small groups, especially once you go beyond Grades K to 2. In Grades 3 and up, the state and national standards, plus our students, call for us to do something different. Our world asks students to do more than regurgitate information. Students need to read and write so that they can connect with the world and its people. They are thinking and talking and creating and doing so that they can navigate and maybe even teach the world something. Practicing what was just learned in whole group, for a second time around, is not always necessary. Figuring out what kids need is a crucial step.

When teachers explain that they pull small groups directly after the minilesson to review what was just taught, it signals to us that what is being taught is too small—that it's sort of dead on arrival. This is because what's being taught is too focused on a discrete skill. It probably isn't directly rooted in what students are reading, writing, talking about, creating, and doing during independent work time. As a result, what's being taught has a slim chance of transferring from knowledge and skills to understanding.

SOLUTION: ASK SOME REALLY IMPORTANT QUESTIONS

Carol Ann Tomlinson reminds us that we should ask, "What do my students need to learn to be successful in a given segment of learning?" (Tomlinson, Moon, & Imbeau, 2015, p. 3). Curriculum wanders when there is absence of clarity on the essential knowledge, understanding, and skills needed for a unit or lesson. If the goal is the students' ability to transfer knowledge and skills into understanding, we should start by asking some important questions:

1. What do I want students to remember 10 years from now (an enduring understanding)?

2. Where do I want students to be smarter (knowledge)?

3. What do I want students to be able to do better (skills)?

4. What do I want students to ponder, wrestle with, and care about . . . which often comes directly from the students themselves (understanding)?

CHALLENGE: TRYING TO SHOEHORN THE GUIDED READING FORMAT INTO GRADES 3–8

Guided reading has a specific protocol based on the premise that books have levels of difficulty, and that grouping based on these levels helps students develop their reading abilities. In the following, we further explore guided reading principles. The challenge is that in far too many schools, guided reading is considered synonymous with small group instruction, and *so it becomes all that is offered to readers*. We know this travesty firsthand. Years ago in our intermediate classrooms, our solution was to try to shove the guided reading structure into the structures that already existed. What we learned is that guided reading is one approach, but it's not particularly indigenous to the landscape of readers in Grades 3 to 8. Let's take a closer look.

How We See It: Some *Similarities* Between Our Approach and Guided Reading

While this book nudges educators to think differently about small group learning opportunities, it's important to draw lines between our approach to small group instruction and guided reading. We believe both frameworks

- Hold student learning at the heart of purpose and process
- Tag voluminous reading as a key to student reading growth
- Prioritize early intervention, even in the middle grades
- Use small group table or small group space as a place to grow new understandings about literacy

How We See It: Some *Differences* Between Our Approach and Guided Reading

Where we depart from guided reading is highlighted in the chart that follows. In the most general light, we believe that time in school is never in abundance, so what we do with the time we have is what matters. Let's look at some differences in the way we see guided reading being implemented compared to effective small group instruction.

Guided Reading	Small Group Instruction
Data typically are focused on students' reading level.	Use of data does not focus exclusively on students' reading level, and includes data collected from interest surveys, teacher observations and anecdotal notes, work samples, and student reflections.

(Continued)

(Continued)

Guided Reading	Small Group Instruction
This approach relies heavily on teacher-selected or program-selected texts.	This approach relies heavily on all members of the group contributing texts to the ongoing reading conversation.
Texts are often purchased as part of a program or boxed curriculum, focused on a level, and used year after year.	This approach uses a variety of authentic text types of varying levels, which change year to year based on students in each class.
Groups are more static than they are flexible.	Groups are nimble and change regularly based on students' interests, passions, curiosities, and needs.
This approach typically includes students meeting in small groups with the teacher present.	This approach includes students meeting in small groups with the teacher, and meeting even if the teacher isn't present.
Running records and reading assessments identify students' instructional reading levels and shape reading group membership.	This approach involves kidwatching so that we know students' interests, and student work and reading goals help shape reading group membership.
This approach does not typically rely on whole group instruction, read-aloud, or shared reading experiences to group students.	This approach relies on studying students during whole group instruction, read-aloud, shared reading experiences, small group learning opportunities, and individual conferences to group students.
This approach places teacher talk, or what's being taught in the guided reading lesson, at the forefront of guiding reading discussions.	This approach places student talk at the forefront of meaning making, reading instruction, and feedback.

Guided reading provides opportunities for teachers to observe students as they read from texts at their instructional reading levels—the reading level that students can typically read with some support. During guided reading, the goal is to help students develop strategies that they can then apply when they read independently. Through small group time, the teacher monitors student reading processes and checks that texts are within students' grasp, allowing students to assemble their newly acquired skills into a smooth, integrated reading system (Clay, 1994).

Individual lessons vary based on students' needs, but the general guided reading structure looks, sounds, and feels like the following components:

1. Familiar Rereading—Observe and make notes while students read books from earlier guided reading lessons.

2. Book Introduction—Ask students to examine the book to see what they notice. Support students as they preview the book and think about the text. Students may notice the book's format or a particular element of the print.

3. Guided Practice—Rotate from student to student while he or she quietly or silently reads independently. Listen closely and take notes. Intervene as needed. Focus on decoding, fluency, and/or comprehension.

4. Teaching Point—Offer some suggestions based on observations made during reading. Teaching points are most valuable when pointing to new things that students are demonstrating or when asking for reflection on how they solved problems.

5. Word Work (optional)—Study words that may or may not be a part of the text students read, often in support of decoding.

The process of guided reading sounds pretty good, right? For younger students, we agree. We believe all students, regardless of age or grade, need a lift. Heck, even adults need a lift at times. The last time Julie and her husband put together a new gas grill, they needed to lean on each other and lift one another's understandings to dissect the technical reading in the manual. Six pages of directions and four hours later, they had a working grill.

Teachers ask us, "Since guided reading works for most of our younger students, carrying that forward to older students (especially if they struggle a bit) makes sense, right?" No. Not always. It may work for some, but we believe it's not the right structure for most—especially given that guided reading is often misused in the upper grades and becomes far more static than it is when implemented well. On the ground, in classrooms, what we see is this well-intentioned use of guided reading but with texts that are too long. Or the texts are leveled, may not be relevant, and do not hold the interests of all readers. Students in upper grades don't really want or need a book introduction, and most students, because of their own experiences and literacy narrative, need different teaching points or nudges to grow their learning muscles. In real time, guided groups in the upper grades usually turn out looking more like a book club gone bad. Imagine a group of kids plodding through a leveled book about pioneers, for example, when really what they want to read—need to read—is a text about their favorite YouTuber. If we want kids to be able to read and understand the world later in life, we have to let them gobble up texts that motivate and inspire them to read the world now.

To a great extent, this issue is tied to the schedule matter we discussed earlier. Too often, "small group reading" may appear as a belief, mandate, or prioritized practice at the administrator level, yet it shows up on teachers' schedules as "guided reading." In Grades K to 2, this autopilot embracing of guided reading makes more sense because guided reading has substantial research support going back to Marie Clay, her miscue analysis, and Reading Recovery, from which guided reading was developed. Beyond Grade 2, it's far less compelling for teachers and students alike. There's less reason for fourth and fifth graders to be in a guided reading group—it's beyond what they need. They need connected and flexible small group instruction around reading and writing projects that have authentic purposes and audiences. For some, this can also be achieved through integrated units of study (see Chapter Eight on planning units of study).

SOLUTION: MEET IN SMALL GROUPS, KEEP THEM FLEXIBLE, AND GIVE KIDS WHAT THEY NEED

While planning, ask yourself,

- What are students consuming (reading, watching, and listening to)?
- What are students producing (writing, making, creating, designing, and talking about)?

Once you can name these things, you can begin to think through what's going to "trip kids up" in their reading—anticipating where they may get stuck—so that you can then design learning progressions (or a series of lessons) during small group instruction to meet their needs. This is the lift that will keep them growing. We are going to show you how to design these progressions later, in Chapters Eight and Nine.

Okay, those were the four challenges you may be up against, and we want you to take stock and take time to see if you can resolve them so you can literally, and figuratively, clear a space in your mind and in your school day to put this new approach to small groups into practice.

One Last Thing

We hope our solutions have given you some traction to move forward with a fresh, optimistic approach to small groups! If we lean into Toni Morrison's words, we can't ignore the idea that if we "wanna fly, we gotta give up the stuff that weighs us down." As you read on, we hope you'll lift small group learning in your classroom by kidwatching, pivoting, assessing, curating, planning, and reflecting so that you aren't so weighed down by the *noise* that comes at you each day. Instead, you'll use these five moves to get lift. Ready to fly? Let's go!

CHAPTER TWO

The Launch

(because who doesn't need beginning-of-the-year strategies)

When we talk with fellow teachers about readers in small groups, they often say, "Teach me the how-tos. How do I know which students go in which groups? How long do groups last? What are the other kids doing?" That's why we decided to call this chapter "The Launch" and show you what those first steps might look like. We will share routines, procedures, and engaging "first" discussion topics. To get you going, we'll frame much of it in terms of swaths of time—first week of school, first months, and so on. However, we want you to remember that there is no single right way to step into small groups. This chapter is all about making sure you have starter ideas so you can ramp up your small group teaching all year, as you see fit.

Small Groups Defined

We define a small group as any gathering with more than one reader. By including partnerships in our notion of small groups, it gives us—and you—the freedom from feeling that heavy-boulder burden of masterminding bigger groups at all costs, at all

Photo by Christian Ford

times. Because pairing readers is relatively easy, partnerships work like a wild card in our deck, giving us important flexibility as we explore small group instruction.

Two Essential Questions
This Chapter Helps You Answer

In reading workshop, small group work fits somewhere between large group lessons and one-on-one conferences. Or rather, small group work wedges in. We typically see in schools, however, that small group work frequently gets squeezed out of the workshop. When we ask teachers about this, they tell us they run out of time for small groups because their whole group lessons often go long, and time set aside for student conferences gets interrupted by off-task behaviors. Their answers don't surprise us because management is key to including small group work in reading workshop. In this chapter, we provide ideas for getting everyone on the same page in terms of reading agreements and behaviors. Two essential questions this chapter helps you answer are

1. How do you get small groups up and going?

2. What are lots of different ways you can use small groups in reading workshop?

> *Effective small group instruction takes more than a level and a kidney table.*
> —**Kari Yates**

Beliefs

Grounding our teaching practice in beliefs helps us place strategies on a firm foundation. Once we name what we believe is true and tie it to research, then we can create the kind of classroom where these beliefs govern our learning.

Our beliefs about small group instruction—changing the groups up regularly and upholding a nimble stance—dates back to our early days of teaching. For both of us, we didn't have the option of sending students out of the classroom for "extra" or "advanced" reading support. We worked alongside the student who struggled with his *b*'s and *d*'s, as well as the kiddo who described the brilliance of a lunar eclipse. We hung together with everyone in the classroom.

We actually miss those days.

Why? Because it was the truest sense of differentiation before there ever was a term. These were our kids. This is what they needed to learn. Small group instruction was the only way we were able to pull it off. Our founding beliefs, which stem back to those days, still ring true today.

We learned how to organize reading instruction into rigid groupings based on the skills and strategies students needed to acquire. Students were assessed at the beginning of the year and then boxed into four groups or whatever the schedule could handle. As shown in the table below, the two lower groups (A and B) met twice as many times each week compared to the two higher groups (C and D). This recommended structure was designed to ensure consistent instruction to students across the week and give a little extra to the students who appeared to have deficits. Here's how it would go:

Monday Group	Tuesday Group	Wednesday Group	Thursday Group	Friday Group
A	A	A	A	Open
B	B	B	B	
C	D	C	D	

While structurally sound and useful for organizing our teaching, we blindly let the structure accommodate planning without reflection and inquiry. There was no room to respond to students—no room at all to teach into their wants and needs. The kids who were in our A group basically stayed in our A group all year long. There wasn't room for movement. If students hit their stride, building their literacy muscles in new ways, it was hard to move them into the next group because each group had its own thing going on.

We are many years away from that rigid grouping, thank heavens, because students deserve flexibility, and teachers deserve breaking free from the notion that small groups are a hot mess of levels, skills, and demands.

Our Beliefs About Small Groups

We believe . . .	How it shows up in our work . . .
Small groups create safe spaces for kids to read, write, think, talk, and create while fostering relationships and collaboration.	After reading a short piece as a class, match up readers and ask them to share their ideas about the text. Using talk as a center for rehearsing ideas supports risk taking and making mistakes, which makes creating new insights safe.
Ongoing, flexible small groups provide time and space to bolster reading volume, access, and choice, which, in turn, grows reading muscles and enhances students' literacy journeys.	During reading workshop time, students have time to read—through either independent reading time or small group learning experiences.
When kids meet and talk a lot in small groups, they feel a sense of connection and belonging.	Kids meet with kids, and kids meet with teachers, two or three times per week.

BEFORE THE SCHOOL YEAR BEGINS:
WRITE DOWN YOUR VISION

Let's begin with an exercise. Take a moment to write down your vision for small group instruction. It's good to go into the year with a clear working definition of what you hope to see. For instance,

> My vision is to use small groups to better engage and involve my students. I want to give students lots of chances to talk about their reading, and I want to learn from what they say. My plan is to use thought partners in large group lessons and to incorporate flexible groups in my reading units of study.

SO, WHAT ARE WE AFTER IN SMALL GROUPS, ANYWAY?

We want students to read—lots of *volume*. We want students to have *access to a variety of texts*. We want students to be *engaged and talk to others* about what they are reading. We want to provide opportunities for students to *think hard* and have a reason and purpose for thinking hard about the texts they are reading. All of this is in service of students growing their independent reading muscles.

You have heard of the snowball effect, right? It's a process where something starts small and grows bigger and bigger in mass and importance. That's what small group reading creates: the snowball effect for kids and reading volume. We meet in small groups so that we can make meaning together—reading, talking, and writing about what the text is trying to say. Since rich, engaging texts are at the small group table every time kids meet, the work inspires more reading—in small groups, during independent reading, and reading at home. Kids read about their favorite YouTubers who do cool tricks, which leads them to several texts about Rube Goldberg and finally to how-to books about pulleys and levers. Since kids are meeting in small groups regularly, they are reading oodles of texts, varying in length and genre. Students' reading takes on the snowball effect, beginning small and increasing reading volume.

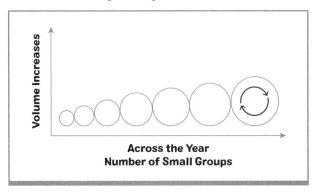

We aren't ignoring the importance of reading skills and strategies. In fact, all that we are doing in small group instruction is in service of those things. We want students to build the whole—build their literacy narrative and lifelong reading habits. And we want students to do this by putting together the parts automatically: the skills and strategies to read all types of books and materials. Here's a list of some skills and strategies that you might focus on during small group learning:

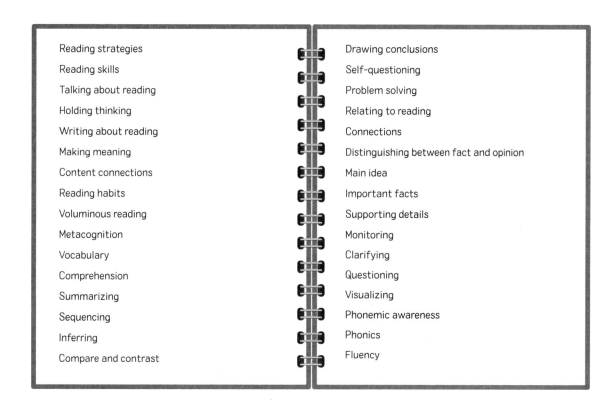

Reading strategies

Reading skills

Talking about reading

Holding thinking

Writing about reading

Making meaning

Content connections

Reading habits

Voluminous reading

Metacognition

Vocabulary

Comprehension

Summarizing

Sequencing

Inferring

Compare and contrast

Drawing conclusions

Self-questioning

Problem solving

Relating to reading

Connections

Distinguishing between fact and opinion

Main idea

Important facts

Supporting details

Monitoring

Clarifying

Questioning

Visualizing

Phonemic awareness

Phonics

Fluency

Ideas for the First Days of School

How do you get to Emerald City? You follow the Yellow Brick Road. You show clear pathways for readers to get them accustomed, so comfortable and clear on expectations that they can handle the flexibility you introduce later on. In this section, we share tools and strategies for establishing norms that help settle students into reading time routines. We show you that even as we are laying these foundations for readers, we are constantly *pivoting*—listening in, joining in, and tweaking—based on what we hear and see from readers about their interests. (For more on pivoting, see Chapter Five.)

Purpose: To quickly build a sense of community and explicitly name shared values around collaborative work

When: First days of school

It's the first day of school, and the fifth-grade students enter the room with a name tag assigned to a table group. Right away they scurry to their new landing spots, and a boy named Josh asks if he can change seats.

"Let's play the believing game, Josh. Trust me. This chair with this table group is going to work out fabulously." The initial message for Josh and others is that we will be intentional in our small group arrangements, we will trust and believe in our enormous problem-solving abilities to get along and share with students different from ourselves, and soon he and his classmates will be asking others to play the believing game. Simply put, we will know more together than we could ever know just by ourselves.

Establish transparent expectations for small groups from the first day of school.

Photo by Christian Ford

Our first order of business is to welcome each other, and we begin with a small group name game. We quickly move to brainstorming what the most important agreements for working together in our room will be. After a short discussion, each student votes for the most important agreement. Fifteen minutes later, students name every student at their table and what is essential to getting along and learning together. For example, all five tables conclude:

- The groups should commit to giving and getting respect as their team motto
- Everyone gets equal airtime and an equal voice in decision making, no matter what
- Each student should be the friend, classmate, and group member he or she hopes to get in return

In Barry's classroom, committing to being respectful speaks volumes about how his class will do good work and learning each school year. It is not by accident that the first class activity emphasizes learning together in small groups. Barry notices his students leaning forward and putting their ideas out for review. They listen, jot ideas, prioritize, agree, disagree, and create shared agreements.

Challenge can act as an engine for small groups, or it can be a distraction. Our second challenge is to come up with a name—an identity—that will unify each group. Heads turn around with funny expressions on their faces, so Julie, Barry's coaching partner, steps in and shares a mentor text that lists all of the Crayola crayon colors. She asks the students if they might borrow ideas from the text to generate group color names. They vote to use the Crayola colors as inspiration; then the groups go about the busywork of choosing a tantalizing and fitting color name that all the students in the group agree on. As the students put forth ideas, argue, discuss a bit, and eventually agree on their group's color, Julie and Barry pay attention to the many ways kids contribute. They take notes and photos for future reference.

The class is buzzing, perhaps a bit too loudly, but buzzing nonetheless, when Julie leans over to Barry and whispers, "This looks like the beginning of a very messy process called democracy." Barry smiles. When asked what worked in this brief activity, students explain that working with others is not easy, and speaking out is easier for some students and more difficult for others. They say that they wonder if everyone will stick to their agreement about giving and getting respect. We culminate this activity by looking over some photos

> Challenge can act as an engine for small groups, or it can be a distraction.

capturing the small group process in action. With the photos beamed onto the whiteboard, we ask students to name what makes their group work well. As they share, we record their ideas:

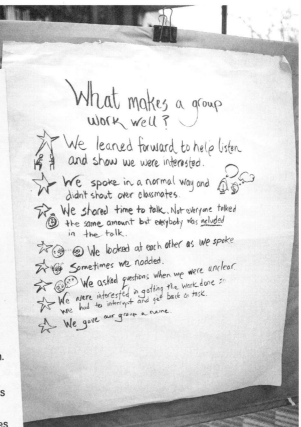

Photo by Christian Ford

"COOL STUFF" BAGS

Purpose: To declare expectations and to "ice break" with an engaging, low-risk activity that lets all readers know they matter

When: Beginning of school year

On the second day of school, Barry's students charge into the classroom with their "cool stuff" bags: bags containing three to six personal items that highlight their curiosities, passions, habits, and needs. The class is abuzz. After placing their cool stuff bags on a specified shelf in the classroom, students head to the carpet. Barry begins by asking if anyone is reading a "can't put down" book. Several different titles are shouted out. Then Barry directs the kids to silently read the notice on the whiteboard:

Today during reading workshop we will

1. Read independently for 30 minutes
2. Meet in a small group to talk about and share things we care about that are in our cool stuff bags

---

Before readers go off to read independently and the color groups begin to meet, Barry pulls out the anchor chart created the day before. He asks the kids to read aloud the shared agreements:

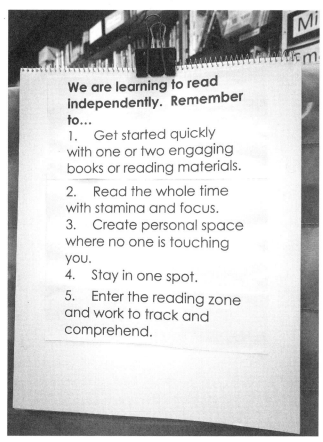

Reviewing shared agreements, written with active verbs, before independent reading leads to more consistent independent behavior.

Photo by Christian Ford

Barry then asks the readers to choose at least one behavior to work on during this reading workshop. He goes over each expectation, and students signal the ones they are going to focus on. Students in the Jungle Green group are reminded that they meet first. Reading workshop works best when everyone is on the same page (figuratively speaking), expectations are clear and agreed upon, students nudge themselves to improve, and the time and routines are predictable. In the beginning weeks of each year, Barry does a lot of explicit modeling and teaching about norms and expectations so that he will have to do less of it once students know what is expected of them.

With cool stuff bags in hand, small groups create a circle in a meeting spot. While Barry will join each of the groups across the next few days, he waits and lets them get started on their own before joining the Jungle Green group. Barry thanks the class in advance, and reminds everyone of the purpose for the small group meeting: "Today we will be taking turns sharing stories and things about ourselves through the artifacts we have in our cool stuff bags." Barry joins the Jungle Green group and asks these students to stick around a little longer than the other groups because part of their work is to develop a tip sheet for future groups. Barry takes out yesterday's list, "What Makes a Group Work Well?" and students make revisions, coming up with a final protocol chart:

1. Meet at the small group within a minute.

2. Sit together so you can see one another.

3. Lean forward and show interest.

4. Speak in a level 2 voice.

5. Share time and involve everyone.

6. Ask curious questions.

We like to co-construct these "agreement" or tip sheets with students because it creates buy-in, ownership, and clarity.

Groups work better when all members know their purpose.

Knowing groups work better when all members know their purpose, Barry writes on the whiteboard, "Cool Stuff Bag Sharing— our job today is to listen and learn as much as we can from our classmates' stories in the next 10 to 15 minutes."

He then places the protocol chart before the group so everyone knows exactly how the meeting is going to proceed. A student volunteers to start, and a timekeeper in the group puts two minutes on the timer. When the timer beeps, kids ask questions for an additional minute. Since Barry is participating, he shares his cool stuff bag, takes notes, and snaps photos.

The students are introduced to a small group protocol that guides them to begin a short discussion about the purpose for sharing their personal items.

Protocol for Launching Small Group Work and Cool Stuff Bag Sharing

1. Sit together so you can see one another.
2. Review the small group work chart and commit to working on these routines.
3. Name the purpose for the meeting (to share and listen to stories and interests from group members).
4. The timekeeper facilitates by placing two minutes on the timer, reminding the speaker to bring his or her talk to an end, and offers a one-minute question-and-answer period. The timer moves to the right so everyone gets a chance to facilitate.
5. The last timekeeper thanks everyone for sharing and brings the meeting to an end: "Thanks for sharing today. I hope we were successful at learning stories and interests about each person in our group. Let's move quickly to our independent reading work."

The beauty of this first meeting is that it puts students in leadership positions. The protocol provides just enough structure so the conversation is meaningful and timely. It also establishes a shared power arrangement where the teacher can sit alongside and observe or participate in the small groups.

Photos by Christian Ford

To Get to What You See Here, **Try This**

1. Ask students to bring three to six personal items that highlight their interests, hobbies, and passions.
2. Write on the whiteboard, "Cool Stuff Bag Sharing—our job today is to listen and learn as much as we can from our classmates' stories in the next 10 to 15 minutes."
3. Review protocol and assign roles.
4. Take notes and take photos for future reference of student interests.

See page 73 in Chapter Three for the Crayola Name and Cool Stuff Bag groups' schedules.

Listening In and Joining In

During the first days of school, a solid practice is to listen in and join in. This is an opportunity to saddle up next to a small group and listen in. You can observe. You can assess. You can take in all of the happenings and interactions individually and collectively. Then, if and when there are opportunities and/or needs, you can join in. Reasons for joining in may include

- You preplanned some instruction around existing or next texts that you want to nudge forward with students
- You see or hear something, in the moment, that you think will lift the group

Let's look at some practices Barry uses at the start of the year to get his students to be responsive. His two main moves are listening in and joining the groups. These group meetings are the intentional and predictable teaching moves that undergird flexible groups. They help define the teacher's role as an anthropologist who digs into the small group for information and ideas that he or she can use to lift the learning from that day forward.

- **Listening in:** Using your listening and observation skills to understand what students know and what they need next
- **Joining in:** Nudging thinking at the table by asking questions, teaching, and inspiring

With notebook or tablet in hand, teachers can create an archive of observations and wonderings from the first days of school. If the intent is to *listen in*, then teachers must do just that. During this time, teachers are doing more listening—much more listening than talking. They are not there to impart new ideas or content; they are there to listen, observe, study, and take note. In short, this is a form of kidwatching as discussed in Chapter Four.

Here are some notes from Barry as he sat alongside the Jungle Green group during one of the cool stuff bag small group discussions. (See page 267 in the Appendix for a full-page Listening In template.)

Listening In

What do I see? What do I hear?	Why does it matter to student learning?	Wonderings
Graysen: loves dance—tap, ballet, and more; has two dogs; parents are from Texas; enjoys camping with her sister and parents; traveled to New York and Universal Studios.	• The round table in the corner of the room is spaced far enough away not to distract independent readers.	• The table is positioned next to the student recommendation display. Will students grabbing a student-recommended book be a distraction in the future?
Devon: loves dance; travels a lot to her older brother's sports events; is close to a few friends; has a huge 140-pound mastiff dog.	• Students are lively and appear to enjoy the independence of asking and talking about their cool stuff bags without the teacher facilitating.	• Familiarity and trust matters. What would happen if this was a mixed-gender group? Would the students be so comfortable sharing their "girl" world with boys?
Nora: loves to read and hike; her father works at a restaurant that serves "farm to table" dishes; her mom teaches.	• The gender grouping of fifth-grade girls is familiar and seems to promote talk and questions.	• What is an effective way for the members of this group to share out their success with the class?
Piper: likes to joke around; she's a big Harry Potter fan, and the middle kid in her family.	• By focusing on writing down insights, I think the kids have given me permission to be invisible.	• Photograph? A "what worked" chart?
Olive: leans forward, listening intently but missing her cool stuff bag of items, and turns to ask if she can share another day.		
Piper begins the small group by welcoming students and asking what they should work on together as a small group. Nora and Olive interrupt each other, laugh, and then say, "Listen and don't interrupt." Piper smiles and goes over procedures.		
Devon asks Piper to talk more about what it means to be the middle kid.		
The two-minute timer is keeping the sharing time quick and clear. Barry coaches the speakers to tell a bit of the story behind their artifacts and to avoid simply labeling (e.g., "These are my ballet dance shoes").		
Devon chimes in and asks, "Graysen, can you tell us more about a time you danced ballet?"		
Then Olive jumps in and begins talking about her own dancing and singing. Sometimes the urge to share is simply too great.		

Because Barry was curious about how the kids in the Jungle Green group conversed, and what they brought and shared, he snapped a photo of each person's cool stuff artifacts and jotted some personal notes about each student. The notes about each student went into his "What I Should Know About . . ." section of his reading/writing student binder.

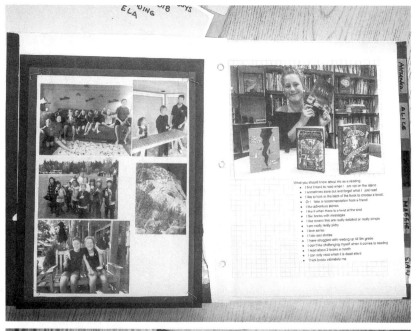

Photos by Christian Ford

In order to make decisions about flexible small groups, we have to understand where they fit into our reading workshop structure. Let's take a minute to examine where we fit in these small groups and how the compelling structure supports independent reading.

EIGHTH-GRADE DIVE INTO NONFICTION

Purpose: To observe and interact with students while reading short texts focused on content

When: Anytime you want or need to integrate literacy across the content areas

Let's take a look at an example of listening in and joining in, from an eighth-grade classroom in New York. The students have gathered at the small group area to begin a student-led discussion on the Triangle Shirtwaist Factory fire of 1911. Julie is busy observing and interacting for 15 minutes in this small flexible group. When she joins in, she goes into it with an inquiry stance, using this as an opportunity to nudge student thinking, to teach, and to inspire. Listening in and joining in yields big results.

Whether we are listening in or joining in, taking notes about our students is an important part of the process because this is often some of the most powerful data we can use to support our readers. Sometimes, just being on the outskirts of a small group, listening in, and taking notes can lead to some interesting inquiries. Take a look at how listening in and joining in complement one another in the following two charts. (See pages 268–269 in the Appendix for two full-page Listening In and Joining In templates.)

Listening In and Joining In

What do I see? What do I hear?	Why does it matter to student learning?	What could/should I do to nudge, teach, and inspire this group now?	Other wonderings for future teaching/ small group learning
• Nick is sitting on his knees, article in hand, pencil behind his ear. • Emily grabs her small stack of sticky notes (sitting next to her work space). • Nafisatu kicks off the small group reading by asking if they can read the first two sections together (she typically takes the lead). • Timothy is looking for his article and decides to share with Nick. • While reading, Nafisatu is stuck on pronouncing a word and understanding what it means in context.	• Comfortable, choice seating matters (standing is also allowed in this class at any time). • Kids are used to taking a few notes or flagging things with sticky notes; having supplies at their fingertips makes things roll smoothly. • Creating protocols for getting started in small groups and figuring out shared agreements about the ways of working creates a productive learning community. • Kids aren't afraid to lean on one another.	• Talk about a protocol for sharing the lead during small group work (rotation system). • Would it help to have a bin where extra copies can be found? • Ask, "Where is Timothy's two-pocket folder?" Maybe the article is actually in there, and he just didn't bring the folder to the small group. • Provide strategies for solving unknown or tricky words when students get stuck.	• Does this classroom need a table lowered almost to the ground for flexible seating? • Do all the kids in this group use sticky notes and other supplies? What's Emily's plan? What is she anticipating she might want to note or keep track of?

During a second small group meeting with eighth graders, Julie joins in as the group reads a second article and an infographic about the Triangle Shirtwaist Factory fire. Students add to their knowledge of fire safety and its changes across the years.

Listening In and Joining In: Next Steps

What questions do I have?	What did I learn?	What could/should I do to nudge, teach, and inspire this group now?	Other wonderings for future teaching/ small group learning
Ask the students: • Do you like the way the small group space is set up? Is there a different table, space, or configuration that would be more helpful? • How are you tracking your thinking over time about what you read? How do you note your questions? Your wonderings? Your connections? Do you use sticky notes for something specific? What other tools/supplies help you stay on top of what you know about what you've read? • Do you switch on and off when it comes to assigning a leader? How, when, and why? • Are your two pocket folders working for your small group? Is there a better/ different way? • What do you do when you get stuck on a word or a section of text?	• Students like the way small group is set up. They said they can move if they get tired of this space. They said that sometimes the room gets a little loud and that makes it hard. • Students showed a variety of ways they track their thinking—highlighter, sticky notes, notebook entries, and so on. All were varied, but none were consistent even for one student. • The group voted Nafisatu the token group leader. She seemed to like it that way too. • Two-pocket folders seem to be a hit. Remembering them is another story. • Three-quarters of the students in this small group explained that when they get stuck, they just move on. • Students are comparing the ideas learned across the texts, and may need some support capturing ideas through student-created note catchers.	• Revisit our volume meter conversation so that everyone has the same idea about noise level. • Discuss different ways students are tracking their thinking over time. Talk through the importance of why we hold our thinking and how highlighting unimportant details can cause more confusion or distraction in meaning making.	• Reviewing "holding thinking" strategies the whole class. We could use these students' work as a model after we discuss it in small group. • Are there other leaders in the group who should emerge? How can we honor Nafisatu's leadership in other ways? • Should two-pocket folders stay in the classroom or travel? • Yikes! Moving on some of the time when you get stuck while reading is okay, but it sounds like this is too frequent of a strategy. Modeling why and how to get unstuck is a must-do ASAP! Will the students do this when I don't join in?

The students in this small group are still interested in the topic of fire catastrophes. This leads to conversation and more reading about what happens in a backdraft, recent gas leak explosions in New York City, and California wildfires. Our conversations and reading snowball into kids reading voluminously.

READING SURVEY DISCUSSION GROUPS

Purpose: To bring together five to six students to share their reading habits and interests with you

When: On days when you can plan to meet with two groups for about 10 minutes, as a forerunner to a whole class celebration

The kids pour into our classrooms with interests and ideas. Our work early on is to find out not only what they can read well but also what they like to read and what kinds of things they are interested in. Reading surveys are a classic routine, but what we consider the powerhouse twist is to have students bring their completed reading surveys to share with you in a small group.

We have noticed that by inviting students to talk about their reading lives, we learn a lot more than the survey alone reveals. Students often add to their surveys during conversation, and we jot down many of the details elaborated on during this small group conversation.

Interest and Reading Survey

What kinds of things do you enjoy doing after school and on the weekends?

What trips or experiences have been the most memorable for you?

What pets do you enjoy?

If you could spend time learning more about something, what topics would you curiously pursue?

What book(s) have you read aloud that you remember with fondness?

What two or three titles stand out when you think about books you have completed?

Which reading categories or genres have you found enjoyable?

How would you describe your daily reading habit? Circle any topics/genres below that interest you.

History	Sports	Art
Animals	Adventure	Teen	Romance
Mystery	War Stories	Poetry	Biographies	Humor
Science Fiction	Horror	Dystopian
Graphic Novels	Fantasy	Science

We conclude the reading workshop time by sharing with the whole class some of the things we have noticed. A fun way of summarizing and connecting the small group survey conversation to the whole group is to ask students to *stand up if they agree* with some of the group's findings:

- Stand up if you enjoy reading fantasy books.
- Stand up if you enjoy reading thin books.
- Stand up if you like baseball.
- Stand up if you like to read in your bed at night.

This "visual survey" primes the tank for the following day's small group survey conversation.

To Get to What You See Here, **Try This**

1. Hand out the reading survey to each student (a template is provided in the Appendix on page 270) and please adapt and add to the survey!

2. Meet with two groups the first day, for about 10 minutes each, to discuss and deepen the students' surveys. Other students can read independently.

3. At the end of workshop time, report the outtakes from group conversations to the class.

4. Meet with two more groups the next day, and repeat these steps until you have met with all groups. (See Chapter Four on kidwatching for more ideas on using student data to inform grouping.)

Photos by Christian Ford

SHARE FAVORITE BOOKS

Purpose: To develop students' identities as readers by visually recording their engagement

When: At the beginning of the school year and again at the start of the new calendar year (January)

At the start of school, most teachers wish they had a photographic memory for students' names and interests. We have found visual records to be very effective in helping us remember key points about our students. They are also engaging to look back at with students to gain a historical reference to how they have grown. Instead of asking kids to hand in a list of their favorite books, we invite kids to meet at the small group area with a collection of titles they love. Each student talks about a book for one minute. These short book talks occur in the friendly confines of a small group. At the conclusion of the small group gathering, kids are asked to point out one book from another person's stack that struck them. The group ends after all members have had a photo or selfie taken of them with their books. The message is simple: When kids talk about the books they love, they motivate themselves and others to keep reading.

To Get to What You See Here, **Try This**

1. Invite students to bring books and lists of their favorite book titles, and be prepared to talk for one minute.

2. Have students talk in small groups.

3. Take photos of the students with their book titles and make the images public (classroom, blog, website, school newsletter, etc.).

4. Consider having students write a goal for increasing their reading volume.

Photos by Christian Ford

What Would You Do?

As the year progresses, students can talk about their favorite genre, author, or even story opening or ending. Based on what you know about your students, what would you add or do differently in January?

_____

_____

_____

_____

Purpose: To get to know students, and have them to get to know one another, while also practicing starting quickly, sharing talking time, and elaborating on their own stories

When: After the core values work, so students have some understanding of reflecting on themselves

We love this activity! Students are asked to place at least five photo images of people, places, and things that are important to them on a sheet of paper. During the small group exchange, students are free to use visual cues to tell stories about themselves. It works best to first offer your own example of what a photo essay looks like and how the visual images allow you to talk from your photos.

During this demonstration, emphasize little tips for successfully transitioning to a small group:

- Keep your photo essay in your reading folder and bring your folder and reading book to your group meeting
- Note when your group is assigned to meet
- When you hear the chimes, collect your things and move quickly to the small group area (remember our goal is to begin talking within 30 seconds)

If your students are unfamiliar with moving from independent reading into a small group, we suggest you practice. Polishing the "getting a small group started quickly" routine early on in the year can make a big difference in saving time. Our experience over the years has been that some students can be a bit nervous about talking about their photos, so they rush through by naming the photos. "This is me on a boat. I am riding my bike. My dad. My sister." We look at this as an opportunity to involve students in coaching each other to elaborate. Prepare "nudging and elaborating cards" ahead of time to aid the process.

On the cards we have these questions:

> "Why is this important to you?"
>
> "Is there anything you want to add about . . . ?"
>
> "Can you tell us a little more about . . . ?"
>
> "Is there anything else important about . . . ?"

We suggest you practice with your own photo essay, giving the students a chance to nudge the teacher to talk more. Barry shared, "This is my son, Keats, and daughter, Isabelle," prompting Stirling to ask, "Can you tell us a little more about Keats and Isabelle?" This empowers kids to facilitate discussions, ask questions, and elaborate when they offer ideas.

Photo by Christian Ford

To Get to What You See Here, **Try This**

The basic guidelines for making the photo essay small group work well are as follows:

1. Thank the group of students for "getting started quickly" with their materials. Remind the group that each student will tell one story before moving on to the next student.

2. The number of stories kids can tell is determined by the 12 to 14 minutes saved for this activity.

3. Ask one student to be the facilitator, whose job is to be ready with a nudge question and to ensure all students talk and listen. The facilitator calls on the first student, and then sharing proceeds around the group.

4. Select a timer to keep track of the 12-minute allotment. A timer helps students internalize the importance of using time efficiently.

5. Take notes about the stories you hear.

6. Do not worry if students do not get a chance to share stories from all their photos. Connecting with your kids and their stories matters most.

The message we want students to get is that small groups are both engaging and timely. We shoot for two photo essay small groups a day, with each group lasting between 10 and 14 minutes. We suggest you skip minilessons, with the exception of a few management tips, so you can fit them in.

"DECLARE YOUR LITERACY" GROUPS

Purpose: To get to know what students love to read

When: At the beginning of the year and at the beginning of each unit of study

The success of our reading workshop rests on how well we get to know each other as readers. It is much easier to recommend a book to students when we know what they love to read, what they enjoy doing, and what kind of text they find meaningful. In turn, students can also recommend and make suggestions to peers if they know what makes their classmates tick. With that in mind, students are invited on the third day of school to bring in books and texts that they care about. We demonstrate by showing examples of sports magazines, food blogs, graphic novels, and books we like—our students need to know that we are on a literacy journey too.

There are really two parts to this engagement. The first is to ensure that all students have books, magazines, or text to share. The second part is to meet in small groups and talk about what they like to read. Let's begin with part 1.

Over the years, we have noticed that some students have little access to, interest in, or understanding of what it means to collect text that they care about. They have problems declaring their literacy and finding texts that represent them. Knowing this, we prepare for our first "in the moment" group. We survey students during our large group meeting time and ask which students have their books and which need extra time to pull their favorite texts together. When a handful of kids raise their hands, we jot down their names and delicately invite them to stay at the carpet for a short planning session.

Creating this "on the spot" small group works because it provides both immediate feedback and remedy to our literacy assignment. The purpose for this small group is not only to build collections of books and texts to share with classmates but also to give students a place to talk about their literacies and interests.

For example, Gabe mutters, "I don't like to read. It sucks." Four other boys nod in agreement. Barry asks Gabe what he likes to do instead of reading. He lights up a bit as he answers, "Skateboard." Barry asks if he ever reads about skateboarding. He has. He prods him further and finds out Gabe watches skateboarding videos. Barry suggests he mark this interest by printing off a screenshot of one of his favorite videos. In the next 10 minutes, this small group of boys begins listing graphic novels, videos, and magazines they find important—literacies often missed in the common canon we celebrate in school. The small group meeting comes up with more read-aloud books they have loved and uncovers other texts not often accepted at school, such as comics, graphic novels, and favorite titles such as *Big Nate* and *Diary of a Wimpy Kid*. Students leave with their shopping list, and while they are assembling their "favorite reads," the rest of the students carry on with reading silently. This small, flexible group provides opportunities for students to validate themselves, to share and stretch themselves as readers, and to potentially add new texts to their stack.

Now that Gabe and his cadre are ready to go, we move into our "declare your literacy" group. We love this group opportunity because it inspires and motivates kids. Across time, this experience helps students learn to lean on each other. This shared responsibility elevates their buy-in and sense of belonging. Making student collections of texts available during reading workshop also helps ensure kids have things to read. At the completion of these small groups, the whole class gathers to talk about where to store our books and how to make them easily accessible.

In subsequent reading workshops, we meet in small, flexible groups and talk about our reading choices and reading history. We often refer back to our stack of personally selected texts. Students make lists of future books to read, and we record insights about each reader. The last thing we do is take a selfie with our books in front of us—both individually and as a "declare your literacy" small group. These photos are artifact placeholders and help define our literacy narratives at the start of the year. The photos, coupled with student reflection, are placed in student portfolios. Kids enjoy going back to see how their tastes have changed and evolved across the year. Some kids even request to have new photos with new books and texts taken. As the year unfolds, these groups get together more regularly. Sometimes teacher directed, and more often student directed, these groups meet as needed—when students need help finding a new book, sharing the inspiration of a new series or author, book swapping, or reflecting about progress—all signs that these kids are shaping their own reading lives. We believe small group interactions of this kind also broaden our definition of reading and what it means to be literate.

> *Shared responsibility elevates students' buy-in and sense of belonging.*

"Declare your literacy" groups start the year with students stating up front what is important reading in their lives and are captured by teacher photographs; this is formative assessment in action.

Students share out their book selections during short whole group debriefing, which happens about four times a week at the conclusion of reading workshop.

Photos by Christian Ford

A Few Weeks Into the School Year

Once the year is under way, small group experiences are focused initially on getting the right book or text in each reader's hand. We meet at a specified area for 10 to 15 minutes. We share ideas for how to choose an engaging text or book. We talk about ways to increase the time we spend reading. We create lists and anchor charts celebrating when we read, where we read, and great books we have read. We even confront fake reading and remedies for lack of reading stamina. These groups are mixed ability and mixed interest by design. We believe that just because you read at a higher level, you do not necessarily think more intelligently. For each small group, we plan meeting times for once or twice a week. The goal is to nudge one another to find and read interesting texts, develop strategies for "sticking with a text," elevate our reading volume, and leverage enthusiasm for reading.

APRÈS-GROUP READING CONFERENCE

Purpose: To provide one-on-one support to a reader on the heels of a small group

When: Anytime you can build in three to seven minutes after a small group meeting

After meeting with a small group, Barry often asks a student from the group to stay back and confer with him about the book he or she is reading. He works to repeat the process with each member of the group. Combining a reading conference with a small group meeting offers time for follow-up with students to ask clarifying questions or to provide some direct feedback to the reader.

It was late September when Barry asked John to stay after his small group meeting to talk more about his self-selected book. John's small group had just generated an anchor poster titled "How can we select the best 'just right' books for ourselves?" During the small group discussion, John suggested that readers pick books where they can read all the words. Barry began the conference by asking John to read aloud his book, *Masterminds* by Gordon Korman (2017). When John began, he read in a choppy fashion, missing a few words. By the end of the page, he had gained some confidence and flow and read with very few miscues. Barry and John talked about whether his book was a "just right" selection. John pulled ideas from the anchor chart and said the book was interesting to him;

he was excited about reading it because classmates had read it. John even retold what he had read just to assure both himself and Barry that the tricky part of this book hadn't interrupted his understanding. Barry and John chatted about the difficulty of knowing when to stick with a book and when to abandon it. This seven-minute conference helped surface the challenges facing many middle school readers: It is sometimes tricky to find a "just right" book because what we read can say a lot about who we are to others.

At the large group sharing time, John asked his peers what they do when they enjoy a book but the book takes longer to read than expected and has difficult words. Alexandra piped in, "I tried to read *The Hunger Games* because it is so popular, but it was definitely too big and wordy for me. I put it away and went back to *Dork Diaries*." John nodded. The next day when Barry checked in on John, he found him cross-legged on the carpet with *Masterminds*. Asked why he stuck with it, John commented, "Now that I get what is really happening in this bizarre town of Serenity, I really want to find out what's next."

The beginning of the year brings about other great topics for small groups to wrestle with.

Here is a list of some of our reading workshop topics that may also be folded into small group work. The key is not prefabricated posters or lists; it's in the magic of co-creating with students. Furthermore, some of these topics lend themselves to building class protocols or procedures to help support students in their literacy journeys:

- How to choose interesting books
- How to check out a book from the class library
- How to return books to the class library
- How to use a bookmark for keeping track of pages turned
- How to keep a reading calendar
- How to make meaningful reading goals
- How to develop keen questions for discussion
- How to find time to read outside of school
- How to get started quickly in a small group
- How to agree and disagree in discussions
- How to abandon a book
- How to take stock of interests/passions
- How to find a thinking partner
- How to match genres and authors to fuel excitement about reading

To Get to What You See Here, **Try This**

1. Choose a procedure or behavior you think would be of great benefit for your students. (In the earlier case, students are developing ideas around how we can agree and disagree respectfully.)

2. Identify the learning target (e.g., "We are learning to respectfully agree and disagree").

3. Record ideas about why this is important to be able to do.

4. In small groups of four or five, ask students to list the things we need to remember to do in order to agree and disagree respectfully.

5. Each group selects one person to share his or her ideas by "tapping" his or her list on the board, turning to the group, and sharing his or her three best group ideas (Tap, Turn, and Talk).

6. Place ideas on an anchor chart for future reference.

Photos by Christian Ford

CO-CONSTRUCTING SHARED AGREEMENTS IN LARGE GROUPS

Take another look at the pictures on the facing page. As you can see, Barry is co-constructing with his students. Julie and Barry work with students to create shared agreements because it gets everyone on the same page. You can create shared agreements about any behavior, routine, or process that impacts student learning. This also includes shared agreements around work products, end demonstrations of learning, and performance tasks.

Note: For more on where large group sharing fits into the architecture of reading workshop, refer to Chapter Nine.

SMALL GROUPS WITHIN A LARGE GROUP LESSON

Purpose: To increase student talk and engagement and start flexible grouping right away

When: You see a prime opportunity to teach something, have students practice something, or open up the floodgates for students to share ideas

Sample Group Configuration

iStock.com/Tiyas

The beauty of tucking small groups inside a large group reading lesson is that it's logistically easy to have students quickly rearrange themselves into groups. We do it whenever we see the need to name and immediately use a very familiar strategy—or want students try one we just introduced. This gives them a trial run so they can more easily apply it on their own, in small groups, and independently. Whether it is Turn and Talk or a small group discussion about a read-aloud, we give power to this interaction by naming it and using it.

You can employ this strategic small grouping in many different ways. One of the easiest ways to envision how this strategy plays out in the classroom is to imagine a teacher-led discussion, where students frantically wave their hands, hoping for a chance to share. Right then, the teacher realizes this is a prime opportunity for a small group discussion—with, perhaps, a recorder to get the group's ideas down. The small group services the learning by affording more students the opportunity to talk, learn, and, at the same time, harness student energy. This is a wonderful example of how a teacher can instantly spin off a large group inquiry or discussion into small group work.

You might see teachers develop a range of different ways of mixing and matching these groupings once they are accustomed to moving large group discussions to small groups. Let's take a closer look at how this might work.

In this case, a teacher starts a reading lesson with a particular strategy in mind, say choosing a good book to read. The lesson begins with the teacher asking student pairs to make a list of ways they choose books to read and then these pairs share their list with another partner group. This group of four then selects three ideas from their "how to choose a book" list and adds it to the class anchor chart, How to Choose a Book to Read. In this example, the partners and groups of four are servicing the whole group lesson. The benefit of this kind of small group work is that it can be facilitated quickly, as simple as a Turn and Talk with a partner, and then to a table group. The teacher holds the controls, and the students work in short bursts. We like to use these types of small groups when we are building class protocols and routines—such as how to read independently, how to find great books to read in the classroom, and how to increase reading stamina. We can substitute out the teacher as a recorder by asking students to record ideas and insights at each table group.

Here are a few more suggested topics for getting up and running with small groups placed inside large group lessons:

- How to choose a great book to read
- How to find a distraction-free reading spot
- How to read independently
- How to partner read
- How to keep a book talk lively and focused
- How to ask curious questions
- How to reread when your brain wanders

- How to read tricky text
- How to write about reading
- How to apply learning from independent reading

SMALL GROUPS FOR GUIDED READING OR GUIDED PRACTICE

Now that we have tackled using fluid small groups in the service of a large group lesson, we thought it best to go after another familiar small group approach: guided reading.

Purpose: To place four to six students in small groups based on instructional reading level text and reteach the large group reading lesson or to zero in on a reading skill or strategy for this selected group of readers

When: You notice a few students struggling with their independent reading time

We think planning reading instruction with small groups in mind helps both the teacher and the students see the aim of the learning and reading work. The key is letting readers in on what they'll gain by getting some extra practice and attention during a small group meeting.

So let's imagine you are teaching students how to talk and write about the main idea of a text or section of text. Students practice by sharing out the "gist" (or main idea) of the text read by the teacher during shared reading. As you listen in, you recognize some students are trying to retell all of the details instead of labeling the main idea. You jot down the names of these students who could use further feedback and practice, and you wrap up the lesson. Next, you invite these students to practice the short text with each other, while the rest of the class moves into independent reading. After reading and talking about the text, this small group disbands and joins the other readers. A small group of this sort might meet two or three times to continue practicing, in addition to their shared and independent reading.

Big Advice

If you want foundational minilessons for readers that beautifully transplant into any reading classroom, see *What Do I Teach Readers Tomorrow?* by Gravity Goldberg and Renee Houser (2017). *Simple Starts* by Kari Yates (2015a) is super practical and abundant with launch ideas.

To Get to What You See Here, **Try This**

1. Kidwatch, and when you recognize students who need more support and practice with a specific reading skill or strategy, gather them in groups of four to six, and plan on meeting two to three times until you see each reader has "got it."

2. Place the meetings on a class calendar and post on the daily reading workshop schedule.

3. Debrief with readers on what they learned or practiced.

4. Choose a student to share lesson insights during large group share-out or with a small group (e.g., "Today we learned how to interpret a character by reading like actors").

For more on guided reading, we encourage you to read *The Next Step Forward in Guided Reading* by Jan Richardson (2016) and *Guided Reading Responsive Teaching Across the Grades* by Irene C. Fountas and Gay Su Pinnell (2016a). We are being intentionally brief here about this approach because we want to give attention to small groups that match learners' wants and needs. We think, as you read on in this book, you will come to see that what we do *is* guiding reading—it's that we are guiding not by reading level but by other factors. For example, one way is to organize students by what they know. Instead of locking students into a level group, a teacher could look at how a group of students could benefit by sharing their synthesizing or inferring skills. Here are other topics students could explore in small groups:

- Finding a favorite author or genre
- Noticing moments of character turmoil
- How to skim nonfiction headings before reading to get one's footing
- Talking about both what a character is feeling and one's own takeaway
- Strategies for reading every day

Here is a scheduling structure Barry uses early in the year. Students work on reading for 30 to 40 minutes, so he decides to meet only once with targeted students.

Monday	Tuesday	Wednesday	Thursday	Friday
After school, Barry reviews student reading calendars and notices a handful of students struggling to find and stick with an interesting book. Focus: talking about new reading titles.	**Minilesson:** Barry book talks two new titles.	**Minilesson:** Barry book talks two more new titles.	**Minilesson:** Saiya and Josh give book talks on two of their recent favorites.	**Minilesson:** Barry facilitates thought partners and groups of four with book talks.
Barry decides to use the minilesson to focus on book talks. He also creates three groups; each group has a mix of students who are adept at finding books and students who have fallen in a rut or are struggling to stick with a book. (Seven students need a lift.)	**Small group:** Group A Students are invited to talk about a book that they enjoyed reading. Observation and student conferring **Sharing time:** Group A students talk about the next book they are going to read.	**Small group:** Group B Students are invited to talk about a book that they enjoyed reading. Observation and student conferring **Sharing time:** Group B students talk about the next book they are going to read.	**Small group:** Group C Students are invited to talk about a book that they enjoyed reading. Observation and student conferring **Sharing time:** Group C students talk about the next book they are going to read.	**Possible small group:** Exit slip: What title or titles are you now planning to read that you heard shared this week during book talks and small groups?

When Barry notices a group of readers are not reading much, he decides to raise awareness of new books and other literature that students in the class enjoy. Small groups are assigned to give time over to each student to talk about their books. Even reluctant readers exchange what they are reading. These groups meet once because Barry wants some flexibility in hearing from different students and time to personally assist reluctant readers with a reading nudge during student conferring.

SMALL GROUPS BASED ON CURRENT INTERESTS

Purpose: To create a compelling focus for students and a clear organizing feature for the group

When: Anytime you want to teach or reteach something, but you want the strategy to take a back seat to student interest—groups often meet for three to four days

As you launch small groups with your students, you will get more and more comfortable with your role as the consummate concierge. That is, as you circulate and listen in on small groups, you'll find that you may notice a *need*—something is shaky or going off the rails—and then your intervention is to discover an *interest* as a way to address the need. Needs and interests overlap!

For example, Julie joined in for a fifth-grade group's share-out session, and noticed they struggled to talk with any depth. Some students tried to chime in without any luck. This was a group of six called "The Admiring Authors Group," where members each read several texts by an author they admired. They already had met two times. The focus and goal of the group were to read voluminously and hold thinking about big ahas, big ideas, and/or connections made within the text. Julie recognized this group's "skinny" conversation presented an opportunity. She did a quick survey by asking students to name their top three favorite animals. The group had common interests of giraffes, elephants, and dogs. Later that day, Julie curated a few short texts focused on the group's favorite animals.

The next day, she met with the group during the first part of independent work time. She asked the students to choose a text from the text set and read it. While doing so, she explained that she'd like them to hold their thinking using a two-column chart in their Reader's Notebooks. The chart focused on the gist of what they just read and captured wonderings/questions that came to mind as they read. Julie gave the group about 15 minutes to read and work while she joined another group. Upon her return, students began their share-out using their two-column charts as a guide. This work both served as a formative assessment to check in on students' understandings and potential misconceptions and gave students something to use as they talked to their group.

Thinking back to the author texts these students were originally reading, Julie wondered if part of the reason that the group was having such a struggle was because the students didn't have enough in common between their books/authors. Their conversations flatlined because they weren't very familiar with the books/authors their peers were reading. Julie also wondered if having a common thread, or organizing features, among their texts was what they needed to help lift their conversations. She gave the group the following survey:

Name: _____

What do you want to read next? Check things that sound interesting. Or, if you prefer, you can rank them (1 = *most interesting* and so on)

- ☐ People
- ☐ Inventions
- ☐ Stories about fictional characters and events
- ☐ Poetry
- ☐ Humor—jokes and funny short stories
- ☐ Time travel
- ☐ Anything sports
- ☐ Other: _____

After reviewing the surveys, it became clear that the way forward was to split this group of six into two groups of three, based on their interests. The survey results showed Julie that one trio was interested in inventions and the other trio thought humor sounded like fun. Julie met with each trio for about five minutes and showed them a few things she pulled from her bookshelf.

As an example, let's focus on the trio of girls who thought inventions were interesting. After Julie showed them some texts, they gravitated toward a book about toys, which launched some interesting work around a common theme. Take a look at the schedule Julie created for herself so that she could create touchpoints with these students to support and nudge their small group work forward.

	Monday	Tuesday	Wednesday	Thursday	Friday
Week 1		**Join in:** Admiring Authors group (6 kids) Give survey	**Join in:** Admiring Authors group Share survey results with the group Show texts about inventions (group of 6 turned into 2 trios: Humor and Toys) • Admiring Authors group disbands, but the students will continue to read their novels for independent reading; they decide that maybe they will all get back together to talk about their independent reading books next week	**Join in:** Humor group **Join in:** Toys group • Read *Whoosh* together • Discuss big ahas and interesting facts	**Join in:** Humor group • Share stack of joke books • Discuss puns • Talk about the fact that what makes something funny to one person doesn't always feel the same to others **Join in:** Toys group • Listen in as the students share out big ideas and how they are holding their thinking about their reading • Suggest that they look across bookshelves (home and school) to add texts to the bucket of resources
Week 2	**Check in:** Toys group • Fill up their bucket with a few short texts about new toys versus old toys and toy companies • Ask them to go on a digital and print hunt for other interesting texts to add	**Check in:** Humor group • Talk about jokes, riddles, puns, and comics • Suggest looking at some as mentors and writing a few Admiring Authors group meets to discuss independent reading books	**Join in:** Toys group • Get out yo-yos and a yo-yo how-to book; encourage students to read a few pages and give yo-yo tricks a try	**Join in:** Humor group • Suggest everyone bring one text (poem, short story, picture book, comic, etc.) that they find humorous and share it with the group	

During this two-week period, Julie met with other groups as well. The schedule highlights her work with two groups of students: the Toys and Humor groups. What's fun and exciting about small group work is that it continually builds on itself. What happens in a small group one day can connect to several days of work. It can also inspire other students, especially if what happens in small group is shared out and feeds readers in the moment. This can lead to future planning and learning across time.

When planning, Julie had a sense of what she wanted to do with each group during the first week. The natural flow of reorganizing the group of six into two smaller groups of three gave way for each group to orient and begin digging into a new text set. Julie had a general plan for what she could offer up the second week, as seen in the schedule, but she knew she would know what to do next depending on the interactions and work at the table. Writing "checking in" in her plans signals to Julie that she needs to be a listener and studier of students, their ideas, their interactions, and their wonderings (see Chapter Eight on unit planning). By listening in, Julie might find that she needs to curate more mentor texts. She might also find that selecting (or having students select) a common text to read and discuss together might lift the group's thinking and ways of holding ideas on paper. Julie might want to help the small group begin creating an anchor chart that shows common themes or big ideas that emerge from the texts they are reading. All of these serve as possibilities to elevate learning at the small group table. (For more about curating texts, see Chapter Seven.)

THOUGHT PARTNERS

Purpose: To have learners share information and knowledge in a setting that promotes risk taking and trust; effective as work that ignites thinking before or after minilessons, read-alouds, and shared reading/writing experiences

When: At times when you want to ensure no one feels left out and to provoke divergent thinking by pairing students for a period of two to three weeks

Pairing one learner with another is powerful. It's great because it's easy to manage at the start of the year, and it's also an all-year strategy, where many learners thrive in partnerships. The trick is to make sure it doesn't become a tired Turn and Talk. To avoid that, let's take a look at the work of business leader Barbara

Stanny (2012). She brilliantly articulates the why behind the practice of thought partners. A thought partner is someone who

1. Challenges your thinking

2. Causes you to modify or change your paradigms, assumptions, or actions

3. Has information or a way of thinking that provokes you to innovate or otherwise leads to value creation in your business, career, or life

To begin, you might want to ask students who their "go-to" is (their thought partner) or who they think could be their thought partner for specific knowledge, skills, and understandings. This doesn't mean you have to always couple kids together based solely on their preferences. Instead, you'll take their ideas into account when you create pairings that could support the learning across the classroom. The key to thought partners is giving students an opportunity to learn with and from someone new, which they may not necessarily choose to do otherwise.

As you think about the two or three weeks ahead, consider the kinds of questions you anticipate asking or learning targets you are going after. One easy way to step into thought partners is to take these questions or learning targets and, instead of talking in a large group, turn them into partner conversations. For instance, we were learning how to check our comprehension by changing a title to a question and answering the question. We placed an article on the document camera and had students dive in as partners to try out the strategy. This really heightened engagement. Instead of one student showing the class how to change a title to a question, partners were busy doing the reading and thinking.

What are the reading skills and behaviors that thought partners explore together? We like to keep anecdotal notes in our notebooks. We record the names of student pairs for various literacy goals. We make observations about what we see and hear kids doing in their partnerships, and the things they are interested in reading. We also informally ask the class to jot down ideas on a sticky note or in their journals. See pages 271 and 272 in the Appendix for two different Thought Partner Planning Grids you can use with both younger and older students.

To Get to What You See Here, **Try This**

1. Pick a text or piece of text that you want your entire class to read.

2. Ask students to sit next to their thought partner and, in the case described earlier, change the title of the article to a question. Then have students share their questions and revise them if necessary.

3. Direct students to read silently with their questions in mind.

4. Ask one partner to read his or her question and have the second partner answer. Switch turns.

5. Discuss how successful and practical the strategy was in helping students understand the article.

Photos by Christian Ford

THOUGHT PARTNERS TO GROUPS OF FOUR

Purpose: To provide students with a fairly high degree of coaching support as they learn the art of talking and listening to one another

When: At the start of the year or anytime you sense the need for students to lower the stress threshold necessary to think bigger

This grouping twofer is terrific early on in the year because it gets kids starting to talk about their lives, hopes, and dreams. Sharing with a shoulder partner is casual and less public. We advise that you list the thought partners on the board so students can sit next to their partners from the get-go. Let students know the groups can change in a couple of days. This predictable arrangement goes a long way to invite cautious learners into the fray and hopefully prevents a less confident kid being left alone during a spontaneous Turn and Talk interaction.

We recommend you start with open-ended questions that build thoughtful but safe conversations. Second, we urge you to give some wait or "think time" before you ask kids to turn and talk. Barry likes to begin the year with "Think of a time you were listening to a story. What are a couple of things you remember from that experience?" Or "Can you think of a character from a movie or book that still lingers with you? Who is it, and what is it you remember about this character?"

Barry listened in on Ruby and Tim. Ruby remembered sitting in her third-grade classroom listening to the tales of Pippi Longstocking and how she fell in love with striped leggings and wore them to school. Tim, a quiet fifth grader, was ecstatic talking about Anakin Skywalker and how he becomes the evil Darth Vader.

Once students had their chance to talk with a partner, Barry showed how partnerships can form groups of four to further talk about the prompt. He asked Noah and Alice to demonstrate by joining Hap and Zephyr. Now that they are a group of four, instead of just repeating their story again, we prefer to have the partners tell the story. So, Alice offered Noah's favorite story, and her three classmates listened while the whole class observed.

To make this a speedy transition, Barry set the timer for 15 seconds and signaled to start. Kids scooted together and began talking.

We find practicing and familiarizing students with this little dance of moving from partners to groups of four at the outset of the year valuable. Students at this time of the year are eager to figure out how the class works. Moving into these groups quickly increases the likelihood that you and your students will draw on this small group strategy throughout the year.

We also like to take photos of the groups of four as soon as they get started. These snapshots become "pictures of success" and are helpful in building agreements with kids later on because they remind the class of what small group work looks and sounds like.

In these initial groups, we enjoy watching kids talk about their favorite books, movies, and videos. The conversations usually have a lot of energy for about 5 to 10 minutes. You might wind up the activity here. However, our preference is to have the class end by watching one group of four model in a fishbowl experience.

Following on from the preceding story, a group of four was selected. The four students situated themselves in the middle of the carpet. The rest of the class encircled them. Kamaria volunteered to talk about Nick's favorite Netflix series, *Stranger Things*. The students were absorbed by Kamaria's details. Students in the outer circle then commented on what Kamaria did well as a listener in retelling Nick's favorite series. Barry quickly jotted down on chart paper tips for speaking and listening.

Then the class turned its attention toward what the other students had been doing while Kamaria spoke. "They leaned forward." "They nodded and smiled." Comments were added to the chart. This timely recap surfaced key behaviors that make small group conversations work.

Our aim is to get these partnerships and groups of four up and running independently. We take time for these brief exchanges where students name what makes these groupings work. While observing, Julie and Barry like to sit with a clipboard and write down things they hear students saying. Notes about partnerships might look like the following:

> "We got a chance to talk about something fun."
>
> "I thought it was nice to talk to a classmate and not have to listen to only the teacher."

And here's what worked in the groups of four:

> "I had to remember what my partner said, and then I had to tell it back, trying to make it interesting."
>
> "We had to listen and not move around. That was hard for me."

We end reading workshop by highlighting student insights. All this groundwork matters as students become more comfortable talking in pairs and in small groups. This ultimately makes it a lot easier to use partners and groups of four in any lesson. See page 273 in the Appendix for a Protocol for Thought Partners and Groups of Four.

Photos by Christian Ford

SMALL GROUPS AS BOOK CLUBS/CLOSE READING CLUBS

Purpose: To bring four or more readers around a common text so that they can more easily support one another

When: Before, during, and after reading the same text

Book clubs are great forums for students to learn and share strategies. For example, the focus might be on remembering what they have read, asking questions of the text, marking up text for future conversations, or finding rich ideas to share about the text. Book clubs can really energize reading workshop. When done well, they give students the chance to dig into a book or text, talk about a writer's little nuances or declare big ideas, and enjoy other readers' insights and company. Many books have been written on book clubs and literature discussions. We simply want to add that reading short pieces for short periods can make your initial steps into books clubs more successful.

During a biography study, we invited students to choose from a variety of short pieces (one to three pages) on inventors. A handful of students chose Ruth Handler, the woman who made Barbie famous. After reading the text independently, we came together to talk about what we had learned and what we were still wondering about. It did not take long for this group to land on a central question worth investigating: Does Barbie encourage girls to be anything they want to be? The discussion time ended before students were satisfied, so they decided to find other reading material to challenge or support this proposition. The following day, this group of five kids met with more material worth examining. Saiya had an infographic on how Barbie's body would look in real life. This prompted the group to look on their iPads for more infographics and even a Barbie blog. After their third meeting, they asked to share their thoughts and opinions about their articles and the role Barbie has played in influencing girls' lives. This group could have met perhaps another couple times, but we think it is more effective to stop while kids still have energy to talk rather than plod along until everything has been said. "End on an upswing" is a good motto.

Curious students search for answers to questions about Barbie's influence on girls.

Photo by Christian Ford

This example highlights a couple of things worth trying. First, how about starting with some short texts or short books when kicking off book clubs? In a science study about biomes, we found some short articles on five different biomes and asked kids to choose from the selection. Second, consider meeting two or three times on consecutive days. These small groups can be highly effective in surfacing important information, getting kids to talk and raise questions, and giving kids purpose for taking notes. Presenting "Did you know?" facts at the end of workshop builds interest for readers.

In the biome study, students in the tundra group shared their fascination with the harsh and hostile environment plants and animals deal with. Students in the rainforest group identified with many of their questions and insights. One student commented, "I guess I'd rather be an animal in the rainforest because they don't have to move around as much."

To Get to What You See Here, **Try This**

1. Find some short articles or books on a topic you are all studying (animals, biomes, inventors, etc.).
2. Provide multiple copies (about six to eight).
3. Give simple and short book club talks about the selections available.
4. Offer time during independent reading to review the selections.
5. Create book clubs based on what is chosen.
6. Schedule meeting times.
7. Meet to talk about what kids learned, what they are thinking, and what they are wondering about; raise questions for a future meeting.
8. Schedule a follow-up meeting.
9. Provide time during the large group sharing time for members to either summarize what happened or, more specifically, outline questions they are going after before their next meeting.

Photos by Christian Ford

GROUPS TO CREATE "WE VALUE" STATEMENTS

Purpose: To explore, define, and refine co-created statements about core beliefs

When: Early in the school year (revisit and tweak a few times a year when the need arises)

Within minutes of starting the first day of school, students can meet in small groups—usually five groups of four students—and decide on your class's top core value. You can do this by brainstorming values and allowing the students to wrestle with different terms. Your students can determine which ones best sum up what they want for each other. The kids prioritize their lists, and a reporter is selected from each of the five groups to share their number one core value for the class.

Here is a sampling of "We value . . ." groups lists:

- We value independent reading time
- We value getting along and making friends
- We value learning and having fun at school
- We value caring for each other
- We value taking care of our environment
- We value respecting others

With agency and enthusiasm, classes we've worked with often agree to commit themselves to the core values of respect and care—for themselves, others, and the classroom. This initiating activity packs a lot of power; it engages students right away on how to negotiate and voice their opinions.

Ah, but here is where the interesting and challenging learning comes in: Each of the five groups may swiftly produce an impressive list of semifinalists, but when it's time to decide their number one choice, groups often get stuck. Instead of solving this for them, we suggest you ask them to think about a strategy for choosing their top recommendation, even when there is disagreement. Asking group members to name what they did when group members did not all agree on a common suggestion kick-starts trust, membership, and problem solving.

We take time to develop agreements because they anchor us to common ways we want to act around each other. We have found constructing agreements with kids sends the right messages. We create a shared agreement tied to respect and know the work will be to create practices and protocols around that value. Over time, the goal is to give students opportunities to grow their understandings of what respectful talk and action looks, sounds, and feels like. Respect is more than a poster in our classrooms. It is a continual co-construction of what the class values and how the students will behave to meet this end.

THE RESEARCH BEHIND NAMING NORMS AND VALUES

Charles Duhigg digs into the research on how effective teams operate in his book, *Smarter Faster Better* (2017). After speaking with members of Google's Project Aristotle, it became clear to him that group norms can enhance a feeling of care and belonging, and group norms can also undermine people's willingness to participate. "There is strong evidence that group norms play a critical role in shaping the emotional experience of participating in a team" (Duhigg, 2017, p. 46). So what norms do we establish with kids, and how do we do this? Google's surveys said these norms were most effective and were all aspects of feeling psychologically safe at work, allowing others to fail without repercussions, respecting

To Get to What You See Here, **Try This**

1. Apply Duhigg's principle of *demonstrating a sensitivity* to what people think and feel.

2. Model kind, respectful talk and tone.

3. Encourage equity in speaking.

4. Catch yourself before you resort to "bad boss" haranguing language.

5. Put a high value on "trading and sharing" what you know so that students see that they are expected to participate yet also know it can be at their own pace.

6. Maintain a standard for group work that in essence lets group members know that they are equal partners, and that being a part of a group means we need to give control to others.

7. Recognize that the willingness of learners to hand over voice and share authority with teammates arises when learners feel fully invited to speak. It is also sustained when learners feel psychologically safe on a daily basis.

Photo by Rachel Langosch

divergent opinions, and feeling free to question others' choices, but also trusting that people aren't trying to undermine you (Duhigg, 2017, p. 51). Our route in the classroom to psychological safety begins with the teacher. Our job of creating a culture of thinkers and risk takers starts with the norming of our class core values. This, in turn, influences the behaviors of our small groups.

One Last Thing

Okay, so now we've given you a sampling of small group practices that are "simple" enough to try if you or your students are new to this. It's by no means an exhaustive list, and in the chapters that follow, you will see many other ideas that you might want to try early in the year. For now, we want to turn to some general principles to apply to small group practice. To quote Sir Ken Robinson (Robinson & Aronica, 2015), "education is a 'human business.'" If we want kids to live up to the demands of the 21st century, Robinson reminds us that we have to create models focused on "making education personal" (p. 53). "All students are unique individuals with their own hopes, talents . . . Engaging them is the heart of raising achievement" (p. 52). These examples foster and support independent reading. By offering students a variety of ways to interact as a group of readers, students not only grow as readers but also gain insights and understanding that nurtures their personal reading lives.

CHAPTER THREE

Scheduling

(because schedules are key for the launch and beyond)

In the last chapter, we gave you lots of ideas for groups that are relatively easy to get up and running. Now let's turn to how to find the time to give them a try. We believe creating a schedule for when small groups will meet is invaluable because when you create a schedule, you commit to making small groups happen. A schedule takes small group work from an idea to action, becoming a relied-upon structure during reading workshop. We intentionally design our workshop around who will meet together, when they will meet, what they will read, possibilities for discussion or holding thinking, and how long they will read. Planning builds predictability and purposely shines a light on small group conversations. This helps avoid disconnected one-and-done small group meetings.

Two common questions we are asked are "I only have 30 minutes, so how can I make small groups work?" and "What if I end up with too many small groups at once and I run out of time to meet with them all?" In this chapter, we give you lots of sample schedules so that you get a bird's-eye view of how small groups are doable regardless of the challenges you face. This chapter is designed differently for easy use.

Photo by Christian Ford

Reading workshop is the key to successful small group learning experiences. How you spend your time each day creates the structure for small group opportunities. Although we don't mean to offend, we are going to state something we value. If you are spending most of your reading time either managing the room or teaching the whole class, pulling off small groups is going to be difficult. If this is your current reality, we know the shift can be tricky, but it is doable and has really big payoffs. Start by defining the time you have for reading workshop by asking, "How many minutes do I have for reading workshop in a day or week?"

WHAT DOES WORKSHOP LOOK LIKE?

Reading Workshop Schedule

Note: This can be spread across two days.

Kickoff/Opening—Launching Reading Workshop (3–5 minutes)

How will you launch the reading workshop? Will it be a quick "Good morning," a formative assessment/knowledge check, or a quick share-out between classmates?

Minilesson—Teaching or Shared Experience (9–11 minutes)

What will you teach?

- Will this be a management minilesson focused on a routine you are teaching (e.g., where to store the books you are reading independently, reading behaviors)?
- Will this be a minilesson about a big idea or concept in text (e.g., ways to hold your thinking in your Reader's Notebook, main idea)?
- Will this be a minilesson focused on content, skill, or strategy (e.g., fluency, metacognition)?
- Will you facilitate this minilesson through direct teaching or a shared experience (e.g., teacher-directed or teacher and students co-constructing the lesson together)?

Work Time—Independent Reading Time and Small Group Learning Opportunities (35–40 minutes)

What will the students be doing?

- What will they be reading, writing, making, creating, or talking about?

- Will they be working independently?
- Will they work in small groups?
    - Will small groups meet with or without you?
    - Which students will you work with, and what will be the focus?

Share-Out/Debrief—Workshop Wrap-Up (5–10 minutes)

What will students share or do to wrap up workshop?

- Will they share with the whole group, with a small group, or in pairs?
- Will you select a few students to share out, or will everyone have an opportunity?

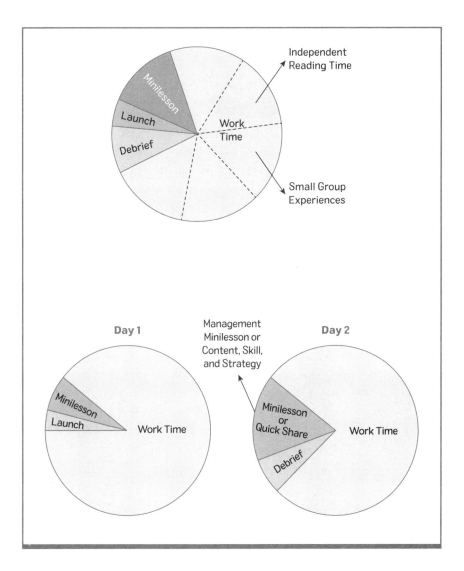

Take a look at your time and compare it to the chart that matches closely to your structure.

45 minutes	60 minutes	75 minutes
Kickoff (2 minutes)	Kickoff (5 minutes)	Kickoff (5 minutes)
Minilesson (10 minutes)	Minilesson (10 minutes)	Minilesson (10 minutes)
Work time (30 minutes)	Work time (40 minutes)	Work time (50 minutes)
Two small groups	Three small groups (stay about 10–12 minutes with each group)	Four small groups (stay about 10–12 minutes with each group)
Debrief (3 minutes)	Debrief (5 minutes)	Debrief (10 minutes)

Note: Remember that the teacher doesn't have to be present in the groups for small groups to meet.

Getting Started, Quick Groups

Crayola Name groups, "Declare Your Literacy" groups, and other groups you read about in Chapter Two can be one-and-done in a day, and so are perfect for the launch at the beginning of the school year or the beginning of your journey into small group instruction. Another great thing is that any of these groups can also be developed into groups with longer duration. For an illustration of this, take a look at these schedules, which highlight some of the groupings described in Chapter Two. As you look at each schedule, you'll notice that the first three groups show an eight-day progression. You could look at this as a model for how to spend the first eight days of launching small group learning (at the beginning of the year or at any point where you want to harness small groups). The schedules are designed for you either to borrow or to innovate and apply in a manner that fits your vision. You might ask yourself, "How can I tweak this model to fit my reading workshop schedule and kids?" Regardless, pay close attention to

Big Advice

Creative scheduling is an art and necessity. Done effectively it assures quality instruction and time to meet with kids in small groups. Leslie Blauman shows how she schedules her workshop time artfully in *The Inside Guide to the Reading-Writing Classroom, Grades 3–6* (2011). *The Cafe Book* (2009) by Gail Boushey and Joan Moser has some excellent schedules and ideas for fitting in time for conferences.

- The number of students in each small group
- Time allocation
- What the teacher will be doing
- What the students will be doing

Remember you can call these groups anything you want (or anything your kids want); the idea is to create an identity (something kids can associate with) for your small group work.

Groups for First Days/Weeks of School

CRAYOLA NAME GROUPS

Note: There are four or five students in each group.

Small groups meet for about 20 minutes each day at the same time	Teacher Time Needed Day 1 Teacher rotates between groups: kidwatching and note-taking	Teacher Time Needed Day 2 Teacher rotates between groups: kidwatching and note-taking
Jungle Green	4 minutes	4 minutes
Mango-Tango	4 minutes	4 minutes
Pacific Blue	4 minutes	4 minutes
Jazzberry Jam	4 minutes	4 minutes
Pink Flamingo	4 minutes	4 minutes

COOL STUFF BAG GROUPS

Note: There are four or five students in each group.

Small groups meet for 15–20 minutes but *not* at the same time	Teacher Time Needed Day 3 (30–40 minutes total)	Teacher Time Needed Day 4 (30–40 minutes total)	Teacher Time Needed Day 5 (15–20 minutes total)
Teacher posts schedule, calls over group to carpet; rest of the class reads independently	Jungle Green	Pacific Blue	Pink Flamingo
	Mango-Tango	Jazzberry Jam	

READING SURVEY DISCUSSION GROUPS

Note: There are five or six students in each group.

Small groups meet for 10 minutes, *not* at the same time	Teacher Time Needed Day 6 (20 minutes total)	Teacher Time Needed Day 7 (20 minutes total)	Teacher Time Needed Day 8 (10 minutes total)
Teacher takes notes as group members share their surveys; rest of class reads independently	Group 1	Group 3	Group 5
	Group 2	Group 4	

Some groups work really well across the year. In order to sustain and maintain small group learning, consider giving some of these groups a try.

"DECLARE YOUR LITERACY" GROUP

Note: There are five or six students in each group.

For the first time the groups meet: Small groups meet for about 25 to 30 minutes, at the same time. The teacher floats between the groups, spending about 5 minutes with each group kidwatching and helping the students document their literate lives.

Group 1	Group 2	Group 3	Group 4	Group 5

For future times the groups meet (various options): You can create a routine where the groups all meet on a specific day of the week or month for an allotted time (20 minutes). These groups can continue to meet across the weeks or months of the school year.

Monday	Tuesday	Wednesday	Thursday	Friday
		Group 1		
		Group 2		
		Group 3		
		Group 4		
		Group 5		

Or, you can ask each small group to make a plan for when they will meet and calendarize it. Make the calendar public, and make sure you prioritize time to make it happen.

Week	Monday	Tuesday	Wednesday	Thursday	Friday
1		Group 1			Group 2
2	Group 3			Group 4	
3		Group 5			

SMALL GROUPS WITHIN A LARGE GROUP LESSON

Note: There are three students in each group.

In the midst of a whole group lesson, pause and ask students to rearrange themselves to form temporary small groups for about two to five minutes. Trios work well for this small group work. The teacher can form these groups "in the moment" or schedule them ahead of time as shown in the schedule below.

Monday	Tuesday	Wednesday	Thursday	Friday
Minilesson	Minilesson	Minilesson	Minilesson	Minilesson
*Small Group	Work Time	Work Time	*Small Group	Work Time
Work Time	Debrief	Debrief	Work Time	Debrief
Debrief			Debrief	

Getting One Group Up and Running

1. Identify one small group (three or four students) and a reason for them to meet. To start, create an interest or inquiry group—finding something in common that the group wants to read or learn about together.

2. Decide (or ask students to decide) *how many times* and *for how long* they will meet during independent work time. (Note: If you want students to have some time for independent reading each day or several times across the week, create shared agreements with the whole class or small groups to determine how to manage time during reading workshop to accomplish both.)

3. Decide (or ask students to decide) how many times the teacher will join the small group.

4. Create a schedule and go!

One-Week Small Group Schedule (Important Inventors Group)

Week	Monday	Tuesday	Wednesday	Thursday	Friday
1	**Inventors**	Inventors	**Inventors**		Inventors

Note: **Bold** indicates when the teacher will join the group.

Week	Monday	Tuesday	Wednesday	Thursday	Friday
1	Inventors	**Inventors**	Inventors	**Inventors**	
2	**Inventors**	Inventors		**Inventors**	**Inventors** Decide if the group will continue to work together; if so, ask students when they want you to join them next week, and try to create your schedule based on their wants/needs
3		**Inventors**	Inventors	**Inventors**	

Note: **Bold** indicates when the teacher will join the group.

Getting Multiple Groups Up and Running

1. Students form small groups (three to six students) based on a focus or an organizing feature according to their interests (author study, topic/content study).

2. Decide (or ask students to decide) *how many times* and *for how long* they will meet during independent work time. Students will either meet with a small group or read independently.

3. Decide (or ask students to decide) how many times the teacher will join the small group.

4. Create a schedule and go!

If small groups are all meeting at the same time,

- In 45 minutes, the teacher meets with each group for about 5 to 8 minutes but spends extra time with one group.
- This process is repeated for four days or until the teacher has met with all groups for an extended time.

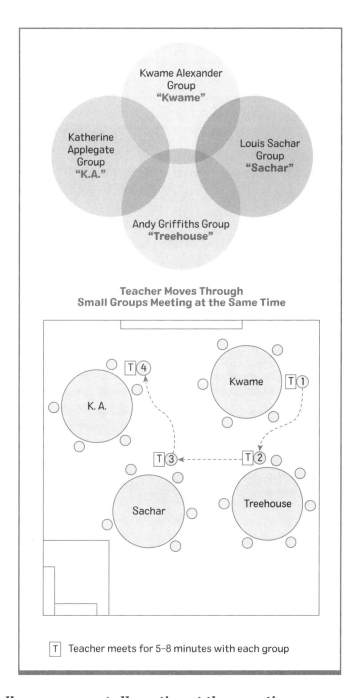

Teacher Moves Through
Small Groups Meeting at the Same Time

T   Teacher meets for 5–8 minutes with each group

If small groups are *not* all meeting at the same time,

- Have students create quick names for their group if the complete text name feels too long (e.g., the Treehouse group was created since the students are starting out by reading *The 13-Story Treehouse* by Andy Griffiths).

Week	Monday	Tuesday	Wednesday	Thursday	Friday
1	**Kwame** **Sachar** **Treehouse** **K. A.**	**Kwame** Sachar **Treehouse**	Treehouse **K. A.**	**Sachar** **Treehouse**	**Kwame** Treehouse **K. A.**
2	**Sachar** **Treehouse**	**Kwame** Treehouse **K. A.**	Kwame **Sachar** **Treehouse** K. A.	**Sachar** Treehouse **K. A.**	**Kwame** **Treehouse** **K. A.** Decide if the groups will continue to work together; if so, ask students when they want you to join them next week, and try to create your schedule based on their wants/needs

Note: **Bold** indicates when the teacher will join the group. Kwame = Kwame Alexander books and short stories group; Sachar = Louis Sachar books group; Treehouse = *The 13-Story Treehouse* series by Andy Griffiths group; K. A. = Katherine Alice Applegate books group.

Other Ways to Give It a Go!

Small Group Monthly/Unit Plans

When we plan small group learning opportunities by the month or unit, we are thinking in a longer chunk of time but also keeping the short term (weekly and daily lessons) in mind.

Biography Unit	Weekly Focus
Weeks 1 and 2	Curating and Building Interest Through Short Biography Texts • Put lots of short biographical texts in front of students and let them explore and read in groups of two or three
Week 3	Reading Picture Books and Other Short Texts • Partners and groups of four select a few anchor texts to read; hold thinking to boost comprehension across texts
Week 4	Reading About One or Two People (Person[s] of Interest) • Partners and groups of four select one or two people to study • Help students select texts that will inspire and push their thinking

Biography Unit	Weekly Focus
Weeks 5 and 6	Becoming a Biographer • Partners and groups of four read independently • Small groups meet to read and write about their person(s) of interest using a two-page-spread format
Weeks 7 and 8	Drafting, Editing/Revising, Publishing, and Sharing • Shuffle small groups for revision and sharing

Small Group Weekly Plans

Small groups need to meet. Small groups can meet with or without the teacher. This could be based on students' wants (sometimes they want more time to finish reading or holding their thinking through writing), or it could be based on students' needs (sometimes the teacher joins in to help clear up confusion). If you honor both ways, you increase the chances for student independence and autonomy. Give your kids the challenge of meeting productively for real purposes in small groups, and then give them time and space to rise to that challenge. A bonus: If you don't believe you have to be present in each small group learning experience, you can then create open slots in the schedule to meet with groups or individual students who need a lift in the moment—because you are either helping to clear up confusion or nudging them forward. In the following we have designed two different examples for how you can organize your small groups across a week.

Example 1

Monday	Tuesday	Wednesday	Thursday	Friday
Introduce the idea of small groups Brainstorm different ways students could break into groups Decide with students how to give it a go Break into groups and read something Reflect: How did it go?	Stick with the same group from yesterday Break into groups and read something Reflect: How did it go? What do you need next?	Switch it up; choose a new group Read something; hold your thinking Find another group; join together and share out Reflect: How did it go? What do you need next?	Switch it up; choose a new group Read a few things; hold your thinking Reflect: How did it go? What do you need next?	Switch it up or stick with the same group Read a few things; hold your thinking Reflect: How did it go? What do you need next?

Example 2

Week	Monday	Tuesday	Wednesday	Thursday	Friday
1	Group 1	Group 3	Group 4	Group 6	Group 1
	Group 2	Open for skill or strategy group	Group 5	Open for skill or strategy group	Open
Week	**Monday**	**Tuesday**	**Wednesday**	**Thursday**	**Friday**
2	Group 2	Group 4	Group 5	Open	Open
	Group 3	Open for skill or strategy group	Group 6	Open	Open

> *Give your kids the challenge of meeting productively for real purposes in small groups, and then give them time and space to rise to that challenge.*

"Just in Time" Skill Groups

The schedule below shows when the teacher meets with "just in time" skill groups. "Just in time" skill groups are focused on checking in on students' decoding, fluency, and comprehension as well as supporting them in elaborating on their quick writes and notes. This group is fluid because even though we can anticipate our students' needs, we will respond in nimble ways through this small group structure. You will notice that there is a small group space unscheduled. Experience has taught us that when students take on a longer-term project or work product, the "in the moment" feedback becomes more important because it helps us lift students in unique ways, ensuring they can cross the finish line. (See Chapter Six on assessing student work for more about how data can inform these "just in time" groups.)

Focus	Monday	Tuesday	Wednesday	Thursday	Friday
"Just in time" skill group	Group 2 Group 4	Group 3 Group 1	Look at student work and begin to pencil out a list of students needing support on elaboration	"Just in time" group focus: elaboration	"Just in time" group focus: elaboration

You may already be thinking about how this small group structure is repeatable across the year based on your students' needs.

How Do I Schedule Meeting Times Over a Two-Week Period?

We all know the adage: An apple a day keeps the doctor away. (And there is truth to that!) We mention it here by way of saying you will find your own sweet spot in terms of how many groups you can comfortably meet with each day, but our advice is to meet with three groups a day as you get up and running each year. Start slow; then keep them going and develop them naturally. As you read the example below, imagine walking in Barry's and Julie's shoes so that you can envision how it can go.

Barry's fifth-grade students form groups around themes such as fitting in, happiness, and trouble. Barry gives each group the freedom to select the books they want to read and discuss over the two-week span and the order in which they will read each text. Barry then meets with *each group* to pencil in meeting times on a calendar. This is an important step for teachers—this deliberate recording-on-calendar—because by outlining which days we will meet with each group, we have our basic game plan.

During this two-week period, Barry shortens his minilesson so he can hold up to three discussion groups in a day. The plan is to meet at least two or three times with each group. Sharing time at the end of each workshop focuses on key reader insights and discussion strategies that are working. Some groups can benefit from an extra meeting, so he likes the flexibility to meet with them if needed. On Friday, the last day of our two-week mini unit, Barry reserves time for reflection conversations about what students learned, what went well, and what they need next.

Here's what a schedule might look like:

Week 1	Monday Group	Tuesday Group	Wednesday Group	Thursday Group	Friday Group
	Launch	Trouble	Fitting In		Happiness
		Family	Happiness	Trouble	Family
			Survival		
Week 2	Monday Group	Tuesday Group	Wednesday Group	Thursday Group	Friday Group
	Fitting In	Trouble	Survival	Fitting In	
	Survival	Happiness	Family		

Julie's fourth graders are fast at work focused on their three-week collaborative inquiry study. During the first week, students are immersed in a variety of texts, on various topics and lengths. By the end of the week, they narrow down their interests and form groups. At first, Julie stands back, notebook in hand, taking copious notes about students' reading behaviors and interactions.

On the second Monday of this mini unit, Julie spends time focused on management minilessons—how groups can roll with their reading, collaboration, and holding thinking about all of their new learning. In order to give as much time as possible for small group work, Julie does not hold any minilessons from Tuesday to Friday during Week 2. This gives time for voluminous small group work.

In her plans, Julie leaves room during Week 3 to meet with the whole group to troubleshoot, affirm new learnings, answer questions, and even share out big takeaways as a way to inspire small group work. Here's what the schedule looked like for the fourth-grade inquiry groups focused on the art of stitching, LEGO mania, New York state parks, Kyrie Irving, and roller coasters.

Week 1 **Monday Minilesson Focus:** Independent reading of lots of texts and peer conversations about texts and new ideas **Julie's Focus:** Study students' behaviors and interactions	**Monday**	**Tuesday**	**Wednesday**	**Thursday**	**Friday**
	Read multiple texts	Read multiple texts	Read multiple texts	Read multiple texts Begin to narrow interests	Choose inquiry groups
Week 2 **Monday Minilesson Focus:** How groups can roll with their reading, collaboration, and holding thinking about all of their new learn **Julie's Focus:** Meet with small groups	**Monday Group**	**Tuesday Group**	**Wednesday Group**	**Thursday Group**	**Friday Group**
	Art of Stitching	New York State Parks	Roller Coasters	LEGO Mania	Kyrie Irving
	LEGO Mania	Kyrie Irving	Art of Stitching	Roller Coasters	Roller Coasters
Week 3 **Minilesson Focus:** To be determined based on students' curiosities, passions, habits, and needs	**Small Group Focus:** To be determined based on students' curiosities, passions, habits, and needs				

Small Group Foundational Q&A

This is just a little refresher to keep your eye focused on the basics of small group learning experiences. Refer to this as you look back across the schedules in this chapter and the other small group moves throughout the book.

What is a small group?

We have liberally defined small groups as two or more students. We have mentioned that they can function as part of a large whole group lesson or as part of a session during reading workshop. The work in this book is to focus more purposely on the small group meetings conducted in a reading workshop structure.

How many students participate in a small group?

Typically, we like to work with groups of four to six, but this changes depending on the purpose of the learning time.

What are other kids doing?

Kids are reading independently most of the time or pausing to write about their reading, and focused on work products related to reading projects or the unit of study.

What do students bring to a small group?

We like kids to bring the book or text they are reading, their reading notebook, and/or something to write with. Some teachers prefer having a reading folder with a notebook or paper inside. If students are reading multiple texts, we use a two-pocket folder and/or a tub to hold materials for easy access and use.

Where do small groups gather and meet?

It is essential that you have a space created for small group work. That space might be on the carpet, at a kidney-shaped or round table, or in a special spot in the corner of your classroom library. In making this decision, consider a spot where all students can see, talk, and listen to each other without distraction. We find that students like to have a say in where their small group works, so giving them the autonomy to create their own productive space is important. One tried-and-true trick is for the teacher to have a stool that he or she can move from group to group. This creates flexibility for the teacher to listen in or join in a small group without hovering or taking a lead seat.

How do kids transition to a small group?

Just as students know how to "get started quickly" with their independent reading, they must also know how to "get started quickly" when meeting in a small group. After demonstrating what it looks like with students, create an anchor chart with your students so that everyone knows the expectations for starting a meeting. It might look something like this:

We are learning to transition to a small group independently. Why? The more time we have to talk and learn from each other and the less time we spend waiting to get going, the more efficient and effective our meeting time will be.

Success Criteria

Get started quickly—bring all your reading tools (notebook, book, pencil, etc.) and sit in a circle in less than one minute, ready with a question or idea to share.

Photo by Christian Ford

How do kids transition out of a small group?

Kids should also know how to end a meeting and what it looks like to transition to independent reading. We encourage you to take the time to work through this with your students as well.

Small group meetings can end in a variety of ways. Sometimes the focus strategy or skill is reemphasized and named by a student; sometimes the group leaves with an assignment; other times the meeting is summed up, and a date is scheduled for another meeting. Sometimes students end by saying one thing they learned or one way another student led them to a new insight or idea. Of course, the ending transition depends on the work of the group. Having some structured conclusion to a meeting will better guarantee an intentional and purposeful flow to your reading workshop.

What's the teacher's role in a small group?

Generally speaking, we believe the role of the teacher is to kidwatch and observe for the purpose of taking in information from the group in order to lead individuals, the group, or the class to new learning. Teachers may find early on they are facilitating discussions and floating ideas. In Chapters Two and Five, we discuss options for teachers to listen in and observe small groups in an attempt to assess and create a focus for instruction for the small group as well as individuals. We also uncover opportunities for teachers to join in the small group so they may nudge and teach. Both give us ways to gradually release or hand off responsibilities of leading the group.

What's the student's role in a small group?

We want kids to openly share their wants and needs in making sense of their reading. To this end, we support and intentionally teach into helping all students learn to listen, talk, confront both their own ideas and others', and be able to learn with and from others.

How long does the teacher meet with a small group during a reading workshop session?

Typically, small groups meet for 10 to 15 minutes during a reading workshop, but this depends on the purpose of the group. Like most questions having to do with time, it all depends on the length of your reading workshop. Once you or your students determine the purpose for meeting and what you want kids to walk away with, you'll know how long you should meet. Sometimes small groups meet briefly: 4 to 6 minutes. Sometimes a small group meeting of 12 minutes or more is focused on content or big ideas in a text that could be shared with the whole class during a debrief.

How long does the teacher meet with a small group across the calendar month or school year?

It depends on the purpose of the group. Examples are as follows:

Time	Small Group Focus
One or two days per week	Talk about reading habits or books we love
Four or five days per week	Book clubs/article clubs
Three weeks	Inquiry groups studying content or ideas

How often does the teacher meet with a group?

Since all students can benefit from small group work, socially and intellectually, we have to be strategic in how we ensure all students encounter chances to talk in small groups. To begin the year, it is essential students have at least two or three opportunities a week to gather and talk about their reading and to build trust and safety in these social interactions.

As your reading workshop time matures and students develop both stamina and focus, it is not unusual to see only one to two small groups a day. A smoothly running reading workshop should offer at least one small group chance a week for each student. To fit in more time for students who need more practice and feedback, we suggest using the minilesson time as a fishbowl small group strategy lesson.

One Last Thing

We start with small groups at the beginning of the year because it capitalizes on student talk. By establishing small group routines, we increase the odds we will use small groups regularly across the year. Small groups create a powerful social energy, especially when kids are reading and talking about topics and ideas that excite them. And when we see our kids motivated and engaged, it empowers us to cultivate small group practice. Ultimately, we want to encourage students to create and schedule their own small groups. Get started with small groups by carving out some time in your schedule. Then, give it a go!

CHAPTER FOUR

Kidwatching 2.0

(because it's all about orient, notice, take stock, *and* inquire*)*

It's Monday morning, and Julie is ready to begin the day. Notebook and favorite green pen in hand, she observes students for 20 minutes in Kristen Bright's fifth-grade classroom. Why is this her first business of the day? Because on Friday, she and Kristen conferred, and Kristen expressed the need for another perspective on how her readers were faring and what they needed next instructionally. Kristen's questions were as follows:

- What can my students do on their own? Can they hold their thinking when they read independently in the same or different ways as they do during small group instruction?
- What do my students need next to help them develop as readers?

When Julie and Kristen met later on Monday to compare observations, here is what their notes looked like.

Photo by Rachel Langosch

Chanaya	Anthony	Ameer
She is struggling with some of the basics—daily oral language, grammar, and conventions. She worked on looking up synonyms in the thesaurus, which led to needing some review of how ABC order works. She is reading a graphic novel and enjoying it. I think it will be interesting to see what she writes on her reading tracker and in her Reader's Notebook.	He has so much fun looking back over his work in his Reader's Notebook. He doesn't like the system of reading logs, so it sometimes looks like he doesn't read, but that's not the case. He just doesn't like filling forms out. I need to figure out a different system for him.	It's his birthday today. He is savoring every moment, which is apparent by his big smile! He has a stack of fiction and nonfiction picture books of different lengths and difficulty levels in front of him. He's enjoying an easy read for him—The Name Jar by Yangsook Choi.
F. J. and Justin	**Daeshawna and Kaylen**	A number of students seem to be struggling with a word ladder activity. I need to build in a small knowledge check and/or model the process again as a whole group.
These students may need some support choosing a book and finding a spot to read. I worry about fake reading going on. Do they need a small group to support them?	These students worked with Julie to uncover some new words and how words go together. They were lit up about their work—they like small interactions, and they are a good pair.	
Many students are using an editing strategy where they are looking for correct usage of capitalization, punctuation, spelling, and whether or not their writing makes sense. Are kids just going through the motion of rereading, or are they really editing and revising, and is it making an impact? Find out!		

Think back to Chapter Two and all the simple starter routines and types of small groups we covered. The fuel, if you will, that makes those groups go and powers new groups is kidwatching. As the observational notes above show, kidwatching *is* the center of formative assessment. It helps you spot everything from the skills you might need to shore up to the social-emotional dynamics that might make the basis for a community-building new group to the reading habits students need to live a literate life.

Educators have been studying students since the one-room schoolhouse, and way back in 1970s and 1980s, Yetta Goodman's work helped give definition to the term *kidwatching* and beautifully described the process of listening and watching as kids "do" (Owocki & Goodman, 2002). Academically, we watch what students know and are able to do in relation to the standards, learning targets, and success criteria outlined in our curriculum calendar and units of study. We can take note of students' understandings and misconceptions about big ideas and essential learnings as we model, guide, and watch them try things. This helps us figure out where kids stand with the "whole." We can also take note of understandings and misconceptions about skills. This helps us figure out where kids stand with the "parts."

Socially, we kidwatch to understand how our students interact with others in the classroom, grade level, school, home, and ultimately greater community. We look for information that will help us know how learners orient themselves each day. Do they have social stamina? When do they lead? When do they follow? Whom do they lean on when they succeed? Struggle? What are students' relationships with the adults in their lives, both at school and beyond? Kidwatching helps us figure all of this out, and once we do, we can provide texts and social experiences around what we believe will *lift* students toward growth.

> *The key is to understand what is going on in each student's mind.*
>
> —John Hattie

In this chapter, we go deeper into *how* to use studying kids as a formative assessment. We walk you through the kidwatching steps of *orient, notice, take stock,* and *inquire.* We explore how to reflect on your data so that you can support students as they grow their reading muscles.

Two Essential Questions This Chapter Helps You Answer

1. What is a kidwatching protocol that captures the needs of students today?

2. How do you use kidwatching and student work to guide small group learning experiences?

Beliefs

Our beliefs about kidwatching are grounded in our early literacy teaching experiences and the work of Yetta Goodman and Marie Clay. Goodman's kidwatching routine and Clay's Observation Survey trained us to pay close attention to significant and observable reading behaviors. Their research and ideas have helped many educators, like us, develop protocols that focus on the moments in learning that have big takeaways for future instruction.

Our Beliefs About Kidwatching

We believe . . .	How it shows up in our work . . .
Kidwatching 2.0 is successful when adults watch and listen carefully, capturing students' assets.	We plan times into our weekly reading workshop to document what kids can do because working off of their strengths gives us a leg up in the work.
Change is a process, not an event. Kidwatching 2.0 requires that we slow down and take stock of what is happening in the right here and right now.	Students change constantly. They deserve us to pay attention, taking note of change on a regular and continual basis.
Kidwatching 2.0 is the purest form of assessment. It requires us to collect data that go well beyond numbers (including students' curiosities, passions, habits, and needs) and then counts on us using those data in our response.	We make instructional choices based on these data. Kidwatching informs our practice, allows us to make flexible decisions on the spot, and partners with our best instructional designs.

KIDWATCHING TO ENGINEER GROWTH MINDSET

As teachers, when we observe students, we live out the tenets of formative assessment best summed up by educator Dylan Wiliam (2011): "The teacher's job is not to transmit knowledge, nor to facilitate learning. It is to engineer effective learning environments for the students. The key features of effective learning environments are that they create student engagement and allow teachers, learners, and their peers to ensure that the learning is proceeding in the intended direction. The only way we can do this is through assessment. That is why assessment is, indeed, the bridge between teaching and learning" (p. 49). We cannot "engineer learning environments for the students" if we don't know our students. Knowing our students helps us connect to them and provides a thousand different ways to talk with them.

We lean on Carol Dweck's (2007a) work on growth mindset to help us think deeply about students' self-concept as readers, and how small group experiences can nudge learners out of fixed mindsets about their ability to read well. We embrace Dweck's idea that smart is not something you are born with, but rather something you can get. In 2015, after the burst of thinking surrounding growth mindset, Dweck revisited some of her ideas because she wanted everyone to be wiser in how the ideas were implemented:

> A growth mindset isn't just about effort. Perhaps the most common misconception is simply equating the growth mindset with effort. Certainly, effort is key for students' achievement, but it's not the only thing. Students need to try new strategies and seek

input from others when they're stuck. They need this repertoire of approaches—not just sheer effort—to learn and improve.

We also need to remember that effort is a means to an end to the goal of learning and improving. Too often nowadays, praise is given to students who are putting forth effort, but *not learning*, in order to make them feel good in the moment: "Great effort! You tried your best!" It's good that the students tried, but it's not good that they're not learning. The growth-mindset approach helps children feel good in the short *and* long terms, by helping them thrive on challenges and setbacks on their way to learning. When they're stuck, teachers can appreciate their work so far, but add: "Let's talk about what you've tried, and what you can try next."

THE PURPOSE AND THE PROCESS

Goodman and Owocki (2002) remind us that "the more we learn about our students through kidwatching, the better able we are to individualize and fine-tune our instruction" (p. 3).

Kidwatching allows us to

- Get a glimpse of the classroom/school community
- Better understand how language and literacies develop
- Study and implement systems, structures, rituals, and routines in a workshop model
- Interact with students
- Observe and document students' knowledge, skills, and understandings
- Put data into context so that it can be analyzed and studied
- Harness student and teacher self-reflections
- Create a focus for instruction that is specific to students' wants and needs
- Put apt, irresistible texts in front of readers to foster their independent reading

Goodman and Owocki (2002) kidwatch by using three simple steps:

1. Taking note of what students know and can do
2. Attempting to understand students' ways of constructing and expressing knowledge
3. Using what you learn to shape instruction and curriculum

In *Mindsets and Moves*, Gravity Goldberg (2016) addresses kidwatching in the "Be a Miner" phase of her four Ms (the other Ms are *mirror*, *model*, and *mentor*). For her, mining is uncovering what, how, and why individual students read, then figuring out what they do by getting into their minds. Gravity nudges us to

1. Set a purpose for what we will be mining for (e.g., what do we want to find out about this reader?)
2. Observe the reader
3. Ask process-oriented questions
4. Listen
5. Collect

To Get to What You See Here, **Try This**

1. Have students spend one or two days reading a text they have chosen or a text they have all agreed to read.
2. Make it clear that you want students to hold their thinking as they read so they can refer to their jots in their next group discussion.
3. Have supplies such as pens, pencils, and clipboards handy for easy use.
4. But here's the kicker: Harness autonomy by inviting students to read where they are most comfortable. Given that they have clipboards, one student in this small group is not pictured because she is off to the side in a beanbag reading independently.

Photo by Rachel Langosch

Our Kidwatching 2.0 Protocol

Our approach is similar to Goldberg's and others, but if we had to distinguish it, we'd say that ours places more emphasis on getting to know readers on a social-emotional level as well as academically. We call it kidwatching "in the round."

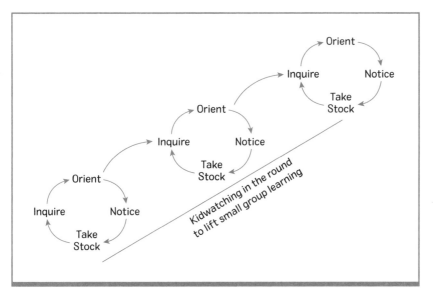

1. **Orient**—Orient yourself and take a pulse to what's going on across the classroom.
   - In general, what are students up to?

2. **Notice**—What do you see or hear academically and socially?
   - Who are your students, both inside and outside of school? What do they do in their free time?
   - What do they like to talk about? What piques their interest?
   - What do students know, and what are they able to do?
   - Whom are students interacting with, and what is the focus of those interactions?

> We ask ourselves, "What are students up to? What do they need, if anything, to lift their learning?"

3. **Take Stock**—What evidence shows that students are knee deep in the opportunities for learning?
   - What are students reading? Writing? Talking about? Creating? Doing?
   - What story does student work tell us about what students can do well?
   - What story does student work tell us about where students need support or extra "lift"?
   - What is the evidence of student thinking in relation to the learning targets and success criteria?

4. **Inquire**—What inquiries do you have about your students?
   - As a kidwatcher, what are you wondering about?
   - What else do you want to know about your students?
   - How do you *reflect* on these data to create a focus for instruction for the whole class, small groups, and individual students?

ORIENT

We read aloud, give directions, deliver that lesson—teachers tend to just jump in and get to it—because we are so pressed for time. What we've noticed, however, is that when we jump too quickly, we may miss important things. That's why our first step is to *orient* ourselves to what's going on across the classroom. This provides us opportunity to take a pulse. We ask ourselves, "What are students up to? What do they need, if anything, to lift their learning?" This takes maybe one to two minutes. Here's when and how this can go:

Orient	
When	**How/Look-Fors** **Focus: Engagement, Tone, Behaviors**
As students are settling into work time—two minutes after you've released them from the whole group minilesson	• Which students know what to do? What are they using to support their efforts? • Who is already settled in and reading? • Which students are lost or confused? Why? What's missing for them? • Who is "milling around" or avoiding? Why? • Who is helping others figure out what to do? • Has the classroom gone from movement, shuffling of bodies and materials, to a quieter, productive hum?
In between the times you are meeting with small groups—as one group goes back to work time and another group is coming to meet with you	
In between the times you are conferring one-to-one with students—as you move from one student to the next	

NOTICE

Then, we kick it up a notch and notice. We nudge ourselves to prioritize studying students, both academically and socially. We *notice* and ask ourselves, "What do students know, and what are they able to do?" and "Whom are students interacting with, and what is the focus of those interactions?" We go after collecting evidence that answers our questions by observing what we see and hear and labeling why it matters to student learning. Eventually, we can mine our data for patterns and trends. Our hope is that our data will teach us what we need to know to provide students with "just in time" instruction and learning opportunities to lift their knowledge, skills, and understandings. Collecting our noticings feeds our instructional moves. This can be as quick as one to two minutes, or it can be longer, depending on how much you want to lean in to observe student behaviors and listen to students' interactions and dialogue. Here's when and how this can go:

Notice	
When	**How/Look-Fors** **Focus: Students' Approaches to Learning**
While students are interacting with you or peers during whole group or small group shared reading and writing experiences	• Which students are actively engaged and independent in their work time choices?
While students are working independently during independent work time	• Which students are not as actively engaged and independent as they could be? Why? What's in their way?
In between the times you are meeting with small groups—as one group goes back to work time and another group is coming to meet with you	• Who needs a partner or small group catch?
In between the times you are conferring one-to-one with students—as you move from one student to the next	

A perfect time to kidwatch is when two friends talk about books they have recently added to their "must read" pile.

TAKE STOCK

Student Work

You can extend kidwatching by looking at students' work. Of course, student work is the stuff kids produce, but it's also more than that. We broaden our definition of student work to capture important "data" about our students by including

- Student talk
- Student silence
- Student writing about their reading (things students make to show what they know)

For starters, push yourself to kidwatch two times during a reading workshop.

Kidwatching naturally leads us to ask questions, inquire, and reflect about ways we can lift our students and help them grow their reading muscles. Our wonderings become the backdrop for how we will study students next because kidwatching is cyclical—it gives us opportunities to have ongoing inquiry and reason for study across classrooms. For example, if two students are reluctant to share in book talks, we look across a few days to note consistencies and inconsistencies. We'll watch in order to sort out if texts are too hard or too easy, how peer interactions are progressing, and where and when interests are piqued. Questions beget questions that lead to the right instruction.

Some Effective Guiding Questions

Because we are "all things literacy" during reading workshop, we know we'd be remiss if we didn't *take stock* and ask, "What are students reading?" Some questions to keep in the forefront of our minds (and sometimes to post in the front of our notebooks!) while kidwatching include

- What do we know about the student as a reader, writer, thinker, creator, and doer?
- What do we want to know more about?
- From our observations, what are some possible literacy invitations that could *lift* the student's knowledge, skills, and understandings?
- What does the student like to read, and why?
- Whom does the student like to talk with and learn from?
- What does the student need that he or she is not getting or may not be able to get independently (without support)?
- What are the opportunities for small groups?

Adding these layers broadens our focus and keeps us astutely aware that if we really want to uncover what students know and are able to do, we need to look across multiple sources of data. If we want students to be working in small groups to develop their reading abilities, we need to widen our lens—especially if we believe that students show us what they know by reading, writing, talking, creating, and doing. Sometimes this is a quick gathering of data. Other times we take our time so that we don't miss important information that would help us create opportunities for lifting students' reading. Here's when and how this can go:

Take Stock	
When	**How/Look-Fors** **Focus: Students' Focus** **While Learning**
While students are interacting with you or peers during whole group or small group shared reading and writing experiences	What are students reading? • What kinds of books? • What genres? • What authors? • What themes? What kinds of issues or topics are students writing about? What are students making, designing, and/or creating as evidence to make their thinking visible?
While students are working independently during independent work time	
In between the times you are meeting with small groups—as one group goes back to work time and another group is coming to meet with you	
In between the times you are conferring one-to-one with students—as you move from one student to the next	

INQUIRE

It's natural for all of this data collection about our students to lead us to *inquire* and reflect about them and their ways of being as readers. We ask ourselves, "What do we see? What did we do today that readers need more of tomorrow? Where are we headed from here?" When we wonder about kids and their learning, we become the kidwatchers who show up every day to connect with kids—by seeing what concoction or elixir we can mix up together. Instead of just wondering or pondering in a light way, we put our knowledge of students all together and determine implications for our next steps *with* and *for* students. Our inquiries and reflections help us create a vision for the future.

Taking Time to Reflect

We almost made "reflection" a fifth step in kidwatching but decided that it's implicit in the inquiry phase. The truth is, reflection occurs in every moment as a teacher responds to learners. Sometimes we reflect *during* an experience or set of experiences in order to plan a focus for instruction or a set of learning progressions. Other times we reflect *after* taking notes, following a classroom learning experience.

Inquire	
When	**How/Look-Fors** **Focus: Create a Vision for** **Future Learning Opportunities**
When you are ready to reflect at the end of a • Minilesson • Small group • One-to-one conferring session • Reading workshop	Look across teacher reflection notes (from whole group, small group, or one-to-one interactions) and/or student work • What trends or patterns do I notice? • What are students' individual and collective strengths? Areas of need? Create a plan • What are the implications for creating new learning opportunities? • How will I plan whole group, small group, and one-to-one experiences going forward?
After knowledge checks that are built in across a unit of study	
At the end of a demonstration of learning (performance task) or at the end of a unit of study	
At the end of a grading period/semester or during progress report time	

You can use a kidwatching template to jump-start your practice of studying students. You can easily create this in your notebook or use the templates provided in the Appendix (pages 282–284). The following is an excerpt from a fourth-grade classroom reading workshop, during independent work time, where students are working in partnerships and wrestling with making meaning of short nonfiction texts. Julie provided the students with three different texts, on three different topics and with three different levels of difficulty. She described the text levels as mild, medium, and spicy. The students were asked to preview them and were given a choice and voice in determining which article met their needs.

What do you see/hear?	Why does it matter to student learning?
Jo and Kelsey look over two of the short texts and determine that they will read the text focused on gorillas.	Choice is important because when students have a voice, they are more engaged and motivated.
Kelsey suggests that they read the article silently before they discuss it. Jo agrees with Kelsey, and they begin reading independently. About two minutes into reading, Jo picks up her pencil and makes some annotations in the margin.	Students have autonomy to determine if they'd like to read together in their partnerships or alone before discussing the text/moving on to working in their Reader's Notebook. Students can determine how they will read and learn best for themselves.
Kelsey settles back in her chair. She moves around a bit and then grabs her article, pencil, and clipboard and moves over to the carpet area to finish her article.	Multiple places in the classroom serve as student work spaces. The more comfortable we are when we read/work, the more productive and invested we are in our task.
After about 10 minutes, Jo joins Kelsey on the carpet and waits for about a minute when Kelsey appears to be finished reading too. They get out their notebooks and begin working on their assignment.	Jo and Kelsey know what to do because a workshop Menu of Opportunities list is on the whiteboard. This is important because it provides a structure for students to build independence.

Tips for Getting Started

We suggest you begin kidwatching and try to make it a routine. You know . . . like brushing your teeth in the morning. You roll out of bed, and part of your morning routine is to brush your teeth. It's not extraordinary—it just needs to get done. Kidwatching sometimes begins like that. So, to get started, set a goal to kidwatch one time during the school day. Decide if you want to sit back with a clipboard or notebook or if you'll stand. Just find a time and a place and play around with it.

FIRST, TRY . . .

First, study kids using a wide lens. When students are reading and working independently, stand back and observe. What do you see and hear? Be general (e.g., "after about two minutes, everyone settled into a spot for independent reading") and move toward more specific (e.g., "Sofia, Adam, Natalie, Ian, and Tomas have all chosen to read the poem about rain"). Kidwatching can sometimes create immediate steps forward (e.g., "Jose has not turned a page in his book for the past eight minutes, so I'm going to confer with him and see what's going on") while at other times looking for patterns over time gives us insight into the moves we should make (e.g., "Camila's notebook entries are not capturing big ideas or main ideas in the texts she is reading; meeting with her in small group or one-on-one to read together and model are my next steps"). Remember that the goal is to kidwatch by *orienting* (engagement, tone, behaviors), *noticing* (students' approaches to learning), *taking stock* (students' focus while learning), and *inquiring* (creating a vision for future learning opportunities).

NEXT, TRY . . .

Once you've given kidwatching a try, kidwatch two times during a reading workshop. You might find your groove quickly. Once this happens, we believe you'll begin to go from a kidwatching routine to a kidwatching ritual. You'll know the difference because

- Your kidwatching ritual during reading workshop will become a meaningful practice. You will feel a real sense of purpose in why you are kidwatching.
- Your kidwatching ritual will lead you to that stage of inquiry we mentioned on page 99—that place where you use your kidwatching to create a vision for future learning opportunities.

USING A NOTE CATCHER

Find a note catcher that supports your efforts and that appeals to your note-taking style. Note catchers are treasures because they give us a space to collect evidence and ask questions, but they have to be personalized.

In the following chart, Barry shows how he uses the note catcher during a reading workshop. The students have just watched a minute-and-a-half video about a teenage graffiti artist who leaves a message on a building for his ailing sister. A small group of five readers has been asked to meet to discuss the video while the rest of the class takes a quick stretch break, chooses new books and texts, and/or reads independently.

Your Move	Noticings
Orient—Orient yourself and take a pulse to what's going on across the classroom. In general, what are students up to?	Students (18) are quickly settling and reading independently. Devon and Graysen are reviewing books to read at the student recommendation shelf. Five readers are situated at the small group table with their reading notebooks and pencils.
Notice—What do you see or hear academically and socially? • What do students know, and what are they able to do? • Whom are students interacting with, and what is the focus of those interactions?	**Whole Class Focus** Graysen and Devon have each found a student-recommended book and begun reading (five minutes from browsing to reading). **Small Group Focus** Sebastian is setting up the group for discussion by naming the purpose for their meeting—to talk about the story they have just observed. The conversation begins a bit haltingly with Sebastian asking for Isaac's take after Maggie, Sian, and Siaya have all supplied their initial insights. Sebastian then injects his thoughts. After about three minutes of talking about what happened, Sian suggests that what the teenage boy paints, a rose, is the symbolic metaphor for the video—a beautifully tragic tale of love and thorny pain. Isaac then says, "Yes, it is about pain." And he lofts the question, "How is it for the mom? What about money?" Is he inferring that having a child on a medical life machine must be costly? Sebastian expertly facilitates the conversation. Each of the five students has contributed at least four times. Sebastian notices a lull and suggests they share their notebook entries about the video. He begins, "Dear Black Night, I do not want to do it … but I have to." Sebastian is writing from the teenage boy's perspective and grasping what the teen is feeling and thinking.
Take Stock—What are students reading? Writing? Talking about? Creating? Doing? What is the evidence of their thinking?	The small group has been meeting for 10 minutes, and Sebastian is checking in to see who will share to the large group. Note: Be sure to have Sebastian recap what these students did so well in their discussions for tomorrow's minilesson. Possibly use Maggie's, Sian's, or Sebastian's notebook entry to highlight an example of how we gain insights into a character's thinking and feeling through writing.

Your Move	Noticings
Inquire—What inquiries do you have? As a kidwatcher, what are you wondering about? What does the whole class need? What types of small groups would be beneficial? What do individual students need?	The notes from reading over the students' Reader's Notebooks suggest that both Sebastian and Isaac struggle to infer motives and make deep insights about how a character feels and what the character thinks. After listening to their perceptive comments about the mom and the teenage boy, I am wondering: Will the way forward for these two be about coaching up their ability to write about their reading and specifically their power to infer or to give them more opportunities to talk about their reading? This also has implications for what I think I know about Olive, Devon, and Tim.

See the Appendix (pages 282–284) for kidwatching templates. We suggest using each as a starting point to create a note catcher that fits your needs, purpose, and style.

Using Your Notes to Form Small Groups

Kidwatch for a week. See what happens. Our guess is you'll have a lot of different notes in a lot of different formats and you'll wonder why in the world you are doing all of this note-taking about kids. Don't give up—this is all part of the process. Use your notes as your guide for making decisions about small groups. Take a look at this kidwatching grid from a fifth-grade classroom. The first three columns name the student and describe what we know and would like to know about the student. This is where *orienting*, *noticing*, and *taking stock* come into play. The last three columns are related to the *inquiry* part of kidwatching—taking everything we have learned and creating a vision for future learning opportunities.

	Orient, Notice, Take Stock			Inquire	
Name	**What do we know about the student as a reader/writer? (asset-based evidence)**	**What would we like to know more about?**	**What are some possible literacy invitations for the student?**	**What does the student need that he or she is not getting or may not be able to get independently?**	**What are some small group opportunities that might benefit the student?**
Joshua	Read comics this summer—*Batman* and *Archie*	Is this summer reading, or is it about a move to more visual entries?	Graphic novel—*The Lightning Thief*	Attention or validity? Support moving from visual texts to more print-heavy text?	Comic strip inquiry group Superheroes group—what makes a hero a hero? Faults or invincible?

(Continued)

Name	Orient, Notice, Take Stock		Inquire		
	What do we know about the student as a reader/writer? (asset-based evidence)	**What would we like to know more about?**	**What are some possible literacy invitations for the student?**	**What does the student need that he or she is not getting or may not be able to get independently?**	**What are some small group opportunities that might benefit the student?**
Holly	Knows all the words to every song from *Hamilton*; reads realistic fiction— "girls and growing up" at school but not at home	Is it the music, the play, and/or the history that fascinates her? What's keeping her from reading outside of school?	Share passion with classmates Lunch time YouTube review of *Hamilton* with a couple of friends	A place to share her enthusiasm for stage, history, and Lin-Manuel Miranda's lyrics and rap Inclusion in a book club?	*Hamilton* lyrics and history study Or author study— Lin-Manuel Miranda Book club—i.e., *Counting by 7s*
Anthony	Ended fifth grade by reading Alan Gratz's *Code of Honor*	What topics interest him that Gratz has written about? War? Baseball?	Read *Prisoner B-3087* Book talk—*Code of Honor* Watch trailer	A chance to talk about an unfamiliar new author in our class?	Alan Gratz author study Partner read *Prisoner B-3087* Short war stories group
Jasmine	Dystopian fan— turns over 500 pages a week; editor to class magazine	She is flourishing . . . What's the next move?	Reviews for the magazine Compare and contrast two different series	Can moving Jaz from the introspective work of reading by herself to sharing with others add new levels of understanding about reading and herself?	Dystopian book club New ground— short story study to inform her writing
Roberto	Loves hockey— dad coaches him	Does he have an interest in reading about sports and hockey?	Hockey cards, websites, writing own sports blog, hockey magazine, hockey history, hockey practice drills	Can matching Roberto up in a team of sports readers give him more purpose for reading on his own?	Sports kids with sports stories or biographies

TAKING TIME TO REFLECT

Once you've done some note-taking, either in a template or by jotting notes in your notebook, continue your inquiry by analyzing and reflecting on what you know.

Ask yourself what kind of notes you are taking that are informing

- Your teaching (whole group, small group, one-to-one)
- Your specific interactions with students (book matching, reading volume, skills/strategies)
- Your conversations with colleagues (curriculum integration, resources, assessments)

EXAMPLE OF USING NOTES TO SUPPORT A READER

Let's take a look at a student from the fifth-grade kidwatching example on pages 103–104 and how that information helps us make decisions about ways to support and push students' reading. Roberto was a hockey enthusiast. While generally quiet in class, he enjoyed sharing his daily notebook entries about his hockey games and love for his favorite team, the Minnesota Wild. Roberto spent a lot of time in the car being shuffled back and forth to the ice rink, a 45-minute drive. Not surprisingly, Roberto found little time to read outside of school. Ninety minutes in the car and two-hour hockey practices can do that. Curiously, Roberto did not see reading about hockey as an option in his daily reading diet. So we pulled together a group of four boys—Keats, a soccer player who had lived in England and loved reading *Match*, a British football magazine; Brett, an athlete who played all sports well and read a ton of "how to" baseball books and sports biographies; Baden, a sports fan who devoured both *Sports Illustrated* and *Sports Illustrated for Kids*; and Roberto.

Big Advice

As you are building relationships with students and gathering data about them, having a system in place for storing and accessing these data is important. If you need some new ideas, see the *Cult of Pedagogy* by Jennifer Gonzalez for more (www.cultofpedagogy.com/relationship-building).

We began by talking informally about what they enjoyed reading. Roberto asked if *Sports Illustrated* ever had hockey stories, and Baden said he thought so but he didn't pay much attention to that sport. We moved back and forth from books and magazines to specific "must reads." Knowing it isn't enough to simply suggest ideas for reading, we lifted the question up to the group—how could we make it easier for kids who love sports to find and read sports stories? The group decided on bringing in their own sports reading treasures, labeling a basket *Sports*, and meeting in a week to talk more about their reading. We ended reading workshop by having the boys talk about their "sports basket" idea and why they loved to read about sports. The sports basket grew in the days that followed from student contributions, and Roberto brought in his *Youth Hockey* magazine. Subsequently, we noticed Roberto's "reading at home" bookmark was packed with sports stories to read in the car.

Kids love to belong. We all do. Instead of making this singularly about Roberto not reading, we were able to harness the unidentified literacy of reading about sports. Students named it. Students supported it. And the work of the small group created a "safe place" for students to both talk about their interest in sports and add fuel to their literary sports passion.

> Kids love to belong.
> We all do.

As one season turns into another, we know that the work of learning about our students is ongoing. We revisit their photos of the books they have read each month, and we continue having conversations with them about how much time they are spending turning pages at home. Our job is to stay tuned in to their ever-evolving interests and literacy habits. And this pool of information will continue to aid us in shaping small groups.

To Get to What You See Here, **Try This**

1. Preview texts with a small group or one-to-one and kidwatch.

2. Study kids and note what texts kids gravitate toward—what they grab and begin reading, how they interact with the text and with one another, facial expressions, and how noisy they are (willingness and interest in talking is a sign of a motivated and engaged reader).

3. Use your kidwatching as an opportunity for authentic, natural formative assessment.

4. Take note of how long students preview before digging in. Don't hurry them up because previewing is a wise choice as a reader. Don't let them dillydally too long because they will need time to read.

Photo by Rachel Langosch

Four-Step Process for Going From Kidwatching to Small Group

Here's a four-step process for taking all of your notes about kids, thinking through possibilities, and creating small groups.

1. STUDY KIDS AND STUDENT WORK

Kidwatching has two parts. First, it's about knowing the kids—their likes and dislikes, what they do in their free time, and what they aspire to do, see, and become. The second part of kidwatching is coupling your observations with students' work when making student groupings. We explore assessment, through collecting and sorting student work, in Chapter Six. Here, we'll give you a glimpse of how to use student work to inform small group learning opportunities.

Deciding what student work to collect—both at the beginning of a unit and along the way—is important in figuring out how to meet students' needs. When we operationalize collecting and using student work, we systematize it. It's not the same type of systematizing as you see in a machine model approach. Rather, it's first building a routine—a must-do—to regularly collect student work and then creating a ritual of studying work that makes students' thinking visible. Revisit the "Our Kidwatching 2.0 Protocol" section on page 94 to dig into this work.

What Would You Do?

Look across your notes about students. Pick four. What do you know about these readers? What are some possible literacy invitations for each student? What does the student need that he or she is not getting or may not be able to get independently? What are some small group opportunities?

_____

_____

_____

_____

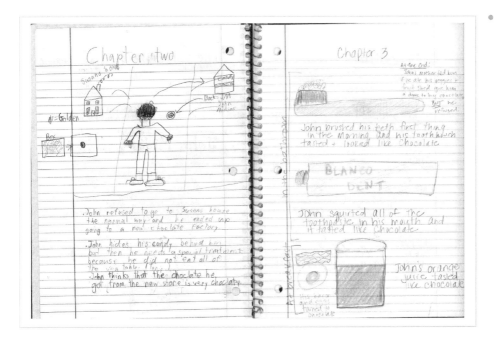

Students will hold thinking in Reader's Notebooks in their own ways.

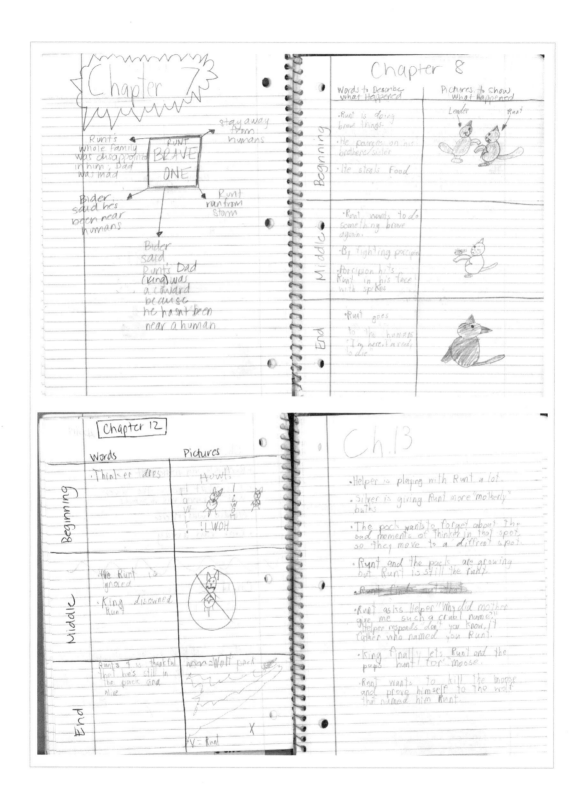

Chapter 7

Runt's whole family was disappointed in him; Dad was mad

RUNT BRAVE ONE

stay away from humans

Runt ran from storm

Bider said he's been near humans

Bider said Runt's Dad (king) was a coward because he hasn't been near a human

Chapter 8

	Words to Describe what Happened	Pictures to show What Happened
Beginning	• Runt is doing brave things. • He pounces on his brothers/sisters • He steals food	Leader Runt
Middle	• Runt wants to do something brave again. • By fighting porcupine • porcupion hits Runt in his face with spikes	
End	• Runt goes to the humans "I'm here, I'm ready to die"	

Chapter 12

	Words	Pictures
Beginning	• Thinker dies	Howl! HOW !LWOH
Middle	• We Runt is ignored • King disowned Runt	
End	Runt's ? is thankful that he's still in the pack and alive	= Wolf pack X ✓ = Runt

Ch. 13

• Helper is playing with Runt a lot.

• Silver is giving Runt more "motherly" baths

• The pack wants to forget about the sad moments of Thinker in that spot so they move to a different spot.

• Runt and the pack are growing but Runt is still the runt.

• ~~Runt finds out that~~

• Runt asks Helper "Why did mother give me such a cruel name?" Helper responds don't you know, ti ? Father who named you Runt.

• King finally lets Runt and the pups hunt for moose.

• Runt wants to kill the moose and prove himself to the wolf that named him Runt

Students discuss text(s) by sharing out big takeaways and wonderings with their group members.

Photo by Christian Ford

Students will articulate how their thinking is changing and/or growing by responding to the following prompt. Using this prompt across time will give insight to the big ideas in texts as well as how student thinking is changing and/or growing.

> I used to think _____.
>
> Then I read/discussed/studied/inquired about _____.
>
> Now I think _____.
>
> I'm still wondering _____.

See exit ticket templates on page 286 in the Appendix.

2. SET GOALS

Kidwatching helps you create goals with and for students. When you lean in to what you learn as you observe and interact with students, you can create big intended takeaways for each student in the small group. Create an overarching goal for students in the small group. Some examples may include

- Reading widely and deeply
- Making thinking about reading visible to others
- Articulating changes in your thinking (about characters, central ideas, theme, etc.) as you read across texts

3. DECIDE HOW OFTEN GROUPS MEET

If you don't have a plan for how often groups will meet, some groups will meet too often, while others won't meet often enough. Planning ahead and making time and space for small groups to meet is an important step. (See Chapter Three to review schedules and Chapters Eight and Nine for an in-depth look at planning for small group learning experiences.)

4. FIND AND USE MENTOR TEXTS

Deciding what texts you will use—in whole group, in small group, and one-to-one with students *and* for shared and independent reading experiences—is an important part of the planning process because it creates direction and focus for the group. (See Chapter Seven for an in-depth look at curating mentor texts for small group learning experiences.)

Example of Small Group Work
Based on Kidwatching Data

Let's take an example from the classroom. Julie was working with a group of fourth graders, and she heard a student conversation about all of the bridges that surrounded the New York area. That sparked an idea! Launch a small group focused on studying all kinds of bridges. Of course, Julie knew that the fourth-grade Bridges group wasn't going to really be just about bridges. The study of bridges was merely a conduit for meeting curricular goals. With students' interests at the forefront, Julie whipped up a plan for content, including frontloading needed background knowledge and new vocabulary. So often, we do the opposite when planning for small group instruction. We outline the content that needs to be taught—such as unpacking a comprehension strategy or reading fluently— before we ever think about the kiddos' interests. Julie and Barry's stance suggests flipping the model. Let us show you what we mean.

At the onset of her planning, here is what Julie knows, and wants to know, about her students in the Bridges group.

Who	Noticings	Wonderings
Aiden	• Sports enthusiast • Oldest of three boys • Likes to put things together and take things apart • Has a favorite green sweatshirt • Appears to know everyone because he says hi to any passerby • Has been simmering (or stuck) in *Sports Illustrated for Kids Year in Sports* books for a long time • Has a personal goal of "reading a really long book"	• Does he have a reading spot and time set aside to read at home? • When he builds with LEGO bricks, does he read the direction booklet or tinker until he gets it on his own? • What is it, specifically, that he likes about the structure/content in *Sports Illustrated*, and would he like some of those features in different texts?
Cameron	• Speaks Romanian in addition to English • Offered up the original idea of studying bridges in a small group • Plays soccer, but doesn't really want to play anymore • Likes to draw/sketch with pencil in his notebook • Interested in trains and building other models • Loves his iPad in his free time • Jumps from book to book in the classroom; can explain the gist of what's going on but only surface-level understanding	• Does he have a special notebook for his sketches, and/or would he benefit from *sketching to stretch his understanding* in reading? • What models has he built? • Does he know about the David Macaulay books? • How do we help him begin and finish a book while monitoring his own understanding along the way?
Jordan	• Best friends are boys • Loves horses • Takes lots of dance classes (hip-hop is her favorite) • Wants to be a teacher when she grows up • *Loves* Kate DiCamillo • When reading independently, she explains that she has trouble staying focused; says she can hear everything going on around the room	• How does she respond to the rhythm of poetry? • Is there something to connect her love of horses to bridges? • How can she take a leadership role and harness her inner teacher? • Should she self-assess her reading atmosphere and study what works best for her style?

(Continued)

Who	Noticings	Wonderings
Jennifer	• Quiet, deep thinker who connects ideas together • Spends her summer with cousins in Maine • "I don't like to read, but I'm not sure why not" • Interested in math and thinks that is her "best subject" because she "knows when she's right and when she's wrong" • Middle child—older sister, younger brother • Hates hand-me-downs! (clothing)	• What bridges are in Maine that might be of interest to her? • How, when, and in what ways should we connect the math behind bridges to our inquiry?

Study Kids and Student Work: While planning, Julie decided that students would hold their thinking in their Reader's Notebooks—some optional graphic organizers would be shared with the students while others would be student created.

I already know _____.

Then I read _____.

Now I know _____.

I'm wondering _____.

See exit ticket templates on page 286 in the Appendix.

See the Appendix for similar versions of this exit ticket template.

What I already know They connect to pieces of land.
Then I read all about the Golden Gate Bridge
Now I know It is 1.7 miles long. It was opened in 1937. More than 1.8 billion people crossed it. Emperor Norton thought about it.
I'm wondering who built it? Was it ever Golden?

What I already know hey normally stand over water
Then I read article about briges
Now I know the Brooklyn Bridge is made out of steelc and it is so old but still strong.
I'm wondering how long it took to build the Brooklyn bridge.

Set Goals: Create an overarching goal for students in the small group. The goal was for students to

- Read voluminously
- Read widely and deeply

Student	Goal(s)
Aiden	• Identify and reflect upon preferred reading spots and times for independent reading at school and at home • Increase access and choice, support as he reads longer texts across time
Cameron	• Work to sketch/annotate across one book to hold thinking and monitor own meaning making when reading
Jordan	• Identify and reflect upon preferred reading spots and times for independent reading at school and at home
Jennifer	• Identify strategies that help her know when she is "right" or ways she can monitor her own understanding of the text

Decide How Often Groups Meet: With the goals in mind, Julie created a schedule for the students.

Details	Rationale
• Sometimes the Bridges small group meets for 25 minutes, while other times they will meet for 45 minutes	• This will give a balance between small group meeting time focused on bridges and time to read independently
• Sometimes the Bridges small group will meet with Julie, while other times they will meet without her	• This will give students time to work alongside of Julie; it will also give Julie the flexibility to meet with other small groups
• Sometimes there is no small group meeting time	• This will give students time to read independently, give Julie time to meet with other small groups or one-to-one, or lengthen workshop time for whole group instruction or share out opportunities

Set a Three-Week Small Group Schedule

(Total amount of reading workshop time = 45 minutes)

Week	Monday	Tuesday	Wednesday	Thursday	Friday
1	Bridges	Bridges	Bridges	Bridges	
2	Bridges	Bridges		Bridges	Bridges
3	Bridges		Bridges	Bridges	Bridges

Note: Blue shows when Julie meets with the Bridges small group.

Find and Use Mentor Texts: What will kids consume? What will they read, watch, and listen to in order to unpack text and grow new ideas? Since Julie's small group's inspiration originally came from a *Time for Kids* two-page article focused on the Tappan Zee Bridge, the kickoff for this small group was a revisit of that text. This short text became an anchor, or mentor text, from which the students would begin to build their knowledge about "all things bridges."

We dedicate an in-depth look at curating your mentors in Chapter Seven, but we will focus on text curation in this example to illustrate the importance of curating with specific students in mind. For the small group described earlier, Julie wanted students to look beyond the long, chapter book type of text or an entire nonfiction book focused on bridges. She wanted to bolster volume, access, and choice through the use of short texts. While some of the texts would be the same for this small group, the two-pocket folders (described below) would also include short texts that might be inspirational for each student and/or springboard new learning based on Julie's knowledge of students through kidwatching.

The website devoted to the construction of the Tappan Zee Bridge (www.newny bridge.com) provided a wealth of resources that students in the small group could dive into depending on interest and inquiry. Some topics were directly related (construction timeline, statistics related to the bridge, time-lapsed video showcasing progress over time) while other topics were an offshoot and provided other opportunities for reading and study (amount of steel used to construct the bridge, the super crane, change in name from Tappan Zee Bridge to the Governor Mario M. Cuomo Bridge, falcons nesting on the bridge, etc.).

Gather Sufficient Texts for a Three-Week Cycle: Curating doesn't mean cutting it too thin! Make sure you have a great range of texts so students have choice. For this study, Julie and her students filled a bucket or basket with books, poems, infographics, two-page spreads, building kits, and other related resources focused on bridges for the small group to dive into each time they met. In addition, each student had a two-pocket folder. In one pocket, the students stored texts (those they were reading with the small group as well as independently). In the other pocket, they stored their Reader's Notebook for easy access and use.

OUR CURATED TEXTS

Finding texts that match students' curiosities, passions, habits, and needs is our number-one goal. Along with this goal are uncovering texts that kids enjoy so much that they don't want to put them down. These are the kinds of texts that students read and read and read because they find joy in what they are learning.

Following are examples of texts that Julie and her students curated for the three-week Bridges group:

Books:

Finger, B. (2015). *13 bridges children should know*. New York, NY: Prestel.

Hurley, M. (2011). *The world's most amazing bridges* (Landmark Top Tens). Oxford, England: Raintree.

Johmann, C., & Rieth, E. (1999). *Bridges: Amazing structures to design, build and test* (Kaleidoscope Kids). Charlotte, VT: Williamson.

Latham. D. (2012). *Bridges and tunnels: Investigate feats of engineering with 25 projects* (Build It Yourself). White River Junction, VT: Nomad Press.

Ratliff, T. (2009). *You wouldn't want to work on the Brooklyn Bridge! An enormous project that seemed impossible*. London, England: Franklin Watts.

Infographics: Bridge infographics can be found in lots of places. Do a search, and you'll see what we mean. Students searched and selected some infographics related to bridges that they thought looked interesting. Julie focused instruction on reading the infographic *and* determining the source and validity of the information presented.

Videos: There is a lot of general information about bridges and a lot of information about specific bridges or bridge types. *Time for Kids* and *National Geographic*, just to name two, are great resources for short informative videos about bridges. Sometimes, depending on the video, purpose, and length, students watch the video more than once. Big ideas and important details from the video can be captured individually or collectively through an anchor chart or note catcher.

Calendars: A big part of our work is mining for texts that teach. One option Julie harnessed for the Bridges group was pictures and text found in wall calendars. Go to any calendar aisle at a bookstore and find a calendar about a specific topic. You will probably find that it's a calendar that teaches through pictures and words. Helping kids know that this counts as text and counts as reading is an important life skill.

Text Specifically Chosen Based on Kidwatching: Aiden was excited about reading *Where Is the Brooklyn Bridge?* by Megan Stine (Stine & Who HQ, 2016), so a copy of this book was added to his folder.

Since Cameron is interested in building, Julie decided that giving him opportunities to tinker around, while reading a set of directions, would be important. This sparked an idea that maybe one of his work products could be focused on gathering some building materials (LEGO bricks, blocks, pipe cleaners, paper, etc.) and writing directions for creating a bridge for others. Julie decided that she would make everyday items such as newspaper, cardboard, and pipe cleaners, along with directions found in books or online for building bridges available in case other group members wanted to do some building too. Julie also encouraged students to consider using Lincoln Logs, LEGO bricks, or K'Nex to build.

Helping Jordan make a connection between bridges and horses was important—but it was tricky. While several chapter books referenced both, Jordan wasn't biting. Julie thought that maybe she could *lift* Jordan's reading muscles and dip into her interests by pairing the Brooklyn Bridge and elephants. She curated two books for her, which included *Twenty-One Elephants and Still Standing* by April Jones Prince (2005) and *Twenty-One Elephants* by Phil Bildner (2004).

To inspire Jordan's interest in rhythm, Julie included some poetry in her two-pocket folder. For example, Shel Silverstein's poem "The Bridge," which begins with the intriguing line "This bridge will only take you halfway there" was a favorite.

Texts Specifically Chosen for Jennifer: Since Jennifer loves math, helping her think about the math behind bridge building provided a fun inquiry. Math is woven throughout the website (www.newnybridge.com) that captures the history and progress of the new Tappan Zee Bridge being built in New York. This site has a lot of information that can be calculated and compared, just Jennifer's style. (For more on curating, refer to Chapter Seven.)

One Last Thing

A friend recently jumped back into teaching after a multiyear hiatus. She had the night-before jitters and said that she wasn't ready. Julie reminded her that she *was* ready because to get started she just needed some important things: (1) her favorite notebook and pen, (2) her eyes and ears wide open, and (3) her curriculum and pedagogy ready to put into action. While these might be good reminders at the beginning of the year, they hold true every day. If we want to know our kids so that we can support them in all the ways imaginable, we have to know that each day brings about opportunities to kidwatch. Whether you jot student observations in your notebook or open a new Word document on your tablet, taking stock of what you see and hear makes all the difference in the moves you make next with and for your students. Find your method. Find your kidwatching way. You'll be better equipped to dive into the work each day because you will know more about your students than you ever thought possible.

CHAPTER FIVE

Pivoting Into Flexible Groups

(because it's the teacher moves that keep readers moving forward)

It was late February. Outside, the sky was dolphin gray, and the weeks of unending cold gave Julie and her fourth graders a bit of cabin fever. Julie looked across her reading workshop; students were reading independently pretty well, despite the usual shuffling of chairs and a whisper or a book dropping here and there. Some kids were snuggled in beanbags, and a couple of small groups were chatting away. As Julie studied her small groups in action, she jotted notes on the "What Makes a Hero?" group. Matthew, Davis, Tessie, and Maddie were showing signs of being "done." Their conversations were dull and stilted. Julie reflected on what she had observed. At the onset of this small group work, her goal had been to create instruction focused on student-generated, compelling questions and topics that would drive the work at the table. Julie wondered now, "Since we aren't finished with the small group experiences we'd planned for the Heroes group, but I sense the students are ready to move on, what does my gut say we should do next? Do I act on the vibe I'm getting from my students? How do I weigh that against my desire to stick with the Heroes mini unit as planned?" Within that very school day, Julie had her answer. We share her decision-making steps on page 127, but

Photo by Rachel Langosch

for now it suffices to say that kids constantly give us powerful feedback—and it's what we do with that feedback that is the focus of this chapter.

[T]ruly successful decision making relies on a balance between deliberate and instinctive thinking.

—Malcolm Gladwell

The point is this: Making decisions about how to move forward is multi-faceted. Students are better served when we marry what we know about kids' wants and needs with our unit plans. We don't want to shortchange it by leaving out the important data we collect by kidwatching and what we learn by assessing kids through their work. Educators Gravity Goldberg and Renee Houser call it *thin slicing*, a term borrowed from research and popularized in Malcolm Gladwell's book *Blink* (2013). Thin slicing is the "ability to find patterns in situations and behavior based on a narrow slice of experience" (Gladwell, 2013, p. 23). In *What Do I Teach Readers Tomorrow?* (2017), Goldberg and Houser assert that teachers "can thin-slice and make moment-to-moment decisions by looking, listening, identifying, and choosing" (p. 7). Our ability to size up a situation, make decisions, and act quickly is what makes small group instruction powerful because we are not statically sorting by ability but by dynamically growing readers.

Two Essential Questions This Chapter Helps You Answer

1. How do I manage to create stability for readers while also regularly switching up small groups, across the school year in order to respond to students' curiosities, passions, habits, and needs?

2. When is it my role, as teacher/facilitator, to listen in versus join in to small group learning experiences? Why does figuring out my role matter to student growth?

Beliefs

In the previous chapter, our beliefs tilted toward a general mindset. We put forth the habit of trusting your power of observation and familiarity with your student readers to help you gather the truest, most valuable information. In short, we taught you *how* to look and listen. Each day. Always. Informally. Here, in this chapter, our beliefs circle around the decision making you often do *in the midst* of small groups as new needs arise. *Pivoting* is the "pocket strategy" Barry pulls out when he suddenly realizes a group needs a clear example of an unreliable narrator; it's when Julie, having read about seventh grader Jose's interest in Tupac Shakur, deftly includes Jose in the biography group that is just forming. Like a poker player who plays the ace, pivoting into flexible groups has to do with timing and instinct. Like the work of a ship captain, it's the work done quickly when a storm comes out of nowhere and re-navigating is needed. Like in basketball, it's the jump cut when a player sees an opening before it's there.

Our Beliefs About Pivoting

We believe . . .	How it shows up in our work . . .
Like a good athlete, we reading teachers are adept at responding in the moment. We create responsive groups to meet students' needs. By assuming a stance of constant curiosity about our readers, we can be quicker on their feet in changing instructional direction.	We study our kids so we know what makes them tick and what they need to grow. This gives us the know-how to group them in ways unique to them. We pivot intuitively and instinctively to meet student needs.
If small groups are static, we risk instruction being static too. Intentionally and regularly switching things up—refocusing and adjusting groups and instruction—yields big takeaways.	Always meeting with the same kids on Mondays or only in response to students' reading levels is filled with missed opportunities. Switching groups up regularly and in creative ways keeps everyone, including the teacher, interested in the work.
Students are highly motivated and engaged by the social energy of their peers, and because peer dynamics are always changing, our groups are often changing.	Kids like to hang out and learn with and from their peers. Flexible grouping motivates and engages everyone in the room.

Now, a confession: This chapter was a bear to write. It took 20 cups of coffee, three conference calls with our editor, and more cutting and editing than James Cameron did when creating the movie *Titanic*. We confess this for two reasons: First, making decisions takes experience, so give yourself permission to get good at it over time. Confidently knowing and flexibly grouping learners truly takes years of teaching. The second reason we admit our own struggle to structure this chapter is that because we know "pivoting" is inherently sophisticated; we decided to organize this chapter in as easy a way as possible.

How This Chapter Is Organized

We start with "The List of Reasons for Pivoting"—a sheer list of reasons you might change up groups—to give you a quick dunk in the possibilities. Next, we provide a section called "Types of Groups to Pivot Into and Out Of." These are engaging types of groups we've done in Grades 3 through 8 that students seem to love wherever we've coached, from Los Angeles to Long Island and everywhere in between. Built into each type of group described are these how-tos for getting started with pivoting.

Signs for when it might be time to pivot into small groups: Generally speaking, look for signs of "want" (what topic, theme, or curiosity is surfacing in student conversation and worth exploring in a small group?) or "need" (what are kids struggling with, and how can we pivot into helping them?). Other reasons include

- To lift the level of discourse about a text that was read during shared reading
- To review unfamiliar vocabulary that is pertinent to texts being read
- To preview texts and activate background knowledge and inspire curiosity
- To clear up misinterpretations

Tips for listening in: Get to know more about what students know, understand, and are able to do to figure out what they need next.

Tips for joining in: Teach into the reading, writing, and talk at the table in order to

- Deepen background knowledge and understanding
- Lift misconceptions
- Support proficient reading behaviors and practices
- Inspire new ideas and learning

Tips for noticing when it might be time to pivot: Change up small groupings based on students' wants or needs.

Signs a small group is ready to disband: Generally, look for evidence that students are ready to move on to something new or to read independently. Some signs include

- Kids tell you they are ready to move on
- Conversation at the small group table decreases
- Your curricular calendar notes that it is time to begin a new unit of study and shift the focus to new content
- The small group dynamics are leading to skinny insights and lacking in energy

Then, we provide a section on "Language for Joining In" to give you some talking points for various scenarios when you are leaning in to make decisions on whether the group can deepen its work or should disband. And finally, in a section called "Troubleshooting," we provide practical solutions for common glitches that can arise with flexible groups.

The List of Reasons for Pivoting

Got your favorite pair of sneakers on? Your favorite sports drink? Ready to hear the squeak of linoleum on your classroom floor? Here we get you moving through the reasons you will want to literally and figuratively pivot amid your readers.

CURRICULUM-CENTERED REASONS

Your unit of study or curricular plan is your playbook for where you intend to go. Like a brilliant coach, you watch over the players, and when you see that the plans need adjusting because the challenge is greater than you'd anticipated, or players are off their game or outplaying your plans, you do not wait—you act decisively in the moment. You pivot to support students with more practice and feedback, with assurance that this small group move will increase the power of the curriculum journey. You might pivot for curriculum-centered reasons when

- You notice students are enjoying a variety of different poems during your poetry unit, so you choose to co-construct poetry topics/categories that fit their interests. These poetry categories veer into student-chosen poetry groups.
- You get new books for your classroom library, and you want to get the literature in students' hands. You create groups so that kids can get up close to the new resources in hopes that they take them and read. Over the next few months, students will gather again in groups to book talk these titles and others.
- You notice some girls are disenchanted at the conclusion of your Ancient Egypt unit, so you match their interest in clothes by inviting them into an inquiry group about beauty and fashion during Ancient Egyptian times.
- You notice in a whole group lesson that students "got it" in terms of understanding a concept, so you decide to collapse the planned three days of small group into a single session.

- You recognize that two of the four small groups comparing and contrasting countries' nationalism during World War I are drowning in a sea of facts and dates, but the other two groups are diving into the texts and finding the big ideas and connections, so you mix up groups so the students who have a good handle on the discussion now peer coach those who need more.

- You notice that kids keep getting tripped up on some content vocabulary while reading about Syria and the refugee dilemma. You "push pause," and invite small groups to read a series of articles with varying levels of difficulty in order to build up background knowledge and unpack new vocabulary that will deepen students' understanding of the issues.

SOCIAL-EMOTIONAL REASONS

Kids often show up wearing their emotions on their sleeves. We read our students, and we pivot, making decisions to support them. This might happen by giving students special attention and encouragement in a small group or by tipping fellow students to help tend to their classmate's tender feelings. Sometimes we even pivot by making space for students if or when they need to step away from a small group. These kinds of decisions help ensure our classrooms are kind, supportive, trusting, and responsive. They lead to a community filled with students who have a great sense of belonging. You might pivot for social-emotional reasons when

- You find out that you are getting a new student, and the school year is already in full swing—kids have settled in, and a community has formed. During independent work time, you hang with the new student and invite four or five students at a time to join you so that students can get to know one another in a small group setting. If you learn that the new student is shy and nervous, you might create groups of three and switch them up a lot in the first week so that the new student gets a chance to meet everyone but in small doses. If the student doesn't speak English proficiently, you might buddy him or her with a specific person for a while, and every time groups switch around, this pair sticks together and joins a new group, which provides consistency and support for the new English language learner.

> *Kids show up often wearing their emotions on their sleeves. We read our students, and we pivot, making decisions to support them.*

- You learn that someone in the learning community has experienced loss or significant change. You carefully select and group students to read literature that gives perspective to the struggle or challenge. Small groups give kids a safe space to discuss and talk about their feelings and opportunities to share some of their writing about the loss or change.
- You spot a pattern in the way kids self-select their own groups, noticing that students have become more exclusive in their choices. You detect that cliques are beginning to form, and you decide that letting kids self-select groups with a few ground rules (e.g., find group members that you haven't worked with in the last few weeks) might help. As the teacher, you could also determine that teacher-selected groups is the way to go for a while, guaranteeing more diversity in group dynamics.
- You look across student work samples and notice patterns that indicate a few students are showing signs of overdependence on other students. You encourage collaboration, so it's not unusual for students to co-construct meaning together. You move kids around and regroup students into new small groups to give them some breathing room and a chance to think and work to their individual potential.
- You see two students who you sense are going to get along, even though they don't hang out together; matching them in a small group might encourage strong peer collaboration between them.
- You notice a significant local, national, or world event occurs that behooves you to jump-start new groups that indirectly or obliquely address the topic and adjacent issues.

INDIVIDUAL READER REASONS

Small groups place readers together for purposeful reasons—skill and strategy work, building on and sharing interests and topics, developing keen inquiries together, enhancing a reading diet, and so many more. These engaging small groups give students opportunities to voice their opinions, insights, and questions. They expose student thinking, and in doing so, they surface individual misconceptions, tangled arguments, and shallow connections. Good teaching involves both pivoting during the small group interaction to untangle and deepen individual understanding and making arrangements for follow-up lessons or experiences. You might pivot for individual reader reasons when

- You notice a student struggling with taking notes, so you invite the student to a small group focused on note-taking and holding thinking where all members of the group share their notes. The students also explain why their note-taking strategy works for them.

- You notice a student who knows a ton about black holes and time travel, and you invite her to create a reading group, share her insights and fascination, and collect reading materials for the group.

- You notice a student's reading volume has decreased over the past few weeks, so you partner him with a prolific reader, who you know is compatible, and decide together on a group reading goal.

- You notice a student dominates small group conversation, so you ask her to be the "conversation counter," keeping tally of who talks. Later you ask this student for ideas on how to involve all reading group members.

- You notice during the knee-to-knee share-out after the minilesson that a few kids are confused about how to identify the main idea of a short story. In order to clear up confusion, you invite the small group to meet with you to reinforce the skill.

- You are meeting a small group of six students to read some high-interest texts about the environment. During the small group, you notice two students are struggling to comprehend the text. You meet briefly with these two after the small group to double-check for understanding, knowing that further pivoting may be necessary.

The Teacher's Role

The previous list is meant not to be comprehensive but to sketch the possibilities for you. As you no doubt gleaned, you have a few roles—lots of observing, pattern seeking, and even physically moving students from table to table in your quest to move their reading forward. Here is a recap of the four roles teachers take on. You are

1. A recorder and reflector of students' growth (mostly done when *listening in*)

2. A modeler of expectations and reading moves (done when *joining in* or during lessons that surround the flexible group when you want to demonstrate a strategy, reading habit, and so on)

3. A staunch advocate for *readers* doing the problem solving, not you (done when behaviors or small groups need a boost but only long enough to prompt student problem solving and thinking)

4. A teacher-mentor who reflects often and even asks students how they are doing in a small group, so you are always ready to pivot (done during whole group, small group, or one-on-one settings and used to make decisions about future learning opportunities)

THE ROLES IN ACTION: JULIE'S DECISIONS ABOUT THE HEROES GROUP

Look back at the chapter opening, and Julie's Heroes group. Remember that she listened in and recorded notes, and here's the decision making that led to her "pivot":

Reflection: "What Makes a Hero?" Group

- Energy is stale. The students in this small group aren't jumping up and hopping into the small group work as they were two weeks ago. There are more off-task behaviors.
- Group members are asking fewer questions about the texts in front of them. Texts are no longer leading them to ask for more.
- Two weeks ago, the group members were talking to think. They are talking less and appear to be in "completing the agreed-upon readings" mode. These students are beginning to feel like a group completing a checklist versus a group meeting to read, talk, and think.
- In past weeks, group members eagerly shared texts they found at the library, online, and at home about heroes. That hasn't happened in over a week.

Asking kids: Julie thought about what might be gained if she asked the students in the small group to reflect about their recent small group learning experiences. Since this was a student-selected topic, Julie reasoned, asking the students what they'd like to do next would honor their decisions and direction. Julie gathered the small group and asked them,

- Do you feel like you've figured out what makes a hero a hero?
- Where do you want this reading work to take you next?
- Do you want to continue with texts about heroes, but take the work in a different direction?
- Do you want us to pull together some new texts that you could take on? Do you want to go on a text hunt and add something new to our text set?
- Are you ready to move away from this topic altogether?

Julie learned that the students in this small group were still interested in reading about heroes, but they wanted to focus in different ways. Here's what Julie recorded in her notes:

Matthew:	He loves sports, and he wants to study a few baseball heroes—comparing and contrasting their stories.
Davis:	He is interested in space. He isn't sure whom to study yet, but he's thinking about old and new people who have had a big part in the study of space.
Tessie:	She is a women's lacrosse follower. She wants to be a professional lacrosse player someday, so she wants to learn more about the 2017 World Cup team. She thinks she might find a hero or mentor by reading more.
Maddie:	She explains that her mom is her hero and she'd like to study her mom. She says her mom's information isn't written down anywhere, but she could interview and learn more about her.

Now that she understood the students' perspectives, Julie knew she could look across the next set of learning progressions in the original unit and determine what could be applied to students' new topics. Classrooms are vibrant works of art because they are dependent on the living, breathing, reading, writing, talking, creating, and doing of students.

Types of Groups to Pivot Into and Out Of

We've listed some groups that you might enjoy giving a go. These are not one-and-done groups—they can be used at any time during the year, as needed and as desired.

GENDER GROUP WRITING AND TALKING ABOUT READING

Writing and talking about reading can be problematic if the only audience is the teacher. So every Thursday, we end our workshop time with students reading aloud their most compelling or interesting Reader's Notebook entries. We gather readers in small groups in order to give them a chance to regularly and consistently share out with their peers. Sometimes we like to invite readers together who share a common perspective. Small gender groupings came about after we noticed more boys were sharing their reading journals than girls. When we invited conversation around possible solutions, some girls explained that they felt safer in a smaller group setting and with other girls. While gender groups aren't a must-do, they are a nice addition to small group learning when students have intent or need for sharing with like gender peers. This is especially true if students have mentioned they like this as one of the possible ways of talking about their reading and writing.

Tips for noticing when it might be time to pivot *into* gender groups:

- Kids express an interest in meeting in like gender groups.
- Kids are processing sensitive themes in a text and want a safe space with like gender students to share their thinking.
- You notice that too many cliques are forming and some voices are being silenced.

Tips for listening in:

- Pay attention to who is talking, what they are talking about, and how much elaboration is taking place.
- When students share, listen in for which notebook entries shine a light into their reading process, understanding of characters, and connections made to other learning, as well as misconceptions.

Our "writing about reading" small groups are set up to give readers a chance to talk and listen to each other. It is also a great opportunity to learn different ways of writing about reading. Generally, we have about six groups going at the same time. When we listen in, we are looking for ways students' notebook entries shine a light into their reading process, their understanding of characters, their organizing of big ideas from the text, connections made among and between texts, and their critical analysis and critique of the text. Sometimes we park ourselves alongside one group and literally make teaching notes about what we hear from the kids. Other times, we zip around the room, listening and looking for how the group dynamics are working. Sometimes our presence is enough to refocus a wayward conversation. Our body language speaks volumes during these listening-in sessions. We also build trust and independence when we hesitate and let the kids carry the weight of the conversation. So sometimes it is enough to be the watchful observer and kidwatcher. Now when a conversation is going recklessly wonky or the opportunity calls for us to "join in," we make the pivot.

Photos by Christian Ford

Tips for joining in: When students in a group—from their body language to their silence or halting, superficial conversation—seem as though they aren't going to pull out of the spin on their own, the teacher pulls up a chair or just leans forward and makes a suggestion. It can be literally 10 seconds of joining in, or 10 minutes, depending on what we sense is needed. With this kind of group, often a redirecting comment with a personal connection works. This might sound like "Isn't it great to have the time to hear our powerful literary insights? I know you thrive on listening to each other's ideas. Who is going to share their character analysis next?" Or it might be a focused question: "Can you find an example in your notebook where you highlight a character's weakness or strength? Let's hear some ideas."

Tips for pivoting: Gender grouping is an example of how we pivot as a result of our combination of listening in and joining in. The message is clear to kids: We care, and we want to invite engaging conversations where everyone has a voice. So it did not come as a surprise when some girls asked Barry during break time if the class could try girl and boy small group sharing sessions. In this case, the kids helped make the pivot.

After gender group meetings have been initiated, there are a few things a teacher might do:

- Ask students what makes these groups thrive and make a list of "what happens when girls share with girls and boys share with boys"
- Provide opportunities for a spokesperson from each group to share thoughts about what big ideas are surfacing—call it cross-pollination
- Ask kids to take what they know about speaking and listening in gender groups and try applying it to mixed groups

READING PARTNERSHIPS

Reading partnerships can be created by the teacher, the students, or a combination when the teacher creates the groups with input from the kids. The purpose for these small group pairings is to create shared reading experiences between two readers with similar interests. Launching reading partnerships during the large group meeting works well because we can highlight our intentions for this small group work and explain how we will use our time during reading workshop. We ceremoniously hand out reading tubs labeled with students' names and filled with a variety of texts.

Similar to our thought partners and groups of four as mentioned in Chapter Two, small group reading partnerships involve two or three reading partners meeting as a group or cohort. Their first job together is to choose a book or text(s) to read from their tub. Once they have selected reading materials, they negotiate with one another about the amount they will read and whether they will read independently or together. They will also consider if and how they will hold their thinking to prepare for discussion.

The most important part of these partnerships is the time spent after the reading where discussion is at the heart of the work. This gives students the time they need to process what they've read and an opportunity to think aloud by talking with a partner about anything that is swirling in their heads about their reading.

Tips for noticing when it might be time to pivot *into* reading partnerships:

- Students need someone they can read aloud to or someone who can model oral reading fluency.
- Students need some support co-constructing meaning; having a partner to practice with is a "just in time" dose of peer instruction.
- Students have been choosing the same types of books over and over again, and they need a fresh outlook on different books or genres they can read.

Tips for listening in:

- Read the room.
  - Listen in across groups as reading partnerships settle in and get started. Take note of partnerships that get started easily and those who may be struggling.

- o Float around the room, listening in for productive reading and talk. Take notes as you go in order to capture patterns across the room.
  - o If/when applicable, ask the whole class to pause. Shout out a positive aspect of a routine or procedure that is working effectively for one group. You may even ask group members to do a quick share about their process.
- Sit down with a group and listen in.
  - o Listen in for evidence of
    - Meaning making
    - Connections among and between group members and other texts
    - Fluency and decoding (if the students chose to read aloud together)
    - Talk and writing that makes thinking visible

Tips for joining in:

- As you read the room, if you notice a group struggling, make your way over to these students and join in. You can ask a few guiding questions to help problem-solve:
  - o How's it going?
  - o What did you decide to read?
  - o Are you reading together or independently?
  - o Can I join you for a bit and kick off our reading together?
  - o Where should we start?
- When you sit down with a group, wait for the right moment so that you don't interrupt reading or thinking. Then, you can ask a few guiding questions:
  - o How's it going?
  - o Can you pause for a minute so you can catch me up? What's going on in the text or your discussion?
  - o _____ is making me think about _____.
  - o What does _____ make you think about?
- Some thinking/talking stems (for both students and teachers) we suggest are
  - o I liked this part because _____.
  - o I didn't like this part because _____.
  - o This part was easy (cool, interesting, funny, strange, etc.).
  - o This part was confusing because_____.
  - o This part reminds me of _____.

- This part made me think about _____.
- If we compare this text to _____, it makes me think about _____.
- The gist of this text/section is _____.
- My big takeaway after reading this text/section is _____.
- I'm still wondering about _____.
- Next, I want to read _____.

Tips for pivoting: Once kids know how to operate within reading partnerships, you can make some further pivoting decisions based on your students' wants and needs.

- The teacher can ask one reading partnership to join another reading partnership, creating a group of four.

For example, when reading partners read aloud to each other, they are working with their reading prosody and oral retelling. When the teacher asks a partnership to join another partnership, it's just another chance for students to give this another try.

- The teacher can build independence by giving kids autonomy to choose if/when to join up with another partnership, creating a group of four.

What Would You Do?

Look at your class roster and pair kids up. Go on a hunt for something they will love to read together. What are your partnerships, and what texts could you put in each partner tub?

_____

_____

_____

_____

When one partnership joins another, it gives students another opportunity to process what they've read and make connections, which deepens meaning making. A good example is Sophia and Zinnia. When they were reading Jerry Spinelli's (2000) *Stargirl*, they were discussing how *Stargirl* had changed her style and name just for a boy. In the midst of their conversation, they turned to Eleanor and Lila to listen to them talk about Suzy, a girl who retreats into herself after the death of a friend in *The Thing About Jellyfish*. The group of four naturally went together, and before long, they were thinking and talking about what these two characters had in common. The two partnerships, through conversation and jotting, had worked out what was happening to both characters in order to analyze what they had in common. Toward the end, Eleanor interjected, "These are two girls trying to figure out who they really are . . . they are trying things on . . . sometimes failing themselves because of outside pressure . . . it's not easy being a girl!"

Two reading buddies, one sixth and one third grader, dive into a self-selected text, taking time to both read a page or two and then talk about what they are learning about and finding interesting.

Photos by Christian Ford

This teaming together doesn't just happen magically. Setting up the parameters ahead of time contributes to students' success. This can be done by frontloading information to students and giving them permission to join together if/when they have connections to other groups or there's an inquiry that fits another group. Another way is to explain that thinking partners evolve out of trying to solve something, so if what they are trying to solve could use the brainwork of more people, joining groups makes sense.

- You might disband the group altogether if/when
  - Students have worked through a text (or set of texts) and indicate they are finished reading the resources
  - Students have read a text(s) that they want to reread again independently
  - Students are inspired by a text in their reading tub that they didn't read in their small group and they want to read it independently

INQUIRY GROUPS

In the next three examples of flexible grouping, we are going to unveil three groups that sound quite similar but have subtle differences. They are cut from the same cloth: the desire to learn and find out more about something. We simply thought you might like hearing how ideas for flexible grouping weave together and create more opportunities for a tapestry of flexible grouping.

Julie and Barry love short texts. Why? Short texts work in our favor because

- Kids can gobble up short texts quickly.
- Kids can revisit them often.
- Kids can find other texts that pair nicely in order to create text sets.

- Short texts are often highly engaging.
- And, finally, there are so many short texts in the world that finding accessible texts is easy.

Let's dip into an example that illustrates inquiry groups. Barry and his students landed on four big topics that the students in his class would enjoy reading and talking about:

Survival	Unfortunate Family Stories
Trouble Fitting In	A Place for Happiness

Barry prepared by making seven copies of three different stories for each topic. The class launched into this two-week study by talking about each topic, then reading aloud a few paragraphs from one article from each topic. Students then recorded their selections on a sheet of paper, prioritizing their first, second and third choices. Barry worked to make sure that all kids had one of their top two choices. Groups were off and reading!

Tips for listening in: Listen in for evidence of

Short texts work in our favor because kids can gobble them up quickly.

- What students already know about their topic
- What background knowledge they link up with the topic
- Student conversation that captures the big ideas in the text(s)
- Wonderings and questions students have about their topic

Tips for joining in: Offer up a new piece of text that kids haven't read before.

- Show enthusiasm for the topic by offering up some interesting tidbit or connection.
- Hand out the text and ask students to preview it so that they can orient themselves to the text.
- Read the opening paragraph. After reading it, you could
  o Ask the kids to discuss the opening with a shoulder partner.
  o Discuss the opening as a group.
  o Partner up and continue reading the text together.
  o Ask the students to read the rest independently.

A small group is poring over some student-written magazines and jotting down favorite articles and ideas on the whiteboard table.

Photos by Christian Ford

Tips for pivoting: These groups met for two weeks. At the end of two weeks, each small group shared out some big takeaways with the whole class. The "Survival" group was on a roll, and the pivot was to not disband but to let the students keep going. Students in the "Trouble Fitting In" group were satisfied with their inquiry and used their small group time to read independently. Because of interest generated during a whole group share-out, a few kids wanted to explore the texts in other small groups. Barry encouraged kids to poke into the texts that were of interest and read them during independent reading time and at home.

MULTIAGE READING PARTNERS/GROUPS

Community is very important to us—classroom community, grade-level community, classrooms that share the same hallway community, middle school house/team community, and schoolwide community. To nurture community beyond the classroom, we suggest working with colleagues to create multiage reading partners or groups. This example of pivoting is the next generation of reading buddies. Two things make this experience different:

1. Partnerships are dynamic versus static (they change regularly).

2. The reasons for creating these types of groups are bottomless.

Take a look at a few examples showing different configurations and reasons for multiage partnerships:

Partnerships	Third and Fourth Graders	Third and Seventh Graders	First and Fifth Graders	Fifth and Sixth Graders
Reason/Purpose	Read, write, and design a plan for the new playground structure	Read, write, and play around with simple machines science content	Read aloud, do fluency work, and talk about books and authors	Study graphic novels

Barry's school has nonfiction reading partners. Every Tuesday and Wednesday, 74 first through sixth graders meet together to read an article from *National Geographic Explorer* magazine. When Barry and his colleagues, Anne and Todd, were selecting these multiage pairings, they considered student behaviors and reading proficiency, making sure each partnership had a fluent reader. These three teachers were very intentional in their rollout. The first meeting was focused on sparking enthusiasm for the partnerships and examining both why and how to read shoulder-to-shoulder. Together they established a partner reading routine. Several students demonstrated what it looked and sounded like. Familiar with the process, these multiage groupings thrived. Groups got started quickly, and it didn't take long for the younger students to become more and more comfortable talking and reading with their older buddies. These inspiring little friendships led the teachers to keep the partnerships intact for an entire semester.

When Julie taught fourth grade, she partnered with various teachers in the middle school English department. These connections gave students an opportunity to work and learn with students of different ages. Teachers in both elementary and middle school had the chance to talk about vertical and horizontal curriculum. Within these pairings, they created multiage book clubs that were inspired by student choice. Some book clubs were pairs, some were trios, and some were groups of five or six. While this idea was wildly successful, it was a short-lived partnership due to the challenges of middle school scheduling. A good idea doesn't die quickly, and Karen, one of Julie's eighth-grade teaching partners, continues to look for ways to make multiage book groups and hopes that a newly improved block schedule (with longer chunks of time for English language arts) will reinspire this opportunity for students.

Tips for listening in:

- Listen in to see if the content makes sense and note where kids are tripping up.
- Pay attention to the kinds of questions kids are asking.
- Zero in on how students are both tackling and talking about the content vocabulary being presented.
- Keep a chart handy so you can keep track of which students you are listening in on and which students you might be missing each week.

Tips for joining in:

- Talk about how previewing the text helps readers "warm up" their brains and build connections.

- Model chunking up the reading by stopping and talking before each section/page or subtitle.
- If partners seem a bit disengaged, show them how to change the title of the article or text to a question and practice answering the question as they read across the text.
- If older students are doing all the reading, demonstrate how to include the younger readers in the reading of the visuals.

Tips for pivoting:

- If you notice some kids are just going through the motions by passively reading and not talking as they go, pull a couple of partnerships together and talk about what they are reading and what fascinating new ideas or facts strike their fancies.
- Unfamiliar topics sometimes prompt a teacher to pivot even before the groups are initiated. Help build some background connections by spotting, talking about, and elaborating on the powerful visual features in the text as a large group.
- When reading buddies are finding it difficult to get started quickly, make a game of it either for the partners or for the entire class.

MORE GROUP IDEAS

The more success we have, the more open we are to trying on new ways of forming groups.

We have been experimenting over the last few years with flexible grouping, and we have noticed the more success we have, the more open we are to trying on new ways of forming groups.

Here is a collection of flexible small groups that have at times been a purposeful fit with our curriculum and at other times provided nimble choices that have surfaced as a result of listening in and observing kids.

Group Name	Why	Duration	What We Noticed
Hooked on Harry Potter	We noticed four students from different friendship groups all loved Harry Potter, so we socially engineered!	Two months	The kids were more comfortable and respectful with one another from then on; it's not that they ever got to be fast friends, but they had that bond, and their skill at asking curious questions and listening respectfully improved.
Partnership	One fifth grader wrote creative reading notebook entries and had a knack for knowing what kind of note-taking would help her most, based on what book she was reading.	Two weeks	There is no doubt that she could help another student who was struggling to use writing about reading.

Group Name	Why	Duration	What We Noticed
Book Trailers	After sharing a book trailer for the book *Took*, we noticed a group of sixth graders in the library during recess hunting down other trailers and rating book trailers from great to awful. So we organized a lunchtime meeting to explore book trailers with an invitation to show two or three a month.	Twice-a-month lunchtime meetings and once-a-month trailer showings through the year	While having used book trailers in the past, handing off this responsibility to this group built excitement for trailers and books and led both this group and class to learning about some great new titles. We enjoyed a laugh together at the expense of the cheesy trailers.
Hamilton	Two girls were trying to read *Hamilton: The Revolution*. They mentioned they loved the songs and the lyrics. We printed out the lyrics and met to talk about them.	Three meetings	With the songs stuck in their heads, they enthusiastically asked questions about Hamilton and American history.
Character Monologues and Dialogues	Reading workshop needed some changing up, something novel.

We partnered up and practiced reading monologues written for teenagers. | Two weeks | Every day readers grew in confidence reading aloud, switching partners, and making meaning from their oral interpretations. |
Best Dystopian Book	A herd of kids were reading dystopian books, so we created a "dystopian reading club" with the task of agreeing on the top three best dystopian books.	One month	Kids argued and challenged each other in naming the top three, sparking great character and plot debates.
Biographies Are Us	A few kids were abandoning books left and right, so we invited them to try reading from the short bio series "Who was . . . ?"	Two weeks	After one student had read Jackie Robinson's bio in two days and rattled off a list of "did you knows," kids were hooked. The average number of books read from the series was four.
What's In? What's Out?	After listening to some kids talking about a Percy Jackson movie, we invited them to read either the novel or the graphic novel and decide on what was left in and what was left out.	Two weeks	Kids were more than willing to list and wrestle with key events and characters featured in each type of media.
Reading Calendar Groups	Readers met to share their reading calendars and celebrate how much they had read. A student captain recorded the groups' reading for the week—the number of pages read and titles completed.	10 minutes each Monday morning all year; groups stay the same	As students talk about what helped them read and what got in their way, the teacher takes notes and gathers ideas for lessons and conferences. Interesting books are shared, and readers have this steady home front and a shared value that volume of reading matters. You can invite kids to call these groups whatever they wish; sometimes Barry's class gives each group the name of a different college.

Timing Is Everything: More About the Duration of Groups

As the previous chart shows, flexible groups can go from a few minutes to a full year! You will find your own pace—we promise. To get you started thinking about the "How long do they last?" question, we like to use an analogy of running. Runners are not all the same. Sprinters run fast, and marathoners run long. Small group instruction is similar in that some small groups are meant to be sprints—the type of group that, by design, doesn't last very long. Other small groups are meant to be marathons—those are the types of groups that stick around longer because the work at the table needs more time and space in order to accomplish the goals. Both sprint and marathon small groups are important. In this section of the chapter, we illustrate what these two types look like and the reasons for choosing them when lifting students' reading muscles.

REASONS FOR SPRINT GROUPS

1. To clear up confusion about a reading skill or content quickly so that it can be applied to other reading experiences (use of punctuation to make meaning, structure of a text, domain-specific vocabulary, etc.)

2. To preview content before it's taught or experienced

3. To repeat an experience related to something previously taught

4. To meet some social/emotional needs of students (see examples on page 124)

5. To co-construct procedures and protocols with students for small groups

6. To familiarize and hand over the small group procedures

7. To elevate student voice and participation

How Long Do Sprint Groups Last?

Sometimes they are a onetime, five-minute gathering. They could also be two or three short meetings across a week.

REASONS FOR MARATHON GROUPS

1. To create multiple, additional experiences for students to practice and demonstrate mastery

2. To help kids step out of their comfort zone and overcome obstacles (Trying something new takes multiple attempts!)

3. To work on longer-term goals or projects

4. To build connections between and among students and content

5. To build confidence with new learning so that transfer and application happen more seamlessly

How Long Do Marathon Groups Last?

Think of the marathon groups as ones that meet over the course of a three- to six-week unit or, in an intense two-week period, meet four or more times.

Language for Joining In

While always keeping in mind that you want to talk as little and as briefly as possible, and make use of nonverbal gestures—so students know it's their voices and thinking that matters, not yours—you nevertheless will want to coach from the sidelines. This coaching comes in the form of feedback that is similar to Peter Johnston's work around teacher language. In *Choice Words* (2004), he teaches us that the language we use when giving feedback to kids matters. Johnston's work suggests focusing on students' work, eliminating praise, making comments, and providing insights about their process. A focal point is describing students' strengths and then making suggestions for what students can do next to make improvements in relation to the goals, learning targets. or success criteria. You can do this coaching in two ways:

1. Stop and give feedback to all students doing the same work.

2. Give specific feedback to students who are excelling or struggling in the moment.

LANGUAGE THAT SUPPORTS DESIRED RESULTS

Language Supporting Desired Behavior Norms

"Thank you for getting started quickly."

"I see that you are ready to go, books and notebooks in hand."

"I see that this group has already started their stories."

"I am noticing that this group is listening with intensity—just look at how they are leaning forward and their body language is open and inviting."

Language Supporting Desired Reader Norms

"I noticed how your ideas about the character have changed over time. Tell me more about that."

"You underlined two words in the text and put a question mark. Did you figure out what the words mean?"

Language Supporting Strategy Use

"If we are using our questions to push ideas, what question(s) have you heard in today's conversation that sparked a new insight?"

"I noticed you went back to your book during our discussion. Talk to us about how this was helpful for you."

"The doodles and drawings you made in your reading notebook are so detailed and engaging. How is that helpful for you as a reader and thinker?"

Language Supporting Risk Taking

"I noticed _____ has suggested the title of the book means _____. Who would be willing to try out another idea about the title?"

"What question do you think is still hiding that will lift our conversation a bit more?"

Language Supporting Wide Genre Reading

"What might we gain by reading a wide genre of books and topics?"

"If you were consulting our class on the three genres we must all read this year, what would you recommend, and why?"

Language Supporting Inferential Thinking

"What are your own experiences regarding _____, and what do you think the features of this article say about _____?"

"What do you think explains why the character acted this way?"

"What are the clues that tell you how the author might feel about this topic?"

Language Supporting Reticent Readers

"Imagine you have the last word about what this story is all about. Jot down what your final message is on a sticky note, and we'll randomly pick and read a few to end this meeting."

"Write down an open-ended question you are mulling over. Then write down your best answer to your question. Hand your card to the person on your left. Now the person reading the question will be the last person to answer the question."

"What is one thing the main character did that you wish you could do?"

Language Supporting Synthesizing Across Curriculum

"When you first started reading, what did you think this story was going to be about, and how did your thinking change after you finished the story?"

"Has this article changed your mind about this topic? Why or why not?"

"What does this text remind you of?"

Language Supporting the Lone Wolf

"Think about what was shared today in our conversation. What did someone else share that surprised you the most?"

"What question was shared today that still lingers with you?"

"How does hearing different opinions and ideas on a story help a conversation?"

We simultaneously mesh teaching into flexible reading groups with the art of questioning, the nudging of sticking to our routines and protocols, and active kidwatching and reflection to drive our "next" steps.

Troubleshooting

We believe a well-managed reading workshop starts by building connections and relationships with our students. That's why we invest time and energy into learning about them in many different ways. We want our students to feel that they can succeed, that they belong, and that they are trusted to make wise choices that meet their own defined literacy needs. To this end, we begin by establishing agreements and procedures for how we will operate and act together. The most effective reading workshop classrooms are self-managed and designed with and for kids. If you find that things are going off-course, work to diagnose what it is that is making it clunky. Here are some examples.

IF: YOU NOTICE UNEQUAL TALKING IN GROUPS

Try This: Share air time. One way to harness participation in a small group is to raise the question, "How do we ensure that everyone is engaged and the airtime is shared?" By asking small groups to develop strategies for "sharing airtime," we again put kids in the pilot seat. One of our favorite suggestions is to have group members keep track of the number of times they speak by penciling a tally mark down. Groups will even come back and wonder aloud whether the tally marks have to be even or whether asking questions demands a tally mark. Problem solving is a dynamic and ongoing process.

IF: YOU FIND YOURSELF DOING MOST OF THE TALKING

Try This: Ask students to share in small group leadership roles. Giving students the job of reading the small group question prompt or explaining the purpose of the small group by reading a card or agenda puts kids talking first.

- Trust students to be timekeepers. Doing so invites both shared leadership and responsibility for running a smooth small group and takes away one more way we assert ourselves (the adult) into discussions.
- Reflect on who is doing most of the talking. We also suggest you ask students to reflect on this question. The more we share in the responsibility of making talking accessible to everyone, the more likely we will all find solutions.
- Commit to devising ways throughout the year to increase the amount and depth of student talk.

IF: STUDENTS IN GROUPS KEEP GLANCING AT YOU FOR RESCUE

Try This: Be a mime. Since we are shooting for everyone to participate, our work is to facilitate contributions. This might be by modeling asking curious questions to less willing students and naming the strategy so it can be handed over to the kids. We also share control in our groups by nodding, repeating what we have just heard, and showing we care by leaning forward and jotting down notes. "When we defer to others' judgment, when we vocally treat others' concerns as our own, we give control to the group and psychological safety takes hold" (Duhigg, 2017, p. 70). Remember that what happens in these first meetings counts toward establishing group norms. Our actions, as teachers and students, speak volumes in what norms are most valued.

IF: YOU FIND YOURSELF GROUPING BASED PRIMARILY ON STUDENTS' READING LEVELS

If the only way we group students is by their reading levels, we've really missed the opportunities to build off of students' interests and passions. Grouping by reading level isn't going to drive student motivation and engagement through the roof. Instead, you might lose kiddos in the process.

Try This: In Chapter Two, we mentioned having students complete a reading survey. Instead of taking the surveys home and mulling over them late into the night, how about using the surveys as short texts to talk about? We have found that kids enjoy meeting in small groups and talking from an interest survey. They tend to elaborate because they find topics and books in common with other readers. Doing this means straight away you have grouped kids to listen to them share their interests and passions and you have moved beyond reading levels. By keeping an ongoing list of things you have learned about your kids, by reviewing the student photo essays and looking over their "book selfies," we think you will have curated a number of ideas for future small groups.

IF: ANY SMALL OR BIG ROUTINE GOES OFF TRACK

Try This: Teach or reteach the protocol. We have spent some time pointing out that norms are deep-seated. What the leader of a group or team does establishes or undermines the work of the group. So we begin by noting that how a teacher responds determines the legitimacy of whether the norm of respect will be carried through. That said, we believe that when we co-construct agreements and protocols with students, we establish a collaborative decision-making process that is crucial to holding students accountable for their behavior. One tactic to help with this is to have a student model reading silently or to show a photo of a student reading independently. Naming what the reader is doing while he or she reads ensures that it is clear what the behavior looks like. Students usually come up with a list similar to this:

> ### Goal: We are **learning** to read independently.
>
> We agree to
>
> - Get started quickly
> - Read the whole time with stamina and focus
> - Create a personal reading space
> - Stay in one spot the whole time
> - Read silently or very quietly as to not distract others around us
> - Read to understand and learn more by the end of reading time than before we started

Once you and your students have named what reading independently looks like, be sure to take time to assess each agreement. If "getting started quickly" is a challenge, you can always make it a class goal. If a group of students is struggling with finding a spot to read with stamina, you can offer a small "problem solving" group to address it. As the year rolls on, students will fall in and out of their pursuit to be independent. This is natural. When things get out of hand, go back to the chart and make the work clear. Who doesn't want to be independent? Let's get clear with kids so everyone knows the path forward. Celebrate their independence and encourage kids to take on the small actions of being independent.

Here are a few quick mock-ups of independent charts we have created in our classrooms:

	We are learning to research independently.	We are learning to meet in small groups independently.	We are learning to track our reading work independently.
Purpose	To collect and learn new information	To gather and share our own ideas and insights about what we read *or* to figure out/make meaning of text	To show our own personal reading progress and reading effort
Remember To/ Look-Fors	Record new information • Record questions • Cite resources • Reread • Ask questions • Talk to others	• Move in and out with ease • Get started quickly • Bring your reading tools (book, notebook, pencil) • Lean in/participate • Speak and listen respectfully • Stretch your own thinking	• Jot down the page you started reading on your bookmark • Jot down the last page you read on your bookmark • Add up and record the number of pages you read during reading workshop • Be ready to share your ideas about your goals, progress, and areas you would like to pay more attention to

One Last Thing

We've shared ways grouping can be done in the moment, like partners and groups of four, and we have suggested that the servicing of students in these flexible groups builds coherence, trust, and responsive teaching. More than anything, we want you to widen your scope of how and why small groups are formed. Loosen your reigns, let kids decide, and don't be handcuffed by students' independent reading levels. Give yourself permission to let kids dive into talk—into the trying on of new ideas and thinking—and then pull up your chair and kidwatch. So much will be revealed!

CHAPTER SIX

Assessing Student Work

(because looking at our readers' work lifts their strategies, skills, and thinking)

Spread out across the tables were students' Reader's Notebooks. The room was quiet, students were gone, and Julie knew that the answer to what they needed next was tucked inside their work from this week's independent reading time and small group learning experiences. Keeping the learning targets front and center, Julie was looking for evidence of students' thinking about the main ideas they read in the text. The focus of the fiction unit was on making meaning by asking questions, noticing an author's new ideas and themes, and making connections.

Julie sorted work in fewer than six minutes. She made three piles:

- Who can teach others
- Who is almost there
- Who is not quite there, *yet*

This chapter is about how to sort through students' work, like their Reader's Notebooks, and organize small group sessions based on these selections. Our goal

Photo by Christian Ford

is to help you move from "What will I teach in a minilesson?" (we think you are already good at that!) to "What small group learning opportunities will I create with and for kids?" It's not enough to teach skill- or technique-based minilessons. Your readers need something more personal and relevant to make learning stick.

First, let's look at the big picture:

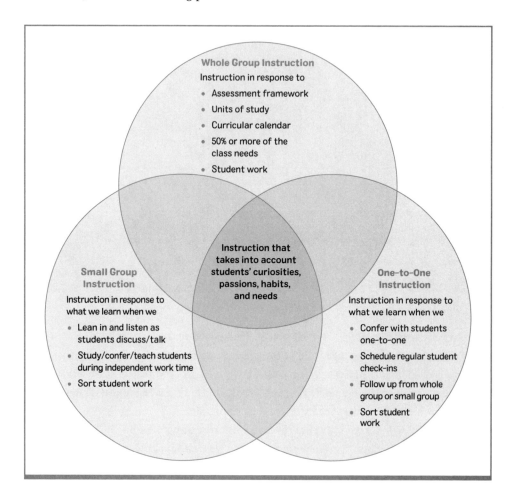

We are guessing the first circle looks different from many of the assessment frameworks you've seen. That's because traditional frameworks aim students toward mastery of certain benchmark levels. Instead, we want to harness units of study and curricular calendars focused on students' interests and needs as our areas of focus. Curriculum directors often remind us that if we didn't have standard reading benchmarks, units, and calendars, we would most likely have misalignment, lack of clarity, and overall gaps in students' academic experience. We don't necessarily disagree, but we believe the issue of alignment (or the false sense of security that saying we are aligned creates) has an unintended consequence—it leaves out what students themselves bring to the table.

The graphic's second circle conveys small group instruction generated from leaning in and listening to students so that we can take this knowledge and weave it into required curriculum and assessments. Both small groups and one-to-one conferences provide "live time" feedback and give direction for future work based on students' wants and needs. We don't lose sight of curricular goals and grade-level benchmarks—it's that we are aligning with student motivations as well!

The third circle of this graphic prioritizes the time we spend with students one-on-one, in short chunks of time. We use the information we gain from whole group instruction/shared experiences and small group learning to inform what individual students need and then work to meet those needs through conferring.

It is only through the analysis of student work that we can truly know what students did or did not learn from a given lesson. With this up-close view we can direct instruction to target students' specific needs.

—Diane Sweeney and Leanna S. Harris

One brain-friendly way to think about assessing as the basis for small group instruction is to imagine it as an invitation.

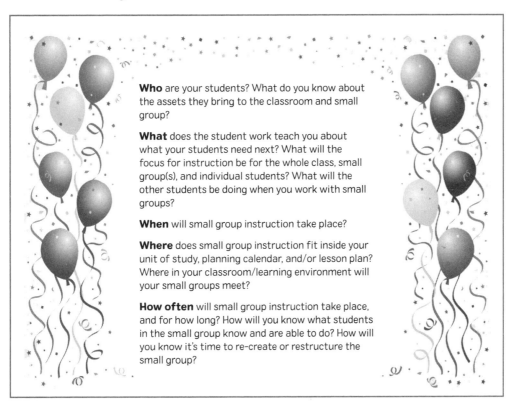

Who are your students? What do you know about the assets they bring to the classroom and small group?

What does the student work teach you about what your students need next? What will the focus for instruction be for the whole class, small group(s), and individual students? What will the other students be doing when you work with small groups?

When will small group instruction take place?

Where does small group instruction fit inside your unit of study, planning calendar, and/or lesson plan? Where in your classroom/learning environment will your small groups meet?

How often will small group instruction take place, and for how long? How will you know what students in the small group know and are able to do? How will you know it's time to re-create or restructure the small group?

In Chapter Eight, on unit planning, you can learn more about the *where* and *how often*. Here, we want to focus on becoming comfortable with evaluating readers' work.

We are going to take you through these facets of formative assessment:

- Assessing With Learner-Centered Benchmarks
- What to Look At
- How to Sort Student Work
- Planning a Focus for Instruction and Putting It Into Action

Two Essential Questions This Chapter Helps You Answer

1. How do you get to know your students through their work?

2. How do you plan small group learning experiences using students' work to guide decision making?

Beliefs

We use student work to assess because it makes sense to use the stuff that kids create daily, weekly, and monthly to guide our understanding of their understandings. More important, using their work sends our learners a very important message—what they create matters.

Our Beliefs About Assessing Student Work

We believe . . .	How it shows up in our work . . .
Student work counts. We, students and teachers alike, review work samples to appreciate understandings and unpack misunderstandings.	What students make and create counts. Assessing the day-to-day—via knowledge checks—informs us so we know what to do next. Assessing toward the end of a study—culminating experiences or performance tasks—provides opportunities for students to put their understandings together and show what they know.
The most authentic form of assessment happens by listening in and joining in small group learning experiences. Through this, we uncover and discover a focus for what students need next.	Sitting near a group of students, with our notebooks in hand, gives us time to observe and take note of student talk, student work, and student interactions.
Student self-assessment brings metacognition and plan of action together.	Students self-reflecting, setting goals, and creating plans of action to move forward is not optional; it's essential.

Assessing With Learner-Centered Benchmarks

According to Fisher, Frey, and Hattie (2016), "Given that teachers judge students based on their performance, it seems only fair that students should know what they are expected to learn, why they are learning that, and how success will be determined . . . Clearly articulating the goals for learning has an effect size of 0.50. It's the right thing to do, and it's effective" (p. 27).

We agree, and these are the primary three tools we use to bring about that mutual clarity between teacher and student around expectations for reading growth. While these conditions of transparency are often cited in relation to whole group and individual learning, we assert that they apply in the same manner to the work students do in small group reading experiences. We show how this plays out in small groups later in this chapter.

When you lean in to what you know about students, coupled with curriculum objectives, you can create big intentional takeaways through individual *goal-setting* conferences. You can create big-picture goals, such as pumping up your reading volume (amount of time or pages read), and/or focus on discrete skills such as paying attention to punctuation during oral reading as it affects meaning.

The *learning targets* of a unit or lesson tell students what they should know, understand, and be able to do. This can be tied to a series of lessons, also referred to as *learning progressions*. *Success criteria* help teachers and students decide if they have achieved the goals behind the learning. "The term 'success criteria' was coined in the UK. It is synonymous with 'assessment criteria' but, instead of reminding students of their (perhaps negative) experiences of being assessed, this term focuses (much more positively) on students' ability to succeed" (Assessment for Learning, n.d.). Sometimes the success criteria might be a list of bullet points outlining what success looks like in relation to the learning targets. For larger or lengthier assessment tasks, rubrics can be used, often with different levels of performance in relation to the success criteria (Assessment for Learning, n.d.).

Big Advice

If you want examples of ways to move from surface to deep literacy learning, in relation to student work products, see *Visible Learning for Literacy* by Douglas Fisher, Nancy Frey, and John Hattie (2016).

Example for Fifth Grade

- Determine two or more main ideas of a text and explain how they are supported by key details; summarize the text.

- Engage effectively in a range of collaborative discussions (one-on-one, in groups, and teacher-led) with diverse partners on *Grade 5 topics and texts*, building on others' ideas and expressing your own clearly.
- Come to discussions prepared, having read or studied required material; explicitly draw on that preparation and other information known about the topic to explore ideas under discussion.

Sample Success Criteria

- I can read and figure out at least two main ideas in a text.
- I can explain how the main ideas are supported by important details.
- I can summarize the text through discussion or writing.
- I can come to discussions prepared and use what I've read to add to the discussion.
- I can engage in discussions in small groups, building on others' ideas and expressing my ideas clearly.

Shared agreements are a way to create mutual understanding between and among students and teacher. Shared agreements can be focused on behaviors, routines, or processes. You can also create shared agreements for student work products, demonstrations, and performance tasks.

OUR ASSESSMENT GUIDELINES

- Share with and/or co-create goals and success criteria with students
- Create shared agreements among and between students and teacher about what counts and the different paths that can get us there
- Nudge one another to stay focused on the goals
- Reflect and self-reflect about the learning process
- Remind students to ask themselves, "When I think I am finished, I check myself against the shared agreements/co-constructed rubric and see if there is anything more I'd like to do/say"
- Focus on giving feedback on what is working

What to Look At

Cris Tovani (2011) stated, "Teachers don't need any more numerical 'data.' What they need is validation to use the data that matters most . . . like student work and student talk—to help figure out next steps for learners in their educational care" (p. 12). With the amount of information and text being generated and put into the world for kids to grapple with, we believe this is even truer today. This type of assessment is easy to get your hands on—it's all the stuff students produce (the work products they make and create) and all the conversations and interactions they have that you note as evidence of their learning.

We say that all the *stuff* students make and create counts. That doesn't mean you have to look at everything kids make and create. It just means that if it's worth their time in class, it counts when we are deciding what work to sort and assess. We also define student work as what kids say, how they act, and how they interact. This is a sweeping definition. That said, think about it. The narrowest definition of student work focuses on what students *produce*—project, literary essay, notebook entry. Widen the lens and notice what else you can capture. Below is a quick list we include in our assessing of student work:

- **Student reading calendars** reveal reading volume for individual students. This can show when students read and when they don't, books completed and abandoned, and genre preferences.
- **Anecdotal records** capture students' actions and interactions. This can show reading stamina, who takes the lead, who takes notes, who engages or disengages, and so on.

This student, in a comfortable reading spot, is the first to read a new book that he "special ordered" through his teacher for the classroom library. He has logged a lot of hours in that beanbag, building his reading stamina and volume.

Photo by Natalie Guerrero

- **Reading surveys and inventories** allow for logging of students' reading choices in a given time. This can show interesting information/data that can feed small group learning.
- **Student talk** invites you to take note of what kids talk about. This can show how students share their thinking, and what they share, with others.

These seventh graders are making meaning of the text and challenging their own assumptions about the amount of sugar in chocolate while reading an excerpt from *How Many Guinea Pigs Can Fit on a Plane? Answers to Your Most Clever Math Problems* (Overdeck, 2017).

Photo by Natalie Guerrero

- **Reader's Notebook entries** showcase students' thinking through writing. This can show how students make meaning of texts and how their thinking changes within a text or across texts over time.
- **Margin notes or sticky notes** provide students with a place to hold their thinking, capturing wonderings, new ideas, and connections made. This can give us insight into students' thinking.

This third grader is holding his thinking about Harriet Tubman's contributions on sticky notes.

- **Highlights or underlines** allow us to notice the words, phrases, and sections that students highlight or underline. This can foster small group discussion and target instruction.
- **Entrance or exit slips** provide a knowledge check at the beginning, middle, or end of reading workshop. This can show us what kids know, what they are able to do, or what they need next as readers, writers, thinkers, creators, and doers. It can be as simple as this:

The teacher hands students a blank index card (lined or unlined, 3 × 5 or 4 × 6) and asks students to respond to two questions:

- Side 1: What were your big takeaways or ahas from your reading today?
- Side 2: Based on what you read and did today, what do you need next?

- **End demonstrations of learning** often involve a performance-based task to wrap up learning at the end of a unit of study. This can show big takeaways across multiple weeks of learning experiences.

It goes without saying that when students have a voice in how they show what they know and are able to do, their motivation and engagement toward the task or learning progression increases. Sorting student work is successful when the work is process oriented—no one-and-done, or the work tends to be too "skinny." The following list, in addition to what we've just described, is a great place to start as you think about the different ways kids can demonstrate their understandings.

Student Work
Ways Students Can Demonstrate Their Understandings

Anchor Charts	Google Classroom (surveys, writing, chats, discussion board)
Annotations	In-Class Discussions
Book Clubs (questions, research, speaking and listening contributions, pacing)	Large Group (monologues, plays)
Book Projects/Book Celebrations	Large Group Discussions With Thinking Partners
Book Reviews	List of Titles: Books Completed
Book Talks	Note Catchers
Discussion Boards	Note-Taking Artifacts
Entrance Slip Questions	Notebooks
Essays	Performance Tasks
Exit Slip Questions	Presentations
Fluency Checks (one-to-one, partner reading)	Projects Based on Learning
	Process Logs

Quick Writes	Small Group Discussions
Quizzes/Tests (teacher and student created)	Small Group Repeated Reading Experiences (choral reading, reader's theater)
Reading Calendars	
Reflections	Sticky Notes
Responses	Surveys
Self-Assessment (thumbs-up, fist to five, checklists, rubrics, goal sheets)	Work Products (drafts and final)

To Get to What You See Here, **Try This**

1. Pick a text or piece of text that the whole class, a small group, or an individual student will read.

2. Give students margin space around the text or a note catcher—designed by the teacher or co-designed by the teacher and students—asking the students to write the gist of what they are reading.

3. Encourage students to write important details around the margins or to write about the beginning, middle, and end of the text on a note catcher.

4. Collect the student work and sort. Look for patterns across students' thinking.

5. Decide what the whole class, small groups, or individual students need based on students' responses. Students pick a text or part of a text (in this case a short story) and determine where they will stop along the way to hold their thinking. Students mark the spots with sticky notes.

6. Here's the thing: You can ask students to do this process with the same text or different texts.

Photo by Rachel Langosch

How to Sort Student Work

Now let's talk about the *how* in sorting student work. It can be overwhelming if you don't keep it simple and manageable. *We keep the sort focused on learning targets that are aligned to standards.* Diane Sweeney (2011), and the *Student-Centered*

Coaching model, harnesses sorting student evidence in order to help teachers recognize patterns and trends related to student learning. When sorting student work, first we think about describing the entire student work sample set. This may be a whole class (if you are trying to determine small groups), or it may be a set of four student work samples from a small group. We use the whole student work sample set to explain what we see and what we notice. Then, we look at the student work through the lens of determining the implications for a focus for instruction. What does the student work teach us? What patterns do we notice? How does the work give us a focus for instruction?

> Keep the sort focused on learning targets that are aligned to standards.

There are different subquestions you can ask next, and they can be continually adjusted to suit your intentions, ways of processing, and the like. The important thing is to keep them to three—so that you can then sort work into three piles. Any more than that will make you tear your hair out.

We are going to show you samples of three different variations of questions:

What does the _____ need? (This gets at meeting needs via types of groups.)

Who is thinking deeply about _____? (This gets at quality of readers' thinking.)

Who is ready to teach _____? (This gets at peer-led coaching.)

WHAT DO STUDENTS NEED TO REACH THE LEARNING TARGETS?

Sort the work into three piles and think through these questions:

1. What does the whole class/whole group need?

2. What do small groups of students need?

3. What do individual students need?

We encourage you to try this template when planning for whole group, small group, and one-to-one learning experiences by sorting student work. In this example, students were reading about people they consider heroes. They filled out an exit ticket explaining the contributions the hero has made.

Creating a Focus for Instruction

What do you see/what do you notice? Describe the student work.
<ul><li>Students wrote different amounts of ideas on their exit tickets.</li><li>Some had lots of ideas, some had a few ideas, and some were disconnected or confused with the text or the assignment.</li><li>Some students just wrote a list of facts versus why the person is considered a hero.</li></ul>

What are the implications for a focus for instruction? What do students need next?		
Whole Group	**Small Group**	**One-to-One**
<ul><li>Revisit what makes a hero a hero through a shared reading experience (Temple Grandin, *Rad American Women A–Z* by Kate Schatz, 2015)</li><li>Co-construct a statement about what makes Temple Grandin a hero</li></ul>	<ul><li>Host invitational small groups for any students who want to work on revising their exit ticket with a collaborative group</li><li>Privately suggest that Jamal, Aria, and Viv join in the small group</li></ul>	<ul><li>Meet with Luca, Jayleen, Karina, and Kai</li><li>Check in on texts chosen for hero work (curate others if needed)</li><li>Read part of the text together to assess where the breakdown is happening—is it about the reading or about writing about the reading?</li></ul>

Note: See page 288 in the Appendix for a blank template.

WHO IS THINKING . . . ?

Sorting work helps us answer important questions. Here is another template that sorts work by depth of knowledge and comprehension.

Sort the work into three piles and think through these questions:

1. Who was thinking deeply?

2. Who needs more strategies, examples, or time to wrestle with the content?

3. Who is not showing evidence of the learning targets yet?

In the example that follows, students worked to finish a series of responses in their Reader's Notebook entries related to their independent reading texts. Many students were also reading and discussing their responses in small groups, so it was a good time to collect notebooks and look across students' work. Here are the results.

	Students	What will you do next with/for these students?
Who was thinking deeply?	Mateo Jake Mya Gabriel Sonjay Elijah Christina Pia Tyrese	Meet together or in smaller subset groups to do some hot reads—selling the books students have fallen in love with. Many of these kids are stuck in a series and could use some nudging to add variety to their reading lives.
Who needs more strategies, examples, or time?	Jimmy J. T. Alejandro Cindy Angel Maggie Stefan Raj	Use some entries from other students to show different ways to make thinking visible. Divide this group into smaller groups and create a schedule to meet and work together.
Who is not showing evidence of the learning targets?	Nick Alexandra Tate Jared Brianna	Make sure book matching has been done with a keen eye for student interest and genre variety. Meet in pairs or one-to-one to assess further.

Note: See page 289 in the Appendix for a blank template.

WHO IS READY TO TEACH?

In this next example, the agenda tilts toward discovering those students who can actually step in and teach peers. Julie sorted Reader's Notebook entries where kids read and determined two main ideas with a few supporting details. She looked at the students' work and then sorted it into three piles.

1. **Who can teach others?** These are the students who are ready to move on to harder or more sophisticated texts, who are ready to go deeper in their meaning making by trying on other companion texts, and whose work could serve as models for others.

2. **Who is almost there?** These are the kids who are on the right track and need a little lift.

3. **Who is not quite there, *yet*?** These are the kids who need more time to wrestle with the text, may need some support rereading and making meaning, and may need more models and experiences.

Here's how it looks when Julie sorts.

Here's an example of "could teach others."

Wonder   the Bleeding Scream

The top 5 things:

- Auggie says "This was going to go down as one of the most awesome days in the history of my life.

- The boys were all huddled and comparing Auggie to bad things

- Auggie overhead Jack say "He always follows me around. What am I supposed to do?"

- Julian said "Just ditch him."

- Auggie left and nobody even knew he was there. He was crying under his costume.

I feel very bad for Auggie and hope he will forgive Jack.

Here's an example of "almost there."

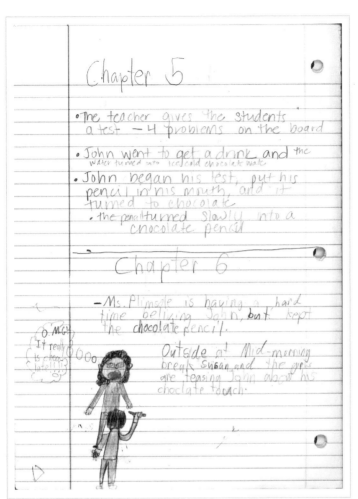

Chapter 5

- The teacher gives the students a test — 4 problems on the board
- John went to get a drink and the water turned into ice cold chocolate milk
- John began his test, put his pencil in his mouth, and it turned to chocolate
  - the pencil turned slowly into a chocolate pencil

Chapter 6

- Ms. Plimsole is having a hard time believing John, but kept the chocolate pencil.

O.MG! It really is chocolate!

Outside at Mid-morning break Susan and the girls are teasing John about his choclate touch.

Here's an example of "not there yet."

Dupercalaraquinstic

charlie and the chocolate factory
    In chapter 5 of charlie and the chocolate factory some important things happen. One thing is willy wonka announces that he is putting gold paper into 5 chocolate bars and if you get one of these chocolate — chocolate bars you win candy for a lifetime! Finally you get a tour of willy wonka's factory.

Here we use a slightly different planning template to focus on who can teach others.

Students	What will you do next with/for these students?
Who can teach others? Bravon, Terri, Da'rion, Taylor, Josh, Kate	Create reading trios—place students with others in this group to read a short text and write two main ideas with a few supporting details.
Who is on the right track? Julia, Zoe, Diego, Christian, Danny, Samuel, TJ, Sammy, Lauren	1. Students will meet in reading pairs or trios. **Bravon** (Diego) **Terri** (Julia, Zoe) **Da'rion** (Christian, Danny) **Taylor** (Samuel, TJ) **Josh** (Sammy) **Kate** (Lauren) 2. Students will meet with me, and we will read a longer excerpt from *The One and Only Ivan* and describe the main idea and two supporting details.
Who is not quite there, *yet*? Eli, Josie, Kate, Joe, Shamira, Brit	1. Create two small groups, and I will meet with each group for shared reading and co-constructing two main ideas and a few supporting details for extra practice. 2. Follow up by meeting with the Group 2 students one-on-one to check for understanding and clear up any confusion. **Group 1** Eli Josie Kate **Group 2** Joe Shamira Brit

Note: See page 290 in the Appendix for a blank template.

You can also sort an exit ticket on a half sheet or index card, or student work can be the notes you take when you meet with students in small group or one-to-one. You are looking at student evidence so that you can determine what it is that students know and are able to do so that you can make a plan going forward with their curiosities, passions, habits, and needs in mind.

Planning a Focus for Instruction and Putting It Into Action

Remember, the work you sort can be something students create inside a note-book (as pictured) or on a single piece of paper that you collect. There are lots of ways to make a plan based on the student work you collect and sort. Don't overdo it. Keep it simple. We'll start with Julie's favorite way—making a sticky note plan right on the stack of work. Remember those Reader's Notebooks that she collected? She made a sticky note plan on top of each stack of notebooks. Here's the plan she made.

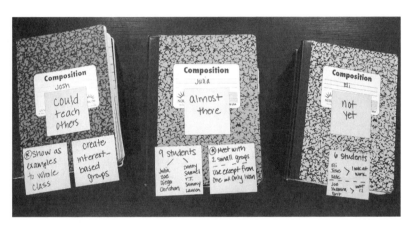

Sticky notes make planning efficient; trusting your instincts makes it rewarding.

Small Group Planning Template

Group: Students who are "almost there"

Texts: Various chapter books (student choice)

Focus/Purpose: Making thinking visible by writing about reading

	What do students need next? (current small group or new small group)	What will students do in small group?	How will students hold their thinking as they make meaning? Will they share out? • Student created • Teacher created
Planning	Extra models of holding thinking through writing (other students' notebooks)	Shared reading: Excerpt from *The One and Only Ivan* Shared writing: Holding our thinking together	Co-created on chart paper

(Continued)

(Continued)

Small Group Workshop	Minilesson	Work Time	Debrief
	What will I show, model, and talk about with students to lift the work at the table?	What will students read, write, talk about, create, design, or do?	How will we wrap up/share out?
	Teacher: Shows a few student exemplars under the document camera Teacher: Reads the shared reading excerpt	Teacher and students: Co-create a response on an anchor chart	Each student will make a plan for how he or she plans to hold thinking during independent reading tomorrow.

More Examples of How to Use Work to Inform Grouping Decisions

If the goal is to sort student work regularly, you have to find ways to simplify it. Otherwise, it won't become a regular part of your practice. Through a series of pictures and captions, we'll show you different ways to think about using student work to create a focus for future instruction. As you look across the following pages, think about the work your students create and imagine how you can collect and sort work too.

> *If the goal is to sort student work regularly, you have to find ways to simplify it.*

BLUE-STAR YOUR CALENDAR

We are often asked, "How often should student work be collected and analyzed?" The answer is *as often as you need to*. You sort work whenever you need to figure out what to do next with and for your students. Collect, sort, and analyze student work to find a focus for instruction

- Regularly
- Consistently
- As often as needed to know what students can do and/or what they need next

We use our unit plan or small group instruction plan as our guide to figuring out the "bends" in students' learning progression based on the work products they complete. For example, looking across the first two weeks in the six-week fiction unit, Julie earmarked the following days to look at student work:

Focus for the Week	Monday	Tuesday	Wednesday	Thursday	Friday
Shared and independent reading experiences and holding thinking	Shared reading and holding thinking with whole group	Shared reading and holding thinking with whole group	Independent reading and holding thinking*	Independent reading and holding thinking	Independent reading and holding thinking*
Independent and small group experiences and holding thinking	Independent and small group reading and holding thinking	Shared, independent, and small group reading and holding thinking*	Independent and small group reading and holding thinking*	Shared, independent, and small group reading and holding thinking	Independent and small group reading and holding thinking*

Note: *indicates collecting and sorting student work

OBSERVE A SMALL GROUP

By listening in to a small group discussing a short story from Ellen Oh's *Flying Lessons and Other Short Stories* (2017) and by looking across some student work, Julie learned what students needed next to flex their reading muscles. Opportunities for student learning with this small group included more clarity or experience focused on

- Recognizing that an anthology is a collection and doesn't have to be read in order
- Using the table of contents to help you navigate what you want to read based on familiar authors or interesting titles
- Reading the foreword to help you orient to the entire piece and better understand the individual stories
- Investigating text types (narrative, expository, technical, persuasive)
- Using text structure (sequence, problem/solution, compare/contrast, description, cause/effect)
- Exploring author's craft

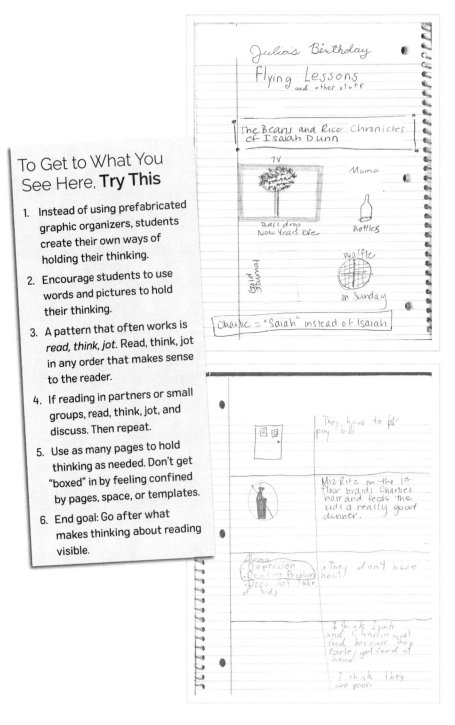

To Get to What You See Here, **Try This**

1. Instead of using prefabricated graphic organizers, students create their own ways of holding their thinking.

2. Encourage students to use words and pictures to hold their thinking.

3. A pattern that often works is *read, think, jot.* Read, think, jot in any order that makes sense to the reader.

4. If reading in partners or small groups, read, think, jot, and discuss. Then repeat.

5. Use as many pages to hold thinking as needed. Don't get "boxed" in by feeling confined by pages, space, or templates.

6. End goal: Go after what makes thinking about reading visible.

OBSERVE ONE-TO-ONE

We spend our time as teachers creating theories about what we think we know about kids' understandings and misconceptions. Listening in and joining into small group learning helps us uncover new knowledge about either proving or disproving our theories, and giving way to "just in time" instruction that will serve students' needs next.

If you are new to kidwatching and formative assessment, start by observing one learner. Build from there. Then, as you get comfortable theorizing about several kids or the entire class, remember to keep coming back to the one-to-one lens because looking closely at one student helps us understand the story all student work is trying to tell.

Looking at this picture, you wouldn't necessarily know that this fourth grader used to avoid books that look big and long. Careful kidwatching helped Julie know that he loves art, and a book that incorporated both words and images in a beautiful and unique way might be just what he needed. Putting lots of different types of books in this student's hands, including graphic novels, was the key to helping him find a book that piqued his interest.

The following template is a tool for digging into

- What we notice—the moves a student is making along the learning journey
- What we learn by conferring and uncovering new knowledge by asking open-ended questions and listening

These observations inform the implications for our work going forward and impact future whole group, small group, and one-to-one instruction.

Here's what it might look like in Grades 3–5:

Student	What do you see/hear?	What is the student working on?	What are the implications of this work for teaching and assessment? (whole group, small group, one-to-one)
McKenzie	• Spent six minutes reading a graphic novel from her book box. Didn't settle in; did more leafing through the pages. • Moved to the rug area with her book box and chose a picture book to read; sat back and rocked and read. • Once finished, she checked out the workshop job board and then moved to the bookshelves to reshelf a few books from her box and select a few more.	• Managing her own independent reading • Book selection • Finding places to read that make her comfortable and productive	• Meet with the student to discuss book choices. • Match knowledge gained from developmental reading assessment data to book choice and small group instruction texts. • Confer with student about graphic novels or create a small group interested in graphic novels.
Trevyn	• While writing an entry about his book, he used different-colored pens for each idea. While his writing was unconnected, he had the beginnings of lots of great openings (marked by the colors) that could be expanded. • He liked to sit on his knees while he worked and organized his work space depending on what task he was working on.	• Getting ideas down on paper and going from the brain (thinking) to paper (producing)	• Discuss how to develop ideas in writing by taking one of his big ideas and writing some supporting details. • Do some shared writing about a text used during shared reading; model how to take an idea and have it come to life through details. • Create a "Writing About Our Reading" small group.
Alex	• Went on a word hunt in his independent reading book for words on his individual word card. • Spent too much time hunting, didn't have a big payoff, and didn't get the bulk of important work done during reading workshop.	• Fulfilling a word study job on the workshop job list and completing the task	• Pull students together for a small group to work on word work, play a game, or look at words and their spellings in context, all while being social and using language and words in context of talking, reading, and writing.

Here's what it might look like in middle school:

Student	What do you see/hear?	What is the student working on?	What are the implications of this work for teaching and assessment? (whole group, small group, one-to-one)
Parker	• Wears glasses, but takes them on and off. • Slow to ignite during independent reading, but once he settled in, everything around him sifted away. • Sat next to a chatty kiddo and turned his body slightly away to create a barrier while reading. • Gobbled up a bunch of pages in 18 minutes.	• Reading volume and stamina • Independence • Self-advocacy	• Inquire or observe more about when he needs his glasses and if the prescription is up to date. • Spend some time conferring and figure out if his reading rate has an impact (positive or negative) on his ability to comprehend or interpret texts.
Drew	• Smiled nonstop during independent reading. • Moved across the room to work in a small group with the special education teacher; started out happy and talkative, then became quiet.	• Reading some passages and then answering comprehension questions	• Does he need something different for small group? • What happens if you throw some new faces together for small group time? How will he respond? • Is the read/answer questions piece something he needs? Is it pushing him forward?
Marissa	• Read some books out of the Who Am I series (explains that she is rereading some because her younger brother loves them). • Taking ideas from her Reader's Notebook, she moved to her Writer's Notebook to begin some biography writing about her great aunt. • Family is very important to her.	• Reading and writing about biographies	• Create a culture of "It's okay to read books that are more like vacation books just because you want to," which is not always popular in middle school. • Find some biography books at a more complex level that she may find intriguing (connecting with the library media specialist). • See if she can bring in some photo albums or pictures of family members—developing some stories from artifacts.

OBSERVE ACROSS SEVERAL STUDENTS

At other times, we can get a bead on what the class needs by looking at a few students at once. We create theories based on patterns we see across several students' work. Take a look at one student's work, which represents several students in this small group.

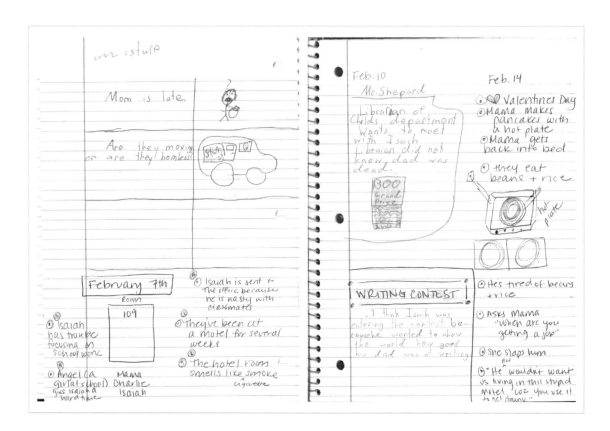

What Would You Do?

Saddle up next to a small group and listen in. What do you see and hear? What are students working on? Based on what you learn, what will you do next?

_____

_____

_____

_____

Our job as facilitators of small group learning is to create theories based on small group discussion and work at the table. Then, we use our theories to guide our decision making for next steps in small group learning experiences. Here are some decisions Julie made based on her theories:

- Discussion about why the bottles were lying around (a gentle reference about someone who may have struggles with alcohol abuse).
- Use of language in the text that signaled the bottles were not soda bottles.
- Significance of the length of time it takes to braid hair and how spending their time not with their mom made them feel.
- Visualizing what it feels like to hang out, relax in a peaceful environment (different from their own), and eat a good meal.

- Several group members asked, "If the car is full of their belongings, does that mean that the family was moving or that they no longer had a home?" This signals that the group might benefit from revisiting that section of the text with Julie joining in and talking through it. In this particular case, it signaled to Julie that she should back up even farther in the text and make sure everyone understood the "notices hanging on the door" (eviction notices) and what a reader could infer about the meaning behind that piece of information.
- Having resources (computer or tablet) in close proximity would be beneficial so that unfamiliar ideas or words can be researched quickly (e.g., *hot plate*—looked it up, drew a picture to create a visual image).
- Students held onto their thinking with the natural flow of the story. Dates are used in the short story to show time. Students used the same structure while holding their thinking, which made reading their ideas easy to follow. This work serves as a nice example to share with the whole class during a debrief or the next day's minilesson to fuel different ways to hold thinking while reading. This also serves as an anchor for students when they are retelling, summarizing, or creating a timeline of events in the story.

STUDENT MOVES AND TEACHER MOVES

We don't typically read a text in the real world and preassign stopping points for where we plan to stop and think. However, this can be a valuable strategy to teach kids as they learn to monitor their own understanding. What we ultimately want is for that process to happen automatically and naturally. Until that happens, we provide scaffolding so that kids learn how to do it as they read.

> Our job as facilitators of small group learning is to create theories based on small group discussion and work at the table.

Student Move: Students can pick a text or part of a text and determine where they will stop along the way to hold their thinking. Students can mark the spots with sticky notes. When they get to a sticky note, they pause and ask themselves, "What is the gist of what I'm reading?" Sticky notes are just a guide. Students do not have to stick with their original stopping point if a better spot naturally fits as they are reading. Take a look at the following example, where a student marked a short story using four different sticky notes.

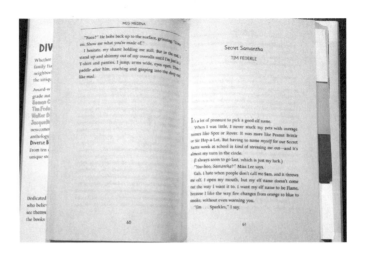

Student work can come in all types of formats. Gone are the days (we hope!) where kids have to write five-paragraph essays to show understanding. We want kids spending time doing things that will help them in their literacy journeys 10 years from now. Making thinking visible should be personalized. Take a look at the work sample titled *Secret Samantha*.

Teacher Move: Allow students a freestyle form for holding their thinking. By modeling and allowing kids to model different ways of thinking, we are actually encouraging and valuing their personal styles and choice.

TAKING TIME TO REFLECT

So, if we want kids to make their thinking visible and use that student work to make future plans, we need to pause and reflect on our practices, coupled with what kids have to say about the process. This helps us provide the right instruction (or scaffolding) at the right time. Here are a few reflection questions that work for both teachers and students—at almost any time, within any content.

- What were your big takeaways from _____?
- What do you notice about _____, and what will you do next?
- After today's experience, what will you do the same? Different?

The information you gain from reflection provides the *fuel* and insight so we know what to do next with and for students.

One Last Thing

Why is it that we've spent the last several decades trying *not* to teach a class as though all individuals in it were basically alike? It's simple. Because doing so just doesn't have an impact on student growth. You teach to the middle, trying to hit as many kids as possible who fall into that category, and at best what you get is a few kids getting stronger and smarter. But, if you work to discern what you know about your students through your interactions with them and the work they produce, you can place that alongside what they need to grow their curiosities, passions, habits, and needs. Couple that with designated standards and learning targets, and you can form nimble small groups that maximize opportunities for student growth. Go ahead—what are you waiting for? All you need are your eyes and ears, your students, your anchor documents, maybe your notebook and some sticky notes, and the determination to use student work to plan for the kids right in front of you. Have at it!

CHAPTER SEVEN

Curating

(because selecting the right texts inspires readers to be connoisseurs)

Casey was a self-proclaimed "non–reader and writer." You've met the type, haven't you? The kiddo who comes through your classroom door and knows school for the struggles it brings. That was Casey on the first day of fourth grade. While his backpack was still swinging from being hung on his hook, Casey approached Julie and said, "I'm Casey. I'm not good at reading, and I hate to write." Then, he strolled away to read the morning message with the rest of the crew. He looked relieved. It was like he was saying, "Whew, got that out of the way." Julie figured that Casey thought this status update would debunk any intentions she might have for his reading and writing that year. As she stood there watching him talk to the other kids while finding his seat, all Julie could think of was "Game on, buddy . . . game on."

This admission of "I don't do literacy" got Julie to jump-start two things: (1) creating a theory for how this attitude and self-perception came to be and (2) beginning the very next day with an inquiry that would help Casey change his mindset. And spoiler alert: 9 times out of 10, it's a matter of finding the right book or text set for the "nonreader."

Photo by Rachel Langosch

During the first few days, Julie did her typical kidwatching moves. She surveyed, listened in to pop-up small group conversations, observed and talked with Casey and other kids while hanging out on the playground during recess, looked across parent surveys she sent home on the first day, and so on. (Refer to Chapter Four for more tips on kidwatching.) She was building a profile of each child, not to label her students, but to mark a starting point. Think of the profile as a sidewalk—a pathway that represents a year. You collect information that will guide you, and off you go on a journey. Here's a beginning snippet of what Julie collected in her notebook about Casey:

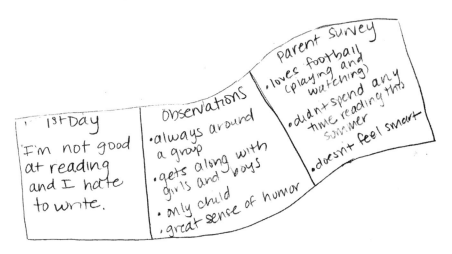

As an experienced teacher, Julie knows that sometimes kids need us to affectionately "pull rank"—to let a child who seems to be calling the shots on what he is willing to learn know he's not going to be able to coast or "hide out" all year. She knew that was true for Casey. In order to figure out the experiences that led him to these literacy woes, Julie met one-to-one with him the second week of school. Here are Julie's notes based on what Casey explained:

- Reading is really hard for Casey and always has been.
- The last book he read that he remembers enjoying was *Curious George* (he says that was a long time ago).
- He hates being pulled out of his classroom by the reading teachers. He feels like it's dumb because they have you read these little books that are boring; he also says that they give you books that look like little kid books and it's embarrassing to get them out so he just keeps them in his backpack.
- He doesn't like his handwriting and says he has nothing to write about, plus he doesn't know how to spell a lot of words.

When you look at what Casey shared, how does it make you feel? Can you relate? Do you have students who feel that way? What Casey was experiencing is what a lot of kids experience. The solution is most often this: Curate. In this chapter, we use Casey and other student and classroom examples to show you how a museum mentality works for every kind of reader. Because it's not about the reading level—it's about the match. Finding texts for individual and groups of students matters. And like in a museum, it's about selecting the finest representations you can get your hands on.

> *Give a reader a book, and he reads that one book. Teach a reader how to choose a book, and he reads for a lifetime.*
>
> **—Adapted from a Chinese proverb**

Two Essential Questions This Chapter Helps You Answer

1. How do I curate texts with students' curiosities, passions, habits, and needs in mind and that inspire new learning while at the same time addressing my instructional plans?

2. How do students curate texts for themselves and others?

Beliefs

Our Beliefs About Curating

We believe . . .	How it shows up in our work . . .
There is an art and a science to curating texts for small group instruction.	Staying current by reading voluminously and widely, with our students in mind, is a *must*!
While a developmental reading assessment can tell you a student's reading level, that dipstick measure doesn't tell you what types of texts are going to create "fires in the bellies" of your students. We curate by knowing students' needs and wants.	We practice kidwatching and asking kids what they want to read or learn more about. If we ask, they usually tell us.
Cultivating students as curators builds a shared vision for a literate classroom, increases student motivation and engagement, and galvanizes student independence.	We invite students into the work and give them a role in curation across each unit of study or learning progression, and we ask them to bring or suggest different types of texts that can support their work and the work of their peers.

Teachers *and* Students as Curators

Many hundreds of professional books and articles have been published on choosing books for read-alouds, shared reading, and so on. As we were writing this chapter, however, it hit us like a thunderbolt that too little attention has been given to exactly how teachers can more intentionally and intuitively cultivate the book-selection savvy in students. Once again, as teachers, we've got to push our readers out the door, so to speak, and make it clear sooner in the school year that they've got to be their own curators. So, we are dividing this chapter into two sections that reflect that. The first is about teachers curating texts with their students in mind. The second section is about students becoming masterful curators for themselves and for others. And you know what? It's the more important section, frankly, because when students curate for themselves, it means they are in charge of feeding and nourishing their own reading. When readers are fully independent, it means they have a say in what they are going to read, how much, and what types. Self-curating readers are able to know and find *what's next in their reading pile.*

THE LIFE SKILL OF CURATING FOR OTHERS

Being able to curate for others means that you habitually listen to and learn from others; you know the kind of reading material that others might find interesting, so you are on the lookout for it. There's an inherent, warm social contract in the air around the concept of curating for others. In education, we often talk about reading as a way to develop empathy, reading as a social act, reading as a gateway to civilized discourse, and so on. It all begins with curating for others in small groups. It's a life skill even deeper than empathy because it implies an intimacy with others' ideas, and a connectedness.

Teachers as Curators

Museums are curated with great thought. Curators anticipate movement; they deliberately choose which pieces to hang and in the best order. Exhibits are planned spectacularly for impact. When we curate as teachers, we act with a similar mindset. Text curation is an art and a science. That's because we choose with our students and curriculum in mind. The art of curation involves matching texts that will inspire and fuel students' curiosities with the science of finding texts that also can be used as teaching tools for the content we need to teach. In this next section, we zero in on daily ways to curate great text for our kids.

Why

- To meet individual students' social and emotional needs
- To stoke students' personal interests and passions
- To nurture students' knowledge development and/or conceptual understandings
- To address curricular demands
- To differentiate instruction/for responsive purposes

When

- During whole group instruction, minilessons, shared reading, or read-aloud
- During small group learning opportunities through shared models or as individual reading in the small group
- During a one-to-one conversation to demonstrate or practice a strategy or to inspire an independent study

CURATING TO STOKE STUDENTS' INTERESTS

Stoking students' interests starts by compiling dynamic texts together. We think it goes way beyond matching a fiction book with a nonfiction book. It includes bundling poetry, novels, infographics, picture books, lyrics, magazine articles, blogs, illustrated calendars, videos, and the like. It's like the food delivery companies that provide you with all of the ingredients to make an amazing meal. Or the clothing companies that send you a complete outfit and all of the accessories in one box. While meal planning and outfit selection become easier, having all the needed items bundled also helps you grow your cooking abilities and sense of style, respectively. Curating texts with and for students is like that. Bundling a bunch of texts with students' wants and needs in mind will support them (access, volume, deeper meaning making, wide reading, etc.). For example, a biography study might house portraits, quotes, and ballads alongside a range of picture books and *Who Was?* biography books. Or a study on bridges might be complemented with models, famous photos of bridges, and poetry by J. Patrick Lewis.

In the last few years, companies like Google and IDEO have stretched the concept of the workweek by giving 20% over to playing with ideas. We wholly embrace this concept, so let's look at a few of our favorite classroom practices that honor creative thinking and problem solving. The first is "Genius Hour," which has caught on in many schools. Genius Hour is the turning over of one hour a week to develop kids' passions and interests. The other is "Passion Projects," which provides kids with time, space, and resources to study and noodle around with, in order to learn more about topics and ideas that interest them, tied to an actionable, tangible outcome. Let's take a closer look at how we might curate an environment of curiosity and invention.

Genius Hour: A time and space for students to focus on projects that interest them. Genius Hour has three steps. Students will engage in

1. Asking meaningful questions

2. Research

3. Sharing their project with others

Check out www.geniushour.com for more information.

Passion Project: A creative side project that has deeper meaning and tangible outcomes. The purpose is to inspire and enable a world filled with people who follow their passions. Students will

1. Brainstorm—find/define their passions!

2. Take time to work on and develop their passion project

3. Share their project with others

This is open curriculum with kids' interests driving the way. For both practices, a teacher's job as a curator is to pivot on the spot. We listen, we nudge, and we act like the experienced librarian who nods and says, "I know just what you need to find out more about . . . "

If you plan to prioritize time in your schedule and space in your classroom to harness these opportunities, you can get a head start by finding out as much as you can about your students. In Chapter Two, we shared two of our favorite ways of getting to know our students: cool stuff bags and photo essays. You might also try this survey that will help you get to know your students in new and interesting ways. See the Appendix (pages 292–293) for blank survey templates.

Take a look at Olive's survey results. While her responses are a bit bare in comparison to her classmates', Olive packs a lot into her few words and shares even more when asked in a small group about her interests. She prefers to read graphic novels, specifically those by Raina Telgemeier, but opts for YouTube star

Spice it up a bit. Ask kids about things that are relevant to their lives, and you'll know exactly what things they will want to read about, which becomes your source for curating.

Name OLIVE!!!!!

Tell us your thoughts…

	LOVE it! 5	4	Kind of 3	2	Not really 1
Building things	✓				
Coloring, designing, making creations		✓			
Watching/playing online games			✓		
Being outside		✓			
Diving right into something without a set of directions					✓
Picking your own groups to work with at school		✓			
Working with 3 people vs. 6		✓			
Reading short vs. long texts (books, poems, articles, etc.)				✓	
Fruit instead of candy	✓				
Staying up late even if it means I'll be tired the next day	✓				

A little bit about Olive

Favorite pop star, Youtuber, singer, band, movie or author? Tell me anything that you want me to know!

Liza Koshy
Raina Telgimate
the things I love are so many yah

How would you describe how/where you learn best?

Bed watch a book on Rock'em I phone open door

If school let out a few hours early and your only job was to have fun for 4 hours, what would you do?

Watch T.V. While I get a puppy

Eating junk food or go shopping for clothes

What do you want me to know that I haven't asked you?

Do you want a Dog? Yes Do you want one? YES!!!
Exactly!!!

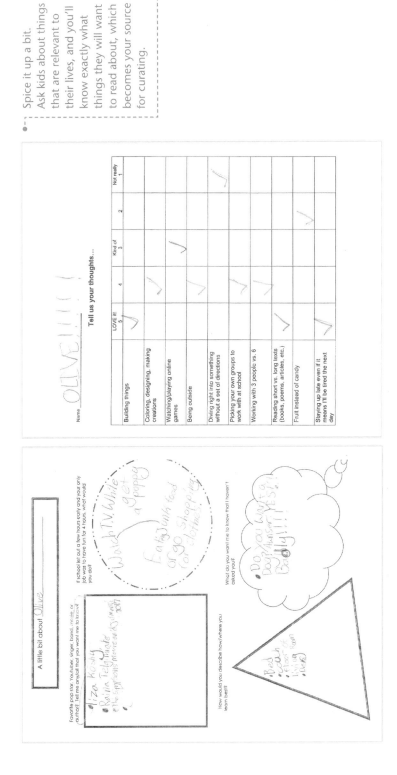

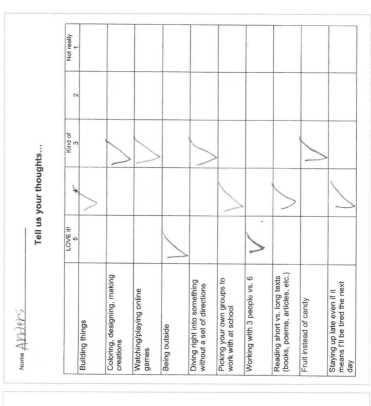

Name _Anders_

Tell us your thoughts...

	LOVE it! 5		Kind of 3	2	Not really 1
Building things		✓			
Coloring, designing, making creations			✓		
Watching/playing online games			✓		
Being outside	✓				
Diving right into something without a set of directions			✓		
Picking your own groups to work with at school					
Working with 3 people vs. 6	✓				
Reading short vs. long texts (books, poems, articles, etc.)		✓			
Fruit instead of candy					
Staying up late even if it means I'll be tired the next day		✓			

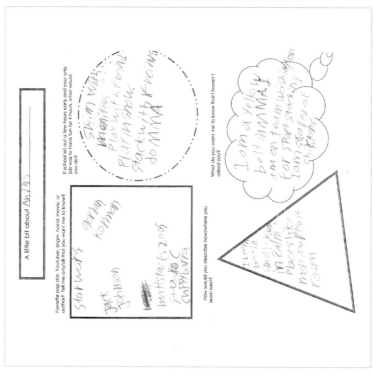

A little bit about _Anders_

Favorite pop star, YouTuber, singer, band, movie, or author? Tell me any/all that you want me to know?

Star Wars
Jack Johnson
Gordan Korman
Matt Stateof staufec Cuppabatta

How would you describe how/where you learn best?

I work best in small groups or in calm places like medium/push room

If school let out a few hours early and your only job was to have fun for 4 hours, what would you do?

Swim with Manatees
Play with a friend
Playin snow
Start with Kicking do MMA

What do you want me to know that I haven't asked you?

I am a yellow belt in MMA. I am on team Washman for spart-spacking. I am a fan of chicken.

Liza Koshy for "after school" fun. Olive makes us think about the importance of YouTube in our kids' lives. We also know she's a "snacker," so giving her options for when she eats her morning snack (it's usually at 10) might be helpful. Maybe Olive wants to nibble on her snack during reading workshop or save a snack for read-aloud time after lunch.

Now look at Anders's survey responses on the facing page. He mentions that he is a yellow belt in martial arts and a member on Team Washington, a sports stacking team. When beginning a study of nonfiction, we make a note that he might enjoy working in a small group reading and writing about martial arts or sport stacking. Maybe he would enjoy the new *Star Wars* graphic novel or investigate the "how to build snow forts" book in our classroom library.

Last, notice both students have a preference for working in small groups. We have found that the more familiar students are with small groups, the more highly students rate them.

CURATING MENTOR TEXTS TO TEACH SOMETHING POWERFUL

Whether you are a teacher looking for a text to meet a curricular need or selecting one for a read-aloud, at heart you are always doing one thing: making a choice that will help you teach your kids something *powerful*. We know that's kind of a subjective word, but we assert it's not more or less subjective than saying we want to teach something *complex* or *challenging*. By wanting our students to have a powerful experience, we find a text whose ideas and quality are worthy models. The authors and their works will mentor readers. Readers will feel the power of mentorship. So we lean on these texts as mentors. Imagine sitting around a circle with mentors like Ralph Fletcher, Penny Kittle, Stephanie Harvey, and Anne Goudvis. We would not only learn alongside them but would also be lifted by the collegial conversation and interaction. The same is the case with our students. We want them to "sit around the table" with Jacqueline Woodson, R. J. Palacio, Angie Thomas, John Green, Matt de la Peña, Jandy Nelson, and Rainbow Rowell.

Steps for Curating

As you can see from the following graphic, curation begins by kidwatching because knowing our kids' curiosities, passions, habits, and needs helps us know what will fuel their reading. Once we know what kinds of things kids will enjoy, we begin curating by selecting texts with that in mind. Decision making is a big part of the curation process. Teachers match texts with purpose by determining when students will use the texts—during whole group, small group, or one-to-one learning opportunities. The fun part, from our vantage point, is drawing kids into the texts we have chosen by sparking interest in texts in preparation for kids to read and construct meaning. Just as learning is never done, there are endless ways to curate more texts. We use reflection to replay the effectiveness of our curation and instruction and determine next steps.

1. **Kidwatch** to learn about your students' reading interests (see Chapter Four) and ask your students what kinds of things they want to read (see interest surveys on pages 39 and 270)

2. **Curate and select** texts that fit students' wants and needs

3. **Decide** how you are going to use the text(s) (whole group, small group, one-to-one)

4. **Spark** students' interests by sharing the texts and your reasons for choosing them

5. **Read and construct meaning** (teacher and students *or* students and students)

6. **Invite** students to curate for themselves and others.

7. **Reflect** so that you can determine if you need to curate more texts (you may need to meet with students in the small group or one-to-one to determine next steps)

Zooming In on Step 2: Curate and Select

Let's jump ahead to Step 2 because the kidwatching step is covered in Chapter Four. By zooming in on curating and selecting texts, you focus on finding texts that you love and can't put down. It also means going beyond texts that are directly related to kids' curiosities and making sure we find amazing texts that support the skills and strategies that kids need to grow their reading muscles. Curating texts targeted to skills and strategies for small groups could include a focus on

- Author's purpose
- Building background knowledge
- Cause and effect
- Comparing and contrasting
- Drawing conclusions
- Inferencing
- Main idea, important facts, and supporting details
- Making predictions
- Questioning the text and answering literal and inferential questions about the text
- Retelling
- Sequencing
- Summarizing
- Text features
- Text structures
- Texts that support an integrated unit of study (such as blending literacy skills with science, social studies, or math content)

KINDS OF TEXTS TO CONSIDER

There are so many texts in the world—so many at our fingertips. So where do you begin? We try to think beyond the typical combination of a fiction book

Big Advice

For a fresh new round-up of read-alouds for K–3, check out *The Ramped-Up Read-Aloud* by Maria Walther (2018); for how to gather and organize a best-in-kind classroom library, see *It's All About the Books* by Tammy Mulligan and Claire Landrigan (2018).

paired with a nonfiction book (infamously known as a text set), and curate lots of resources that look, sound, and feel different from others selected in the set so that students have depth and variety in the collection. We believe that will help students make connections, lift their knowledge and skills, make them question and ponder, and feed into what gets them excited about learning. Here are some of the types of mentor texts we curate when designing units of study, learning progressions, or companion text sets for small group learning experiences.

Examples of Mentor Texts

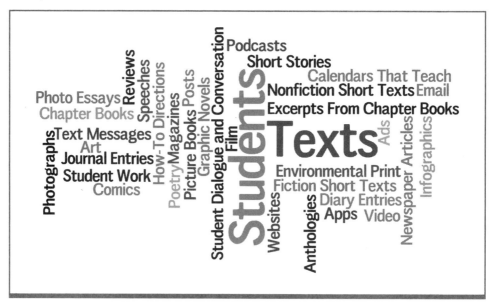

Wordle.net

To go a step further, the following table shows how we start with a rich text and use it to create meaningful small group experiences. We outline some big takeaways as an example, but keep in mind that your big takeaways may differ based on your approach, length of time using the mentor text, and instructional moves throughout the learning experience.

Small Group Mentor Texts in Action

Examples of Mentor Texts	Examples of Small Group Mentor Text Experiences	Intended Big Takeaways
Rad American Women A–Z: Rebels, Trailblazers, and Visionaries Who Shaped Our History . . . and Our Future! by Kate Schatz (2015) (nonfiction book filled with one-page biographical spreads about women leaders)	• During a biography unit, a small group meets to discuss self-selected biographic sketches from Kate Schatz's *Rad American Women A–Z.* Students share how they took notes and what information struck them. • Students take a few minutes to study the format and author moves. What does Kate Schatz do to make a memorable one-page biographical sketch? How is it organized? • These insights are recorded on a chart. • Students are invited to read a couple more one-page biographies to see if Kate Schatz has some new moves they didn't identify.	• These short one-page biographies give kids a chance to dive into a text, take notes, and name important details of a person's life (mentorship in capturing important information and taking notes). • Students can retell facts and choose to research more (mentorship for curiosity and research). • Small groups will notice organizational aspects like the number of words, paragraphs, opening sentences, endings, and craft like word choice and voice. • It also provides a great starting point for students to study what Kate Schatz does in narrowing the facts and story of important people's lives to one page. • This "accessible reading text" becomes a friendly writing model for students to borrow from and create their own one-page biographic sketches. • By making a chart—"What does Kate Schatz teach us about writing one-page biographies?"—we subtly move from reading for information to reading to learn about writing. • Students learn to "read like a writer."
"The Most Beautiful Goals" infographic by John Grimwade and Jeong Suh (2014; from *The Best American Infographics 2014*)	• For five to seven minutes, ask students to dig into the text. (Create a jot list of all the things you notice about this two-page spread.) • Have students share out their noticings. (What did you notice? Where do your eyes go? What grabs your attention, and why?) • For five minutes, ask students to take a second read of the text. (How do the orientation of the text, use of color, labeling, charts, and illustrations help you make meaning of the text?) • Have students share out their noticings. (What moves did the author make that lifted your meaning-making muscles?)	• Depending on whether or not students play soccer or are familiar with the game, they anchor into the text in different ways—some flip the book around and go right to the infographic that spans two pages while others read from left to right, beginning with the informative paragraph. • The picture provides the reader with a lot of information, but the chart (including use of color, movement of the ball, angles, directionality, and labeling) is necessary to make meaning of this text. • If the small group has read about soccer before or is studying infographics, this text becomes relational. Furthermore, if students are writing nonfiction and/or using infographics to share out their own research, this text could be inspirational as students aspire to create/produce content for the world.

Examples of Mentor Texts	Examples of Small Group Mentor Text Experiences	Intended Big Takeaways
The Hero's Trail: A Guide for a Heroic Life by T. A. Barron (2007)	• In a character study unit, T. A. Barron's *The Hero's Trail* can be used to look at ways to define and compare and contrast what makes a hero. • Begin discussion by asking students to define a hero. • After co-constructing a definition, ask students to name potential heroes that they know or have read or heard about. • Record each hero's name on a card. • Generate categories to classify each of the heroes listed. • Go back to T. A. Barron's book and list the kinds of categories he has placed heroes in (mentoring ways to name the world—or categorize). • Revise categories to fit the groups thinking about hero categories. • During the study and further reading experiences, go back to the categories and see if they can be revised to fit the group's ongoing understanding of heroes. • Read short passages from *The Hero's Trail* to better situate T. A. Barron's categories for heroes.	• After co-constructing a definition for *hero* and generating categories to fit heroes in, debate whether famous people are heroes or celebrities or both. • Using the different categories, have students find example figures in their community who fit as heroes and invite them into class to speak. Generate questions to ask the speakers and ways to record their stories. • Leave questions for T. A. Barron on his website about how he researched people for his book. • Have students borrow from T. A. Barron's style of telling the hero's story in a few paragraphs and write their own hero books fitting categories of heroes to hero stories.

Keep in mind that your big takeaways may differ based on your approach, length of time using the mentor text, and instructional moves throughout the learning experience.

Zooming In on Step 3: Decide

Making decisions about *how* to use texts is the messiest part of the process because there are lots of ways to use texts. There isn't one right answer; it really comes down to your purpose and sometimes amount of time.

Curating Texts: Steps for Decision Making

	Whole Group	Small Group	One-to-One
Curating text(s) for shared reading	**You can** Read the whole text together OR Read part of the text, then stop (this gets your teaching point across, but doesn't require any more time or attention to the text) OR Read part of the text, then pause and invite students to read the rest in small groups or individually ⟶	⟶	
Curating a second text for similar reasons to use the same day or the next day	**You can** Read the whole text together OR Read part of the text, then stop (this gets your teaching point across, but doesn't require any more time or attention to the text) OR Read part of the text, then pause and invite students to read the rest in small groups or individually ⟶	⟶	
Curating text(s) for small group(s)		If using a text with a small group(s), **Students can** Read one text together Read multiple texts, but on their own (and come back to small group to discuss) ⟶ Read the same texts, together Read the same texts, but on their own (and come back to small group to discuss) ⟶ Read different texts, but on their own (and come back to small group to discuss) ⟶ **Teachers can** Make decisions for the group Make decisions with the group Let group decide Listen in Join in small group Join in, but confer one-to-one ⟶	
Curating text(s) for individual student(s)			If using a text with an individual student(s), **Students can** Read one text Read multiple texts **Teachers can** Make decisions for student(s) Make decisions with student(s) Let student(s) decide

Steps 4–7: Spark, Read and Construct Meaning, Invite, and Reflect

After you make important decisions about whether you will use the texts you've curated with the whole group, small groups, or individual students, it's important to build excitement about them. If you are reading a text in front of students as a read-aloud or through shared reading, you might spark excitement by sharing some interesting author facts. Reading a short text closely can take more time, but it's worth the investment in close reading with student Turn and Talk because it allows you to anchor back to it again and again. Or, maybe you kick off a small group session by asking students a question related to the text, such as "What is this title trying to say?"

So, let's imagine what we've done so far. You've sized up kids' interests and used that information to curate and select texts that will fuel their reading. You decide whether or not you will be working with the curated texts in the whole group, small groups, or one-to-one. Regardless of the decisions thus far, the next step is focused on the whole reason we read to begin with—to make meaning.

Whether you are reading texts in the whole group, small groups, or one-to-one, students are actively constructing meaning. That's the main "work" you want them to be doing. Ways they might show their thinking include

- Creating an anchor chart
- Participating in discussion
- Writing bullet points, notes, doodles, and lists in Reader's Notebooks
- Answering a teacher- or student-generated prompt

The reflection process enables us to go back and forth with our decision making. Curating text for students is a recursive process. The more we work alongside kids and text in small groups, the more we will know about what they can do and what they need next.

CASEY: AN EXAMPLE OF CURATING FOR AN INDIVIDUAL STUDENT

Remember Casey, the fourth grader we introduced at the beginning of this chapter? Julie's next move was to use those data, coupled with current developmental reading data, and get to work. Seeing that Casey was reading independently at the end of a second-grade level, the reading team prescribed four days of guided reading, outside of the classroom, with a group of third-grade students who were reading at about the same level. Julie knew that was not what Casey needed and definitely not what he wanted. She proposed a different plan.

LIFTING CASEY'S READING

1. Create a small group for Casey and some buddies (based on **kidwatching** and common interests/inquiries)

2. **Curate and select** a bunch of texts that they will find interesting (different levels, different genres)

3. **Decide** on how to use the texts and who could benefit in small group.

4. **Spark** small groups' curiosity by briefly sharing and thinking aloud from the text set

5. Have **students read texts** from the text set and **construct meaning** by holding their thinking and sharing out understandings and big takeaways (Julie will join in the conversation about half of the time the group meets)

6. **Invite** students to contribute their own texts to the small group reading work.

7. **Reflect** by meeting with Casey (one-to-one) for a quick check-in to look across his chosen texts and notebook, helping him self-monitor his reading at school and at home; meet with his small group to determine next steps

As Casey's teacher, Julie had to think about what might inspire the small group. Sticking a variety of texts in a bin for quick choosing was a first step. This companion set of texts, focused on sports, which was the topic of interest and choice by the boys in this small group, gave way for authentic differentiation because it could be expanded or contracted based on individual students.

CURATING ACROSS A UNIT: EXAMPLE FROM A FOURTH-GRADE CLASSROOM

Let's see how this played out in a classroom: It was late February, and Julie was working alongside fourth-grade

What Would You Do?

Think about a small group of kids that you want to pull together and what they might enjoy reading. Based on what you know about them, what texts would you put in a basket for them to explore and read?

_____

_____

_____

_____

students who were preparing to read and write texts that focused on writing opinions, and eventually persuading someone to take a stand with them about a topic they felt passionate about. Julie knew that these students were interested in the way things work and the "why" behind what makes things go because she had listened in to their questioning and conversations a lot. These kids were passionate about big topics such as global warming, mysterious stars in our galaxy, the balance of power in government, benefits of organic foods, and a controversial local issue related to protecting green space from city development. Julie knew the opinion/persuasion unit on the horizon would be an excellent landscape to stretch students' reading and writing muscles. She also knew, based on formative writing data, that many of these students had strong thinking and verbal skills, but writing ideas down and using a text to support their thinking were areas that needed lifting.

Julie brainstormed a list of authentic mentors or models existing out in the world for students to wrestle with that would jump-start their reading and writing journey for a unit focused on *going* organic. Here's an example from Julie's notebook that served as a good start:

Chapter Book: *Chew on This* by Eric Schlosser and Charles Wilson (2007)

Infographic: "Big Bad Corn" by Mother Nature Network (Shreaves, 2012; see www.mnn.com/food/healthy-eating/blogs/infographic-big-bad-corn)

Website: Iowa Corn (www.iowacorn.org)

Newspaper Article: "A Pancake Brings Corn and Berries Together" by Melissa Clark, *The New York Times*, August 17, 2017

Picture Book: *The Life and Times of Corn* by Charles Micucci (2009)

Since Julie spent the first part of the year focused on meaty texts through shared reading, using excerpts from *The Omnivore's Dilemma: Young Readers Edition* (Pollan, 2009) as mentor texts for this unit was a great entry point. During this integrated science, social studies, and English language arts unit, the students read a short news article explaining the benefits of organic foods that spurred debate among the students. This hot topic was relevant to the students' current events reading, and many seemed very interested and motivated to learn more about related topics.

A few weeks into the unit, the kids were ready to lean on this mentor text, specifically Chapter 6, "Processed Food, Splitting the Kernel." Julie knew reading the whole book aloud for shared text was not the move her students needed, but using a chapter from the book as a mentor text to engage readers and create a text for discussion would be perfect. Doing her own assignment prior to working with students is a must-do for Julie. For this reading, it was a matter of reading the text and imagining where students were going to get tripped up. That's because if we can anticipate where they might get stuck, we can pause and teach into it in the moment. For writing, it's imagining where students' writing might be too skinny and anticipating where student writers might need to lean into a mentor text (something to dig into to unpack the moves an author is making) so that they can mimic or try on their moves. With this class, the "Processed Food, Splitting the Kernel" chapter was used in multiple ways and for multiple purposes.

Purpose	How was the mentor text used in support of reading?	How was the mentor text used in support of writing?
Using a mentor text through shared reading with a whole class	Making meaning of the text: • Identifying big ideas in the text • Understanding new vocabulary • Identifying facts and opinions stated in the text • Identifying language used to persuade others	Unpacking the moves the author made: • Identifying when, where, how, and how often the author used facts and opinions in the text in order to persuade others • Using infographics and diagrams to present information or show a side of an issue or compare different sides of an issue
Revisiting the whole class mentor text, or part of the mentor text, for reteaching or focus	• Identifying unknown or unfamiliar words • Using annotations or talking back to the text in order to make meaning of the big ideas • Breaking down language that is used to state a fact versus opinion • Identifying sentences in the text that were trying to persuade the reader	• Outlining steps in a process that supports or dismantles a point of view • Using headings to make writing flow and reading friendly • Using language to evoke emotion • Using illustrations to develop a message or further a point of view

Julie leveraged this mentor text and gave students multiple opportunities to use the same text to make meaning. In this example, Julie went from the whole group (shared reading with the same text for the whole class) to the small group (shared reading for a second read with the same text, but with a small group). This deeper dive, across multiple settings, provided students with more than one opportunity to read with different lenses and purposes. These combined experiences helped students get ready to read other persuasive texts and write their own opinion/persuasion pieces.

Sometimes planning for small groups, outside of the whole group, is needed. This is where the biggest impact can be seen and where teachers can say with confidence that differentiation is on the front burner. In order to prioritize small group instruction, Julie took advantage of what she learned by studying students during the whole group and small group work that led her to create these small groups.

Students as Curators

Creating opportunities to support students as they grow into independent, voracious, lifelong readers is the goal. We've made it clear that we believe a high leverage point in accomplishing that goal is through small group learning experiences. Giving kids time to read texts of varying lengths (say good-bye to kids only reading chapter books in the upper grades!) and experience cross-pollination of genres at one time (say hello to narrative nonfiction, YouTube videos, and infographics as top-notch text choices to inspire kids) and diversity in text complexity (say goodbye to sticking with a student's reading level as the only qualifying factor for students reading a text). Instead of perpetuating passive learners, with classrooms of kids depending on us to curate texts, we want kids curating for themselves and for others.

KIDS CURATING FOR THEMSELVES

We want kids to grow up saying things like "I love reading mystery, but I'm not all that excited about historical fiction" or "I saw this sign on the subway, and I can't stop thinking about what it was trying to say" or "Did you see that letter to the editor in *The New York Times* last week?" All of those statements signal vibrant, voluminous readers. If we let kids curate for themselves, we can also model and teach them to live off of Tom Newkirk's (2012) advice: "We can learn to pay attention, concentrate, devote ourselves to authors. We can slow down so we can hear the voice of texts, feel the movement of sentences, experience the pleasure of words and own passages that speak to us" (p. 41).

If we want kids to grow up having opinions about how much they read and what they read, we have to let them practice in school.

This student loved *The Tale of Despereaux*, which led her to *Flora & Ulysses, Because of Winn-Dixie,* and *Raymie Nightingale*. Self-curating by reading an author's entire body of work is a great way to ramp up reading volume!

Photo by Rachel Langosch

KIDS CURATING FOR OTHERS

This is a skill that is needed across the classroom today and for decades to come. While kids are in our care—if we decide that we don't have to be involved in every small group learning opportunity—we have to trust that kids can and will listen to one another. If we create the right small group culture, we will make it safe for kids to offer up new ideas for their peers to read. They may even comb through their own reading materials or the shelves in the library with someone else's interest or inquiry in mind . . . all in service of being a part of a small group team who looks out for others. We want kids to have that feeling of satisfaction of handing a book or article to a friend and saying, "I thought of you when I saw this." That is how we help support students in becoming great guests at a dinner party. If you are well read and comfortable in curating diverse texts, you will probably have more confidence in small talk about the world during the drinks and appetizer phase.

Sometimes reading volume comes when kids have the opportunities to curate texts for a new "club" they are hosting. These students wanted to create a humor club to investigate joke and riddle books, newspaper comics, puns, and age-appropriate how-to pranks and tricks. They know what they find funny, so curating for themselves and others their age works!

Photo by Rachel Langosch

KIDS-AS-CURATORS PROCESS

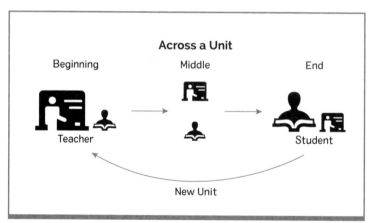

iStock.com/-VICTOR-

You simply tweak the steps for teachers as curators to draw students into the curating process.

How to Gradually Release Responsibility for Curating to Students

Teachers as Curators	Inviting Students Into Curation	Students as Independent Curators
Kidwatch to learn about your students' reading interests (see Chapter Four). Look around and take notes about popular series, topics, authors, and genres.	Ask your students what kinds of things they want to read (see interest surveys on pages 39 and 270).	• Listen actively when working with others • Make connections to self and others related to curriculum • Book talk about what they enjoy reading
Curate and select texts that fit students' wants and needs.	Invite students interested in talking about _____ books to meet at the small group area. Listen sharply to what kids enjoy about the books and their own personal preferences and connections to the texts. Take notes.	• Are always on the lookout for texts and authors that they know classmates will love • Offer up texts to peers that they have • Share texts that have curricular connections • Place books on the "You've got to read this" shelf
Decide how you are going to use the text(s) (whole group, small group, or one-to-one).	Provide a chance for students to "put a shine" on their book selections by sharing out to the large group.	• Have the autonomy to decide how they think a text they curate could or should be used with others • Know the systems and structures in place so that they can curate with individuals and groups in mind (e.g., how to get copies of an article made, or protocols for checking books out from the library for someone else)
Spark students' interests by sharing the texts and your reasons for choosing them.	Find a place to put student-selected books and invite students to add quotes about the books and write/share book reviews, hot reads, pictures of book stacks, or even selfies of them reading the books.	• Have the autonomy to display books across the classroom • Create new tubs with curated texts for others • Know the times that would be great to do a hot read about a book or author
Read and construct meaning (teacher and students _or_ students and students)	Give students the opportunity to find and offer up mentor texts or companion texts to peers and decide if they want to lead a discussion about them.	• Use supplies as needed to hold their thinking (chart paper, extra notebooks, sticky notes, index cards, etc.) • Know when to share their ideas—writing and discussion—with others without being led by the teacher • Have self-chosen book club conversations
Reflect so that you can determine if you need to curate more texts (you may need to meet with students in the small group or one-to-one to determine next steps).	As you reflect, have kids reflect too. Ask them if they think more texts are needed and, if so, who should curate and select them.	• Advocate for more time and resources • Make notes about books they love and abandon • Make stacks of "next in line to read" books. • Keep and/or clear out texts from units in their reading folders

Note: The **invite** step is incorporated throughout the process in this table.

CO-CURATING PROCESS IN ACTION: EXAMPLE FROM SIXTH GRADE

In this example, we show that teachers and readers often, in a sense, co-curate. Barry created the conditions for this, but it was his students who discovered both their voice and the mentor text during a small group discussion.

Barry *kidwatched*, as he always does. Julie was visiting and working alongside Barry as his coach, and she kidwatched too. Their observations made them wonder why there was such a keen interest in graphic novels during reading workshop, so Barry invited a small group of kids who love graphic novels to meet him at the conference table. While many students chose to read silently, three sixth-grade girls sauntered over to the meeting place. They each had their hands wrapped around *Smile* by Raina Telgemeier (2010). They began by talking about graphic novels and what made them so much fun to read. Soon they pointed their attention to *Smile*, and their conversation became more animated. Their enthusiasm was contagious. Ruby was particularly excited. She pointed out spots in the book she loved and how she felt like she was almost reading about herself. She related to being accident prone and how embarrassed she felt for Raina when she knocked her teeth out. Ruby went on to talk about her own experience from when she first came to our school and how nervous and self-conscious she felt. She mentioned it was like she was under a constant spotlight. Clumsily, she said, she bumped her way through, just like Raina in the book.

What had started as an opportunity to hear about the importance of reading graphic novels had emerged as a chance for three quiet girls to use this text to model how reading can launch us into our own personal stories. Barry and Julie gathered at the carpet at the end of reading workshop to hear the three girls talk about both *Smile* and the little stories of their own lives that this book raised.

As the kids went to break, Barry and Julie realized what the promise of this book and the girls' demonstration held for the class. They knew they had to double back and put *Smile* front and center again as a mentor text for lifting stories of their own lives from the connections we make as readers lost in our own books. Thus, Barry *curated and selected*. Then Barry and Julie *decided* just how they were going to use *Smile*: The following day, Barry held *Smile* up and *sparked* interest by asking if anyone had another story of a time when they felt awkward and self-conscious among their peers.

After a few funny tales, the class paused for five minutes and jotted their own stories in Reader's Notebooks. They then took four more minutes and read their short pieces to their shoulder partners. Before sending the readers off for reading, Barry gave students a purpose for when they *read and construct meaning* by asking them to pay attention to these kinds of connections as they read. Barry reminded the class that writers keep track of these thoughts in their notebooks. He mentioned that there would be a time to share their reading insights and stories at the end of reading workshop.

The following day, Barry *invited* students to bring their own favorite graphic novels to store on a special shelf in the class library, and he asked the girls to design a "cool" graphic novel sign. Through *reflection*, Barry and Julie took note of what worked well. They agreed that students as curators helped them see the power of popular tween/teen literacy and how giving students time and space to use a mentor text can ultimately bring out stories that might otherwise never be shared.

Blending teacher and student choice in reading graphic novels builds trust and ownership while inspiring meaningful conversation.

Photo by Christian Ford

Exemplars of Students as Curators

When teachers are metacognitive about curating texts for learners and, in turn, ask kids to be reflective, it helps readers become super self-reliant about guiding their own reading lives. We know that sounds a little pie in the sky, but it's true. We see it year after year. If we don't build rituals and routines for kids to curate, we risk them becoming overdependent on others, always waiting for someone else to hand them things to read. Instead, we want to create a culture of curation for self and for others because that's what we want our students to be able to do 10 years from now. Students play apprenticeships to teachers in the art of curation. There is an intentional hand-over process. First steps are pretty easy. In our argument unit of study, we ask kids to bring in examples of texts that feature persuasion and arguments. In our biography units, we ask kids to bring in examples of people they'd like to read more about. In our character unit, we ask kids to bring in examples of stories with characters they admire. In these initial steps, we ask kids to give us reasons for choosing the books and materials they have brought in. Coupled with book talks, where students are actively sharing books they love, students see their classrooms as places where they participate in building a rich classroom library.

> *Curating helps readers to become super self-reliant about guiding their own reading lives.*

FISH FARTS

Take a look at the photo below where kids have chosen a few poetry books that they haven't ever read before. They noticed a bin of poetry books in the library, and the one about "fish farts" caught their eyes. Before long, they were reading aloud and laughing. While they hadn't planned to read poetry, this excitement led them to small group learning about poetry during wintertime indoor recess.

To Get to What You See Here, **Try This**

1. When kids tell you they want to join a small group with their buddies, help make it happen. Think outside of the box if time feels limited (indoor recess, lunchtime, after school, virtual small group via a tech tool or platform, etc.).

2. Put multiple texts in front of kids that they want to read. Sometimes finding an organizing feature (poetry, heroes, toys, inventors, basketball, Kate Messner books, etc.) becomes the focus for the text set.

3. Decide approximately how many sessions or weeks this group will meet together and give kids the timeline so that they know what to expect.

4. Help everyone stay organized by giving each member of the group a two-pocket folder and a bucket/bin to house their texts in for safekeeping.

5. Add nourishing content to students' reading diets by folding in new texts regularly.

6. Invite students to add texts too.

Photo by Natalie Guerrero

SPOTTING GECKOS

Kids curating is often sparked by student interest. Cameron has an old gecko for a pet. When he found a *National Geographic Explorer* magazine featuring geckos, he pulled a pile and gathered some friends together to read and talk about geckos. Cameron's eyes lit up when he shared with the class how some geckos are nocturnal while others are diurnal. "And I thought I knew a lot about geckos," he chuckled.

Photo by Christian Ford

To Get to What You See Here, **Try This**

1. Students will more naturally curate when they see curation as a possibility. So we suggest you nudge individual students to talk about their horse or soccer interest with a small group with a text at their side.

2. Take a photo of the group, display the photo, and ask the group leader to talk about what happened. How did it get started? How did it end? What did the students enjoy?

3. Create a sign-up for a short, onetime small group focusing on a key interest and a text that will deepen curiosity about the subject.

4. Meet with one of these interest small groups, and after the conversation, co-construct a "creating your own small group" procedure chart.

5. Display the chart and have one of the creators share it with the whole group.

FUN FACTS LEAD TO MORE CURATION

Students were shocked to learn that George Washington checked books out of the library and had overdue charges because he didn't return his books on time. That led to students finding more interesting facts and stories about America's Founding Fathers.

Photo by Rachel Langosch

To Get to What You See Here, **Try This**

1. Give students a basket and let them find texts that excite and inspire them.

2. Encourage them to fill the basket with texts of all sorts of variety, size, length, genre, and range of complexity—and focused on the same topic.

3. Make sure you have all of the tools students might need close by, such as sticky notes, two-pocket folders, pens, pencils, and coloring utensils.

4. Encourage the group to make a plan for reading. Will the students read the same thing at the same time or different? When will they get together to talk about what they are reading and thinking about and writing? Will they bring other texts to offer up to the group, and if so, when?

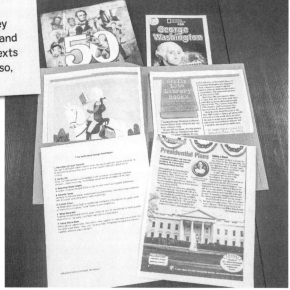

A SEARCH FOR WOMEN IN HISTORY

Seventh-grade students were looking across "women in history" texts. They combed through public library and family-owned resources to create a companion set of texts that included biographies, anthologies, two-page spreads, poems, and sophisticated alphabet books that they would read over a two-week period. Eventually, the texts might inspire some nonfiction writing about what makes a person stand out in history and never be forgotten.

Photo by Natalie Guerrero

To Get to What You See Here, **Try This**

1. Once kids are in reading partnerships or groups of three or four, ask them to read a short text about a topic and discuss main points or takeaways.

2. Give them guiding questions, such as "Why are all of these women being honored as heroes or important figures in history? What were their contributions to society?"

3. Ask them to pick a text to read during independent reading or that evening for home reading.

4. Teacher homework: Curate more texts to put in the bucket for the next day.

5. The next day, get the students in this small group back together to continue their reading and/or discussion.

6. During the workshop time debrief, have group members share out some of their takeaways from the reading and discussion. Ask the whole class if anyone would like to join this group. (If the group gets too big, break the group into subgroups.)

TAKING TIME TO REFLECT

It's interesting to compare our skills for choosing and displaying books and reading materials with those of a museum curator. It leaves us wondering what museum curators and even bookstore owners do to entice. Now think about what you do to match kids with great reads.

- What can you do to promote reading a wide range of fascinating materials?
- How can you hand the curation process over to your students so they are purposely choosing their own books, magazines, and videos and offering them up to their classmates?
- What is your next unit of study? What will you curate for your students, and what will you ask them to bring in?

One Last Thing

We began the chapter talking about Casey, the self-proclaimed non–reader and writer. We would be remiss to overlook the impact various texts and small group learning experiences had on Casey that year and remind you that this is generally true for all kids—those striving and those thriving. As Julie explains it, she knows her teaching and interactions made a difference. But the real growth emerged as a result of Casey having opportunities to read texts that excited and inspired him. With the social capital earned by talking and working alongside peers, Casey gained momentum as a reader. If you recall, Julie wanted to avoid repeating Casey's past reading experience: One book, teacher chosen, guided reading with kids who were younger than him. Just as the Chinese proverb suggests, giving him that one book would teach him to read just that one book. Teaching Casey to read multiple books—through curation of companion texts by the teacher and by students and eventually by Casey himself—gave him the chance to become a reader for a lifetime. Isn't that what every reader deserves? You bet!

CHAPTER EIGHT

Unit Planning

(because small groups are best anchored in a harbor of big ideas)

Barry's story says it all about planning:

> I am embarrassed to admit this, but I did not know how to teach when I began my first year of teaching. I knew a lot of bits about writing a lesson, but I didn't grasp how to organize weekly and monthly plans. My work was day to day. Even my initial preparations for the school year were askew. I spent my whole time decorating the classroom—that's how naive I was. I planned every lesson the day before I taught it, which usually meant I worked late into the night after an exhausting day of trial and error.

Recently, when Barry and Julie were comparing their rookie years, Barry burst out laughing as he described a typical weekend of prep, chewing on ideas from *Scholastic Teacher* magazine and rereading the basal reading guide. Sure, today's equivalent for a newbie teacher might be grazing Pinterest on a Sunday afternoon, but the truth is the same: New teachers don't yet have the experience or confidence needed to take a deep breath and trust their own instincts about

Photo by Christian Ford

how to plan with individual students in mind. In this chapter, we teach you to embrace planning in a manner that quells late-night anxiety, limits random acts of 10 a.m. winging-it minilessons, and cures an overreliance on ready-made commercial curriculum plans. We show you unit planning that can be used to sketch out the whole school year—gulp—so you know just where you want students to wind up. Mapping out the year through unit planning is a must because the success of small group learning depends on it. When we coach in schools that host small groups without a plan for the year, we often find that teachers use the small groups just as skill practice. For example, if teachers don't know the focus for the four weeks to come, they might recall and just repeat the small groups that they offered during the same period in past years. This overgeneralizing happens often, and it causes teachers to wedge skills in haphazardly because some learner at some point may have needed it.

Let's compare overgeneralizing and responsive small group planning. During a nonfiction unit focusing on text features, a teacher does some whole group instruction, and then while the class is reading independently, she calls four students who are not her strongest readers to a small group to investigate text features again, regardless of whether they need extra practice or not. By contrast, teachers with a Civil War–themed unit can be more strategic by intentionally planning for their students. For example, they might select riveting Civil War texts, including a few primary sources, and plan a number of shared reading experiences by earmarking a few battles in the war that might pique the interest of some students they know love reading about the battles in particular. These teachers might also anticipate where reading could break down due to lack of background knowledge or new vocabulary, so they prepare to offer some small group experiences focused on those expected challenges. The teachers' aerial view, like a gliding bird, spots small group opportunities to surround students with beautiful texts and varying complexity, while fulfilling students' curiosities, passions, habits, and needs. (See Chapter Seven for more on curating texts for students.)

Big Advice

If you are looking for the definitive professional book on planning, the go-to resource is *Understanding by Design* by Grant Wiggins and Jay McTighe (2005).

We are big believers in planning backward—the idea of planning with the end in mind has moved our work with students from good to amazing because of the intentionality it requires. Stephen Covey (2013) first influenced educational thinking when he said, "To begin with the end in mind means to start with a clear understanding of your destination. It means to know where you're going so that you better understand where you are now so the steps you take are always in the right direction" (p. 98). Wiggins and McTighe (2005, 2011) put that into action through their extensive work with Understanding by Design (UbD), or "backward planning" as it's commonly named, nudging educators to anchor their planning with the end in mind. We lean on this framework because it focuses on teaching and assessing (see Chapter Six) for understanding and the transfer of learning. Backward design planning rests on three big questions:

1. What should students know, understand, and be able to do?

2. How will we know if students have achieved the desired results?

3. How will we support learners as they come to understand important ideas and processes?

The foundation of this framework recognizes learning is enhanced when teachers think purposefully about curricular planning. UbD focuses its planning design on students' understandings, essential questions, and transfer of performance objectives or tasks (Wiggins & McTighe, 2011).

Chapters Eight and Nine can be read separately or in conjunction with one another. Read them in order or dip into the chapter that you need, when you need it. Both chapters guide you in planning instruction through unit planning and weekly/daily planning. The essential questions and beliefs we outline below apply to both chapters, so please refer to them accordingly.

> *All things are ready,*
> *if our mind be so.*
> —**William Shakespeare,**
> *Henry V*

Two Essential Questions
Chapters Eight and Nine Help You Answer

1. How do you create unit plans that prioritize what's most essential?

2. How do you create weekly and daily plans that include small group learning opportunities to address the unit theme, attendant skills, and students' curiosities?

Beliefs

The standards give us a list of *what* we need to teach, but we teachers still have to do the work of putting it all together to design the *how*. In accepting the responsibility of designing the how, we give our students opportunities to wrestle with the content, work to make meaning, and possibly create something that can be added to the world's knowledge. By contrast, when teachers merely follow a reading program, it's less likely that students will produce meaningful work, because how could basal writers from New York City or any publisher anywhere possibly know what is meaningful to your learners?

So, as you plan, trust "locally grown" yearlong curricular calendars and individual unit plans. Planning takes shape and gains "personality" and relevance because it's unique, not mass produced. Our beliefs about long- and short-term planning, with a focus on small group learning experiences, include the following.

Our Beliefs About Unit Planning

We believe . . .	How it shows up in our work . . .
Unit planning is our guide, or road map, for where we are going. We anchor small group plans to unit plans to ensure cohesive instruction.	We plan with the end in mind—it's that simple. Our planning is dynamic, not static, because we are always matching weekly/daily plans with what we know about our students.
Weekly and daily planning is what makes our units of study come to life. If we plan for every minute across the week, we risk missing opportunities to respond to students' unique wants and needs.	We use templates as a place to write plans and refer to them, but we leave spaces in our weekly calendar to be responsive to students.
Small group plans need to include two types of small group planning: upfront planning that is intentionally designed to support the goals of the unit of study and in-the-moment planning in response to students.	When we create units of study, we anticipate where kids will need extra support and then build in weekly/daily small group experiences to match. We also "push pause" at the end of each week or at the end of a learning progression and use the data we've collected to create responsive small groups for the upcoming days or week.

Planning: The Reality Show

Everybody uses a plan book—where you highlight and pen short-term plans and outcomes, or where you scratch out a two-month-old idea and use a bright marker to add a better idea—right? Wrong.

"Planning is overrated," one of Barry's colleagues, a seasoned teacher, said. For him, meaningful student work springs from looking around the school or borrowing ideas from the teaching books he is reading and the websites he enjoys. Teaching, in his estimation, needs to be responsive to student needs and really shouldn't be weighed down by plans written at the beginning of the year. He has a plan book, but it is filled with mostly notes on meetings and coverage of curriculum. For instance, his math block has *place value* scribbled in it. He said he pencils in when to start a reading group or if word study is changing to a different time in the day, but it is not really an essential document in his teaching arsenal. Barry asked him how he knows what to teach and when. He said he watches the kids, mostly follows the math and reading curriculum pacing guides, and draws off his years of experience. He mentioned that he feels

Notice in Barry's planning book how work time is Monday–Friday. That's when flexible small reading groups meet; you want to doggedly preserve that time. On Tuesday and Wednesday, Barry planned for *National Geographic/Gecko* groups made up of multiage reading partners.

teaching is much like improvisation—you respond to the moment and what is being given to you. This teacher, while not a planner, brings good things to the classroom each day. Students learn the basics, they enjoy school because things are organic, and the classroom community and culture appear to thrive.

What's absent, though, is strategic thinking around what kids need to grow and support their interests and curiosities and, in turn, how small groups come together to support these needs. We gained a lot of insight by asking other teachers about their planning. Their responses included the following:

- *I am a pretty good teacher without all the hassle of figuring out "best-laid plans." What is there to gain if I give my chapter tests, go with my gut, refer to the curriculum calendar, and teach lessons that balance a bit of creativity and lesson plan objectives?*
- *My students are doing fine. I use the district curriculum.*
- *I organize my lessons from the district-adopted curriculum that has standards labeled, provides tests that match the lessons and standards, and fits with what my colleagues are doing. Are you asking me to be a curriculum designer now, without resources or professional development?*
- *I plan, but I don't write it down. My principal stopped collecting my lesson plans a long time ago.*
- *Writing it out is a lot of work. Plus, I have a lot of other things I'm responsible for during the school day. My planning time is usually filled with meetings.*

Our colleagues' approaches are a departure from what we live as educators, and we don't dismiss what they do as less effective—but we think it's riskier. In general, very seasoned teachers might not need to write things down as much as less experienced ones do, yet even with experience, we think the precision and the spark of learning is ossified when plans don't change year to year. Why? Mainly because teachers merely doing what seemed to have worked in the past can't be taking into account where their *current* students' perspectives come into play into the development of lesson plans.

We recognize that along about now, you may be thinking you have far too many locked-in important initiatives to add a student-responsive layer. We get it— believe us. But we assure you that the planning structures we offer will help you weigh all of the competing opportunities and work to make them "talk" to one another. Planning for us is a two-part process. First, we develop a yearlong plan. Then, we suggest developing units of study within the yearlong plan, following six steps that provide a method by which you can develop the planning structures we suggest, or use another unit design that you like. We have outlined unit planning steps sequentially, yet we show you that planning can be personalized by approaching the steps in the order and ways that they make sense to you.

PART 1: DEVELOP A YEARLONG PLAN

Whether your district provides you with a yearlong pacing guide or you create one, it is essential that you have a guide that outlines the overarching content that students will explore *across the year*. This acts as your central navigation system and provides the scope and sequence. While there are many organizational structures that could serve this purpose, we offer a few examples for your reference.

Example 1: Fifth-Grade English Language Arts

September	My Reading and Writing Life	Plays, Poetry, and Performance
October–November	Reading and Writing Story	My Reading and Writing Life Outside of School
	Stories and Characters Change Across the Narrative Arc	
December–January	Reading and Writing Nonfiction	
	Becoming an Expert	
February–March	Perspectives in Literature	
April	Testing as a Genre	
May–June	Author Study and Argument	

Once the scope and sequence is mapped out, you can begin to anticipate small group opportunities that will deepen your students' reading. Look at "Reading and Writing Nonfiction" and "Becoming an Expert" in December and January, shown above. The fifth-grade team anticipated that students might benefit from the following small group learning opportunities across the unit:

- Curating resources for individual research projects
- Making meaning across multiple texts, and comparing and contrasting
- Note-taking and going from reading research to synthesizing it
- Brainstorming ideas for end demonstrations of learning
- Drafting, editing, and revising
- Rehearsal/practice for presentation
- Peer feedback and reflection

Example 2: Eighth-Grade English Language Arts

First Trimester	How Things Work: Informational Texts for Procedures and Protocols
	Taking a Stand: Argument for a Better World
Second Trimester	Stories Matter: History, Biography, and Personal Narrative
	True Character: Finding and Naming Character Traits in Ourselves, Our Reading, and Our World
Third Trimester	Celebrating Poetry and Performance
	Imaginative Worlds: Reading and Writing Fantasy

Anticipating when kids might need a lift, through small group learning opportunities, is part of developing a yearlong plan. In this eighth-grade example, the first trimester includes a unit called "Taking a Stand: Argument for a Better World." While many times the content can be delivered through whole group lessons, the eighth-grade English language arts team also anticipated when students might benefit from some of the following small group learning opportunities across the unit:

- Reading types of persuasive writing (e.g., letters, editorials, public service announcements, and political cartoons) by
  - Small groups each reading the same type of text and sharing out
  - Small groups each reading a different type of text and sharing out

- Reading arguments and making comprehension visible by jotting and talking
- Determining and articulating a personal position about a topic or idea
- Reading and talking about counterarguments
- Reading and collecting ideas for taking a stand about something
- Writing and evaluating arguments (drafting, editing, revising, sharing ideas, peer feedback, etc.)
- Mini debate and small group presentations

**Example 3: Third-Grade Integrated Unit—
English Language Arts and Social Studies**

Quarter 1	Exploring Reading and Writing Notebooks What Makes My Community Unique?
Quarter 2	Reading and Writing Stories (Narrative) Who Are the Local Heroes I Should Know?
Quarter 3	Reading and Writing Nonfiction How Can I Improve My Community?
Quarter 4	Reading and Writing to Teach and Persuade How Does My Community Impact My State?

In Quarter 2 of this third-grade narrative example unit, called "Reading and Writing Stories: Who Are the Local Heroes I Should Know?," the team mapped out when students might benefit from some of the following small group learning opportunities:

- Determining what makes a hero worthy of knowing
- Reading short texts about lots of people who have hero status
- Generating character traits about what makes a hero
- Finding evidence and making judgments about characters and their actions
- Talking and jotting about heroes in their own lives
- Writing about a hero in their own life (using a model from your reading)

PART 2: DEVELOP A UNIT OF STUDY

Educational researcher John Hattie, who wrote *Visible Learning for Teachers: Maximizing Impact on Learning* (2012), linked student outcomes to several highly effective classroom practices, three of which jump out at us when we think of unit planning: teacher clarity, formative assessment, and metacognitive strategies. Hattie refers to teaching clarity as making sure students and teachers know the purpose and learning goals and how students benefit by seeing successful visual models such as mentor texts and examples of final student products. We liken teacher clarity to the concept of beginning with the end in mind (Covey, 2013). Covey posits that to provide effective and accurate feedback, teachers need to assess student work frequently in relation to the unit of study learning goals and end product. And finally, he finds student ownership increases when students are given opportunities to plan and organize, monitor their own work, direct their own learning, and self-reflect along the way.

Teacher clarity, formative assessment, metacognitive strategies, and resources are at the heart of unit planning. When we create unit plans, we become clear about what students will know and be able to do. We think through how we will let our students know how they are doing (see Chapter Six for more on assessing student work). We act as demonstrators for our students when we hand over the work of planning and organizing their own learning by having demonstrated our own unit plans.

Two weeks before we begin a new unit of study, we begin creating that unit. This isn't always easy to do because we are wrapping up one unit while working to dig into the next. However, doing so gives us the time needed to map out a unit of study with *our* students' curiosities, passions, habits, and needs in mind. The steps outlined below may appear to be linear, but we would like to encourage you to think of them as fluid, even recursive at times. While we almost always begin with the big ideas behind the unit, we tend to jump back and forth from box to box while we plan because we let our thoughts guide our development versus working so tightly within the boxes.

Our unit plan begins to take shape as we think through a planning template. These boxes are meant not to "box you in" but rather to provide a place to noodle around with learning opportunities that support intended outcomes. When planning, sometimes these boxes become pages in our notebooks or looseleaf pages in our binder. Other times, especially when we are planning as a grade-level team or department, our templates become anchor

> Two weeks before we begin a new unit of study, we begin creating that unit.

What work products
will show that
students got stronger
and smarter about
the designated
learning targets?

What is this unit of
study all about, and
why is it important?
What do I want
students to walk
away with at the
end of this unit of
study? What will
students learn that
they will remember
10 years from now?

What will students
consume? What
will they read, listen
to, watch, or talk
about? What will
students need to
do or experience?
What will I read to
them, show them,
and think aloud with
them?

When would it
benefit students
to meet in small
groups?

What compelling
questions will
students answer
that foster
inquiry, long-term
understanding, and
transfer of learning
to new learning
situations?

What standards will
be included in this
unit of study?

What work products
will students create
to demonstrate their
knowledge, skills, and
understanding—key
projects, products,
performances, and
so on (formative
and summative)?
How will students
demonstrate what
they know and are
able to do in relation
to the learning
targets? How will
they become creators
of content, producing
something that has a
real purpose for a real
audience?

What other learning
opportunities could
this unit include
(field trips, guest
speakers, real-
world experiences,
connections to kids'
interests, reflection,
feedback, work
products from
previous year's
unit, etc.)?

Long-term targets
are tied to the what
and why of the unit
of study and to the
standards. Short-
term /daily targets,
listed below long-
term targets, are a
set of scaffolded
instructional targets
used on a daily/
weekly basis that
describe the learning/
steps that help
students achieve the
long-term targets.

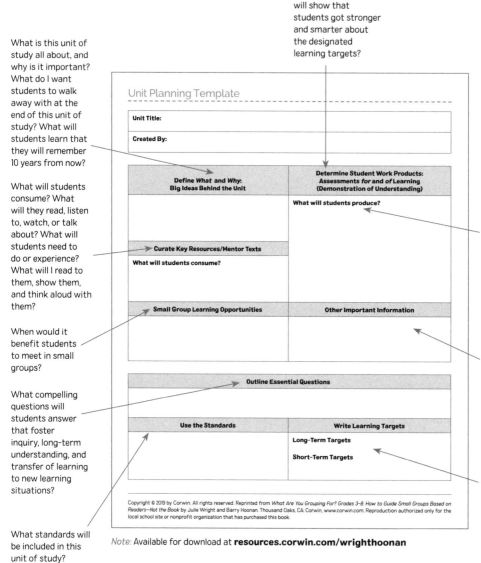

Unit Planning Template

Unit Title:

Created By:

Define *What* and *Why*: Big Ideas Behind the Unit	Determine Student Work Products: Assessments *for* and *of* Learning (Demonstration of Understanding)
	What will students produce?
Curate Key Resources/Mentor Texts **What will students consume?**	
Small Group Learning Opportunities	**Other Important Information**

Outline Essential Questions

Use the Standards	Write Learning Targets
	Long-Term Targets **Short-Term Targets**

Note: Available for download at **resources.corwin.com/wrighthoonan**

charts around the room. There is no one right way to use these templates; they are meant to be changed, so add boxes or categories that fit your purpose.

We will walk you through each planning step, but the facing page shows the planning document in its entirety.

Six Surefire Steps

1. Define what and why (big ideas behind the unit)
2. Use the standards
3. Outline essential questions
4. Write learning targets
5. Curate key resources/mentor texts
6. Determine student work products (assessments *for* and *of* learning)

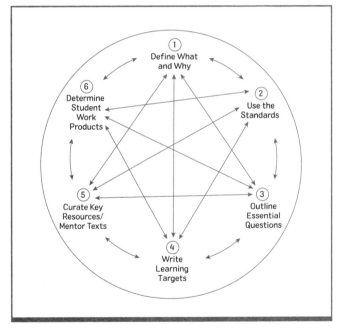

See Chapter Nine for developing a unit calendar and weekly/daily lesson planning.

Note: Steps 1 through 6 can be done in any order.

STEP 1: DEFINE *WHAT* AND *WHY*:
BIG IDEAS BEHIND THE UNIT

When we sit down to begin designing a unit of study, we launch into our work by defining the *what* and the *why* behind the unit. This gives us an opportunity to write what the unit of study is all about. We do some free-flow writing and ask ourselves,

- What do we want students to walk away with at the end of this unit?
- What will our students learn that they will remember 10 years from now?

This process helps us outline the big ideas behind the unit of study. Oftentimes, we find that teachers, like ourselves, get caught up in the standard language and lose sight of what they want the long-term takeaways to be for their students. Working on this piece at the beginning of our planning helps us stay focused on those big takeaways.

Here are a few from some units:

Fifth Grade: Who Am I? A Peek Into My Past, Present, and Future

Who we are, where we come from, our family values, our family history . . . it all matters and helps define and shape who we have been and who we will become. When we can identify with our background, our heritage, and our family histories, we know ourselves more deeply. When we know about others, it helps us make connections, builds tolerance and empathy, and helps us appreciate our similarities and differences. Ten years from now, I hope others will remember me for who I am and what makes me me. And 10 years from now, I hope that others will have impacted the American I have become.

Seventh Grade: Reading the World

Ten years from now, I hope my kids can say that they walked away from this experience saying

- They loved reading informational texts and found nonfiction to be pleasurable and a rich part of their reading diet
- They understood ways to record and remember the information they studied

- They found a writing voice, style, and structure to transfer their thinking into published work
- They could identify when informational text is credible and useful

Sixth Grade: My Reading and Writing Life

In this unit, students will explore their own identities as readers and writers. Students will reflect on

- What types of texts (genre, format, size, shape, etc.) they enjoy
- What texts they haven't really given a go because of time or past interest

This unit will emphasize that reading is an active process—a dialogue between the reader and the book, and sometimes other people. Students will work to develop this internal dialogue through practicing the active reading strategies of predicting, questioning, visualizing, and connecting. Students will make this thinking visible to others through use of sticky notes, highlighting, and annotating. Students will be encouraged to form their own opinions on these strategies and reflect on which strategies are most and least helpful to them as well as when they are and are not helpful to use. Students will view annotating as a process through which to deepen their understanding of a text, not a required method that slows down their pace and hinders their reading experience. Students will also learn to identify moments when they are confused, lost, bored, or "zoned out" during reading and what steps they can take to remedy this situation, including rereading, accessing graphics, and reading ahead. Students will share this journey with their families and peers through written products and visuals at a family reading night called *The Living Reader Museum*, the culminating activity at the end of the unit. Ten years from now, students will be able to articulate their reading interests and experiences and act upon them through their voracious reading diets and habits.

STEP 2: USE THE STANDARDS

We like standards. To us, they are like the skeletal system to our full-bodied curricular design. They give us "the bones," a frame for how we will shape the learning for our students. That's it. They tell us *what*; they don't tell us *how*. It's the how that we love to design, and it's the how that makes us jump out of bed each morning so that we can learn with and from our students.

Our units of study are almost always filled with too many standards. That is the nature of the work these days—too many things to cover and not enough days in the school year or even interest by us to get through them all. Instead, we take an approach that you may find helpful. The following list outlines our thinking process related to determining which standards are most important:

- We list all the standards that are tied to the unit of study.
- We look across content areas and list standards that are related (we are big believers in integration!).
- Once we've determined our formative assessments (knowledge checks) and summative assessments (way[s] students will demonstrate their understandings at the end of the unit), we look back over the list of standards and highlight those that are most directly tied to what we will assess and what students will remember 10 years from now. Those standards then become the focus in the unit of study.

Note: In the past, standards were deemed "essential" or "power standards" if they were a major focus for standardized testing. We want to dismantle the thinking on that by redefining why you put a standard on the front burner. The process we described earlier does just that.

Since we aren't "one and done" educators, it's assumed that numerous standards will be revisited a few times across a school year. This process gives us a blueprint for making sure our units are tied to standards that help us determine the "what" in our units. Refer to the graphic on page 219 as a reminder that Steps 1 through 6 can be done in any order and in any colors or templates that suit how your mind works and your students thrive. We know planning is personal, and making this process your own is important.

STEP 3: OUTLINE ESSENTIAL QUESTIONS

During our time in New York City, when we worked at Harlem Village Academies, we had the unique pleasure of working alongside the late, great Grant Wiggins. His role was advisory in nature, but ask anyone who knew him, and you'll learn that while he advised, he also inquired. The inquiry around our work together is what made it so interesting. We have applied many of the teachings of Wiggins and McTighe (2005, 2011) over the years, and our planning template highlights an important aspect of theirs. As we plan a unit of study, we pose essential questions that keep us grounded in the work with our students. The work of Understanding by Design helps us write essential questions by paying close attention to seven defining characteristics. According to McTighe and Wiggins (2013, p. 3), a good essential question

- Is *open-ended* (i.e., it typically will not have a single, final, and correct answer)
- Is *thought-provoking* and *intellectually engaging*, often sparking discussion and debate
- Calls for *higher-order thinking*, such as analysis, inference, evaluation, and prediction, and cannot be effectively answered by recall alone
- Points toward *important, transferable ideas* within (and sometimes across) disciplines
- Raises *additional questions* and sparks further inquiry
- Requires *support* and *justification*, not just an answer
- *Recurs* over time (i.e., the question can and should be revisited again and again)

For example,

- What makes writing worth reading, and why should we do it?
- How are stories from different places and time about me?
- How can we make a convincing case about a problem that inspires people to take action?
- Is there ever a "just" war?
- What is worth fighting for?

While we plan, we work to organize compelling questions that will foster inquiry, long-term understanding, and transfer of learning to new learning situations. This, we believe, will help push the thinking behind what we want students to remember 10 years from now.

STEP 4: WRITE LEARNING TARGETS

Once we determine the standards for the unit of study (both those on the front burner and those on the back burner), we can take a closer look at the standards we've marked in bold (front burner). For each of those standards, we write learning targets that help us revise the standard language into student-friendly learning targets. We do this in two ways:

1. **Long-term targets** are tied to the *what* and *why* of a unit of study and its standards.

2. **Short-term/daily targets**, listed below long-term targets, are a set of scaffolded instructional targets used on a daily/weekly basis that describe the learning or steps that will help students achieve the long-term targets.

We outline our learning targets and tie them directly to our formative and summative assessment process. We make sure that our students have an opportunity to show what they know and are able to do related to each learning target (both long-term and short-term targets) by outlining what work products will serve as our assessments of and for learning.

Learning targets are

- Written as a goal for *students*
- Created from the standards
- Written in student-friendly language
- Understood by students and teachers
- Used to assess growth and achievement
- Tied to formative and summative assessment
- Focused on learning (process-oriented, not task-oriented)
- Easily measured

For example,

- I can read a variety of texts and make meaning about immigration (past and present).
- I can hear, read, and retell immigration stories (through talk and writing) from the past and present and connect the stories to what it means to be an American.
- I can interview my family members to learn more about my own family heritage.
- I can write and revise a poem or piece of writing about what it means to be an American.
- I can share my poem/writing with others when we visit Lady Liberty and at our Family Literacy Night.

Steps for Creating Learning Targets Aligned to the Standards

1. List all the standards that are tied to the unit of study.
2. Look across content areas and list related standards (we are big believers in integration!).

3. Determine formative assessments (knowledge checks) and summative assessments (way[s] students will demonstrate their understandings at the end of the unit).

4. Once we've determined our formative assessments (knowledge checks) and summative assessments (way[s] students will demonstrate their understandings at the end of the unit), we look back over the list of standards and highlight those that are most directly tied to what we will assess and what students will remember 10 years from now. Those standards then become the focus in the unit of study.

5. Use these standards to write learning targets.

STEP 5: CURATE KEY RESOURCES/MENTOR TEXTS

A founding belief is that while students need to produce work, they also need to consume. As we plan, we think about what students will read, listen to, watch, talk about, and experience in order to deepen their knowledge. We ask ourselves a few questions to help guide our planning:

- What will we read, listen to, watch, or need to talk about?
- What will students need to do or experience?
- What will I read to them, show them, and think aloud with them?

We mentioned that our unit plans are always dynamic. Many times, we come across something mid-unit that will feed our students what they need to move forward. These learning opportunities cannot always be anticipated when we initially plan our unit. Good teaching and learning always produces even more good teaching and learning. As a result, as we naturally teach into something or share something new based on what we know about our students or that we had not originally intended to do, we revise our plan so that we capture the new information. Taking the stance that our unit plans are always developing gives us the opportunity to design before, during, and after the unit. This gives us another reason to always think of our unit plans as dynamic. (See Chapter Seven for more about curating.)

STEP 6: DETERMINE STUDENT WORK PRODUCTS (ASSESSMENTS *FOR* AND *OF* LEARNING)

Samantha Bennett, a good friend and mentor, pushed Julie to think and rethink how to plan for students' work time. Asking questions about students' work

What Would You Do?

List the standard or set of standards that is tied to an upcoming unit of study. Think about how kids will demonstrate their understandings. Then write two or three student-friendly learning targets.

_____

_____

_____

_____

products has become a focus area for Julie when she supports teachers and administrators. As teachers, we often think we need to focus on our own teaching when, in fact, we need to focus more on guiding students in creating work products. We think about what students can produce that demonstrates their knowledge, skills, and understanding of what they've learned. To that end, in our initial planning sessions, we focus on student work products. First we generate a list of brainstormed ideas; then we shrink the student product list to a workable number (see the examples that follow). A key to our work is determining what work products will serve as formative assessments (assessments for learning) to be used as our guide for determining where students are across the unit of study (see Chapter Six). Julie refers to these as knowledge checks. Don't let the language trip you up because this is the same thing as checking progress through formative assessment structures. In simplest terms, it is any type of work that students are creating day in and day out that helps us know what they understand and where their understandings need lifting. This preplanning work, before we even launch the unit, helps us get our heads around possibilities. It helps us create "can do and must do" opportunities because sometimes our ideas are good but too many in number. If we determine ahead of time those things that must be done, it provides accountability but also leaves room for some can-do items if time and interest permit.

> As teachers, we often think we need to focus on our own teaching when, in fact, we need to focus more on guiding students in creating work products.

Note: An even more important part of developing formative assessments is asking the kids to add onto the list. Once the unit is launched and kids get a sense of what the learning is about (maybe a week into it all), we tell the kids about some of our ideas for "showing what we know or have learned" and ask if the students have ideas for how they could demonstrate their knowledge, skills, and understanding. Kids always add great ideas to the list of opportunities!

Next, determine how students will show their knowledge, skills, and understanding by choosing a summative assessment (assessment of learning). This summative or culminating demonstration is commonly named a unit project. We brainstorm and determine how students will demonstrate what they know and are able to do in relation to the learning targets. We like to think about this in terms of how students will become creators of content and produce something that has a real-world purpose for a real audience. Remember, involve students in this process because their voice is very important. Sometimes students come up with ways to show what they know in more interesting and meaningful ways compared to our original ideas. Having students work with us sets the tone for our learning community. In other words, we plan with a pencil so that the assessment ideas can drive us forward and we can be receptive to what surfaces during the unit.

Possible Student Work Products

Students could

- Make a two-page spread of "Who Am I, and What Can I Contribute Now?"
- Write an original poem about what it means to be an American
- Go to the Statue of Liberty (stand in front of Lady Liberty and sing/recite poems)
- Share out during Family Literacy Night
- Study an admired American and write about him or her (include answers to essential questions)
- Share reading responses (read-alouds, shared reading passages, independent reading, etc.)
- Interview family members
- Make a scrapbook page to add to the class scrapbook about family heritage
- Complete a "change over time" graphic organizer related to specific texts (I used to think . . . , Then I read . . . , Now I think . . . , I'm still wondering . . . , etc.)

A Unit Plan in Action

Example: Unit Plan

Unit Title: My Reading and Writing Life
Created By: Barry Hoonan and Julie Wright

Define *What* and *Why*: Big Ideas Behind the Unit	Determine Student Work Products: Assessments *for* and *of* Learning (Demonstration of Understanding)
This unit is designed to launch students into naming what is important about their reading and writing lives and developing goals to help them chart their own journey. This also gives them an opportunity to note growth and improvement along the way. • Students will learn ways to grow writing ideas through a Writer's Notebook. • Students will develop and share reading strategies through their reflective Reader's Notebook.	**What will students produce?** • Reader's Notebook entries • Writer's Notebook entries • Reading calendars • Reading goals **What will students do?** • Students will select reading entries to share with classmates and explain how their work shows their reading understanding.

(Continued)

(Continued)

Here's what we hope students say about their reading and writing lives after this unit:

- Reading and writing has a purpose in my life.
- By reading, I discover more about myself and the world I live in.
- By writing, I can reflect, connect, create, and inspire.
- My reading habits and goals guide my reading behavior.
- My reading improves by spending time reading and reflecting on my reading.
- My writing improves by spending time writing and reflecting on my writing.
- My writing improves when I study the kind of writing I want to produce.
- Building a tool kit of writing strategies gives me more control over my writing.
- Building a tool kit of reading strategies gives me more control over my reading.

- Students will reflect on their reading goals and make plans to shape their reading growth.
- Students will select writing entries and research and show how these ideas led to a finished piece.
- Students will use their Writer's Notebooks to write a short piece on demand in one writer's workshop block.

What will students publish and celebrate?

- A narrative story for the class magazine or blog
- A narrative poem for a video presentation at open house
- A reading calendar highlighting the amount of pages they have read and texts they have completed
- A reading reflection sharing what others should know about them as readers based on evidence in their reading notebook

Curate Key Resources/Mentor Texts	Other Important Information

What will students consume?

- *First French Kiss and Other Traumas* by Adam Bagdasarian (2002)
- *Wallace's Lists* by Barbara Bottner and Gerald Kruglik (2004)
- *My Map Book* by Sara Fanelli (2001)
- *Wilfrid Gordon McDonald Partridge* by Mem Fox (1989)
- "Where I'm From" by George Ella Lyon (1993)
- *A Writer's Notebook* by Ralph Fletcher (2003)
- *Questions, Questions* by Marcus Pfister (2011)
- *The Boy Who Loved Words* by Roni Schotter (2006)
- *Nothing Ever Happens on 90th Street* by Roni Schotter (1999)
- "Watch Your Brothers" by Jon Scieszka (2005)
- *The Best Story* by Eileen Spinelli (2008)
- *Oliver's Must-Do List* by Susan Taylor Brown (2005)
- *Each Kindness* by Jacqueline Woodson (2012)
- Music videos from YouTube

Make available previous class anchor charts on

- Independent reading agreements
- Independent writing agreements
- Student reading goals
- Student writing goals
- How to choose a "just right" text

Make available previous student examples/models of

- Reading calendars
- Pictograph book lists
- Literacy photos
- Reader's Notebook entry ideas
- Reading goals
- "Where I Am From" poems
- "Where I Am From" lists and notebook entries

Co-created anchor charts could include

- Shared agreements for reading and writing independently
- How to conduct writing circles
- How to use mentor texts to inspire writing
- How to conduct writing and reading partner conferences
- How to read tricky texts
- How to set reading and writing goals
- How to choose books effectively
- How to grow reading and writing ideas in a notebook

Small Group Learning Opportunities

- Sharing Reader's Notebook entries (students modeling for others)
- Reading calendars (reading volume, types of texts marked as favorites, what are you abandoning and why, etc.)
- Reading reflections
- Peer editing and feedback for notebook entries and work products
- Responding to exit ticket responses (what do you need next to grow your reading and writing?)
- Citing textual evidence to support thinking
- Determining central idea or theme, including key details

Outline Essential Questions	
• What strategies should I use when I don't understand what I'm reading? • What strategies should I use to deepen my reading understanding and grow new ideas? • What strategies should I use to propel my writing to meet a goal? • How can I chart my own reading and writing journey?	

Use the Standards	Write Learning Targets

Read closely to determine what the text says explicitly and to make logical inferences from it; cite specific textual evidence when writing or speaking to support conclusions drawn from the text.
 	
Determine central ideas or themes of a text and analyze their development; summarize the key supporting details and ideas.
 	
Read and comprehend complex literary and informational texts independently and proficiently.
	Long-Term Targets
	• I can choose and use a reading response strategy that helps me deepen my understanding and grow new ideas.
	• I can choose and use a reading strategy when I don't understand what I'm reading.
	• I can increase my reading volume and read with stamina.
	• I can make and meet challenging reading goals.
	• I can find books and texts that I enjoy reading.
	• I can make and meet challenging writing goals.
	• I can complete writing narratives that matter.
	
	Short-Term Targets
	• I can keep track of my reading volume and use those data to guide goal-setting conversations.
	• I can collaboratively create anchor charts to help guide an effective reading and writing workshop.
	• I can share examples from my Reader's and Writer's Notebooks in order to
	  o Open new possibilities for deepening understanding and growing ideas
	  o Show how lists and insights generate ideas for writing
	  o Show how reading and writing strategies are working

TAKING TIME TO REFLECT

Planning is an important process. Equally as important is building a teacher reflection routine about your plans. Barry and Julie talk to think. Asking questions to figure out next moves is an anchor for them. They often begin by noodling around areas that aren't making sense. For example, they ask themselves,

- Should kids be writing about reading in a journal or on the Google Classroom response page? Should they be composing on paper or on the computer?
- What's impeding reading conferences from being more efficient and effective?

- If engagement is important, how do we keep track of who is doing the talking during discussions and who isn't?
- What was up with _____ today? Is there something out of the ordinary going on that we should be digging into this week?
- Did you see what _____ accomplished today? How can we keep that inspiration going?

One Last Thing

Planning with the end in mind requires intentionality. If we plan by taking into account the curricular scope and sequence and match that to kids' interests, we can create dynamic small group learning experiences. We use our unit plans as our road map but leave time across each week to reflect on and respond to what we believe will help students grow. Without that responsiveness, we risk falling back into static plans that prioritize content over kids.

CHAPTER NINE

Weekly and Daily Planning

(because weekly and daily plans chart the course for small group experiences)

Unit planning gives us our framework for the whole. It gives us the overarching goals for the instructional experiences we will design to support our students' reading growth. Weekly and daily lesson plans focus on the whole group, small group, and one-to-one "parts"—the specific content, teacher moves, and student tasks that will lift students' learning forward. Think about Martha Graham's masterful dance *Rite of Spring*. Graham's envisioning as she listened to Stravinsky's harrowing score is akin to unit planning. We imagine she scribbled words like *primal* and *tribal* in her notebook, and imagined dancers both still and in frenetic motion across the arc of her dance. Her choreography—how the dancers individually and collectively moved across the stage and interacted with one another to tell the story she envisioned—well, those precise moves are akin to what we address here: weekly and daily planning. Readers, like dancers, move about the room, from circles of readers to other circles of readers.

Let's move to the steps in the planning process that get into the nitty-gritty of the Monday–Friday procession.

Photo by Christian Ford

Creating a Calendar for Weekly and Daily Lesson Planning

Here's how we start. We grab a piece of chart paper, section off space on a white-board, or open a Word document, and commit to a template of some kind. The goal is to write down what we plan to do so that we can see the scope and sequence of the week ahead. For us, thinking about this in terms of a calendar works. Here are six steps to consider when planning weekly and daily lessons:

> *I'm not afraid of storms, for I'm learning how to sail my ship.*
>
> **—Louisa May Alcott**

STEP 1: CREATE A CALENDAR PLAN FOR EACH WEEK

Determine the main focus for each week by noting the big ideas or big intended takeaways that students will experience by the end of the week and put that information on a calendar. Ask yourself,

- What is the big idea or intended outcome for the week?
- What is my initial thinking on how small groups might serve this goal?
- Will this be a focus for one week, or might it carry over to the following week? (Try not to put yourself in a box—you don't have to plan Monday to Friday, and you don't have to confine yourself to one week. Based on when your unit of study begins and ends, you might plan Tuesday to Tuesday, or you might plan the focus in two-week chunks).

STEP 2: OUTLINE ANY SCHEDULE IMPLICATIONS

Determine if and when schedule implications will impact planning, and calendarize them. Ask yourself,

- Are there any school breaks scheduled during this unit?
- Are there any other school-related events that will impact this unit (student-led conferences, schoolwide assemblies, half-day releases, etc.)?

STEP 3: PLAN ASSESSMENT

Determine what days you will assess students' knowledge, skills, and understanding and mark them on a calendar. Ask yourself,

- When will I formatively assess the work products students will create? (knowledge checks)
- When are final projects or work products due? (summative assessment)

See Chapter Six for more on assessing students' work.

STEP 4: PLAN WHOLE GROUP INSTRUCTION AND ITS OUTCOMES

Use the main focus you stated in Step 1 to create your lesson plans for the week. This planning is focused on whole group instruction and is, while not a major focus for this book, an extremely important part of planning for students' reading experiences. Ask yourself,

- What minilessons will I teach?
- What mentor texts and models will I show the students?
- What shared reading and writing experiences will we harness together?
- What work products will students create and produce?
- What will students share out at the end of small group or reading workshop?

STEP 5: MAKE PLANS FOR SMALL GROUP LEARNING OPPORTUNITIES

Create weekly and daily plans that focus on small group learning. Ask yourself,

- What small groups will I preplan in anticipation of clearing up confusion?
- How much time should I leave in my plans for in-the-moment small groups in order to respond to student work that I have collected and sorted?
- How much time should I leave in my plans for the in-the-moment small groups that feed students' curiosities?

STEP 6: CREATE SHARED AGREEMENTS

Map out when and how you will co-construct shared agreements or rubrics with students so that they can be part of the assessment process *and* so that they can use what is created (a list of success criteria or rubric) to make their work hit the aim or target of the unit. Ask yourself,

- When should I begin co-creating shared agreements with students about success criteria or rubrics that will be used to assess and self-assess the end demonstration of learning?
- When should we revisit our shared agreements and make sure that nothing needs to be added or changed?

EXAMPLE OF A UNIT PLANNING CALENDAR FOR A SIX-WEEK UNIT

Here's an example of a *unit planning calendar* from our six-week "Art of Argument" unit in which students present soapbox speeches to community members.

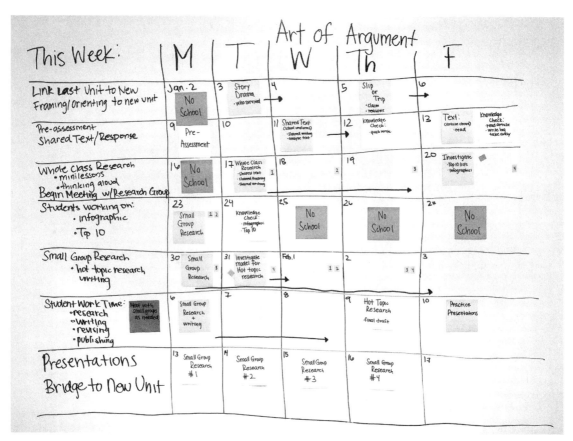

Note: View a full-color version of this unit planning calendar at **resources.corwin.com/wrighthoonan**.

A Guide to the Color Codes in the Chart

Main focus *(Write this information on the left-hand side of the planning template.)*

Blue sticky note: Schedule implications

Green sticky note: Assessment

Yellow sticky note: The day's instruction

Pink sticky note: Small group instruction

Orange sticky note: Shared agreements

Note: The color of the sticky notes is not significant. What is important is that the color signals to you that it's related to a specific area of planning. Change colors as you deem appropriate. While you can plan these in any order, we found success doing them in the order we've listed. The beauty of the sticky notes? They make it so easy to adjust ideas during planning and as real learning unfolds. It's as simple as ripping off a sticky note if the idea no longer applies, moving a sticky note if the timing is wrong, or adding a sticky note if you've neglected something important.

Example of a Calendar Highlighting the Relationship Between Assessment and Small Groups

Here's another example of a unit plan. You don't need to read the writing on the sticky notes; we want you to notice how we use different flags to signal assessment days and small group meetings.

Sticky Notes

Blue: Whole group or shared reading experiences

Yellow: Short texts that will be used

Orange: Small group reading invitations (If one topic is listed, all students read something about that topic in a small group; if more than one topic is listed, students pick the topic they want to read about and join others in a small group.)

Purple: Focus on quick check-in topics

Flags

Neon green: Knowledge checks (when teacher will collect and sort student work)

Magenta (with numbers):   Signals when the teacher will join in the small group

Plan for a three-week nonfiction unit focusing on inquiry research groups inspired by students' curiosities passions, habits, and needs.

Focus	M	T	W	Th	F
Shared Reading Shared Meaning Making	What is nonfiction? • what do you like to read? How do you orient to a NF text? Bucket of NF Texts	Review Text Features Text Structures Eye Witness 50 Americans National Geo.	Shared Reading Shared Meaning Making Think Aloud NYT: Games Arcade	Weird but True	Pop! Invention of Bubble Gum
Small Group Work 4 small groups • same group all week • everyone reads same text	Visit Library • class curation NF Texts	Exploring Ways to hold thinking Dude Perfect Video Infographics	How does reading more about a topic help? Jackie Joyner Jackie Joyner	Misty Copeland Misty Copeland	Misty Copeland Multiple texts about dance/ballet
Pick a NF Focus Small Group Work 6 small groups • same group all week • different texts within topic.	Use student notebooks as examples of writing Brainstorm Topics Visit Library Small Groups • Make decisions about topic.	Lanzo Ball 1 1 Candy 2 2 Hurricanes 3 Drone Tech 4 4 Fidget Spinners 5 Nike 6	Small Group Quick Share 3 5 6	How does reading about a topic lead you to other topics? 1 2 3 4 5 6 Quick Checkin • volume • favorite texts • holding thinking • what do you need?	Big Take-aways

Note: View a full-color version of this unit planning calendar at **resources.corwin.com/wrighthoonan.**

Unit: _____

Things we are wrestling with this week	Monday	Tuesday	Wednesday	Thursday	Friday

Note: See page 295 of the Appendix for a full-page template.

Zooming In on Step 5: Make Plans for Small Group Learning Opportunities

Okay, now we move into the heart of this chapter. When we write weekly and daily plans for small group instruction,

- We want to anticipate content that might be challenging for students and prepare for small groups that respond to those needs.
- We want to plan for our pivots—leave space in weekly plans for in-the-moment small groups based on students' wants and needs. This means that initial plans will have some "unplanned" time; you will use this time by hosting responsive small groups, some of which can be entirely student-led. See Chapter Five for more on pivoting into small, flexible groups.

GUIDING QUESTIONS FOR PLANNING

During the work time portion of reading workshop, students are independently reading, meeting in small groups, or conferring one-to-one with the teacher. Opportunities for building reading volume and reading stamina are at an all-time high. See Chapter One for more information on the workshop model. When we develop weekly and daily lesson plans with small groups at the center, we ask ourselves the following questions:

- Do I anticipate any small group needs? Will any follow-up be needed based on the whole group minilesson?
- Which students will I meet with?
- How many small groups will I meet with? What will be the focus?
- Will any small groups be meeting without me? What will be the focus?
- What will the students be doing while I work with small groups—will they be reading independently or working in small groups?
- What will students be reading, discussing, writing, or making so that their thinking is visible to others?

Some Popular, Proven Models to Guide You

Take a look at the following models for ways you can plan for small group learning. There is no one right model—the idea is to make decisions based on your hopes and goals for students. Ultimately, the more groups you have cooking across the weeks, the more opportunities you have to get up close to students' reading and thinking. If you don't get up close to kids' work, you end up grabbing at straws for what you think kids need. Proximity helps them open up, making it easier for you to uncover their understandings and misconceptions. When you are in the know, you have a greater chance at impacting student learning.

ONE SMALL GROUP DURING READING WORKSHOP

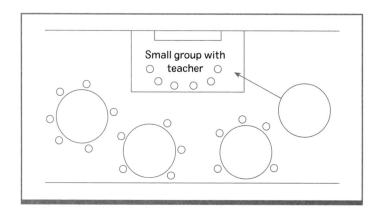

Note: If students are not meeting with the teacher, they are reading independently.

Reasons Why You Might Hold One Small Group

- You recognize that most students still need to build reading stamina; you want them to spend time *reading*, so a single small group suffices.
- Reading workshop time is shortened due to a scheduled school event, so you only have time for one group.
- One group of students needs extra time to work together, so you join them for most or all of the allotted small group time.

Here are a couple of samples:

One group a day reading fiction: Let's say you are studying characters in texts. You could meet with one group a day and focus on noticing character complexity in Week 1; in Week 2, your one group a day could address secondary characters; in Week 3, . . . Get the picture? Yes, one group a day is a starter pace, but hey, slow and steady wins the race.

One group a day reading nonfiction: Imagine an integrated literacy and social studies unit where students read about different types of rocks. You could meet with one group a day and investigate texts about igneous rocks in Week 1; your one group a day could address sedimentary rocks in Week 2, metamorphic rocks in Week 3, and so on until students read all the important content.

TWO SMALL GROUPS DURING READING WORKSHOP

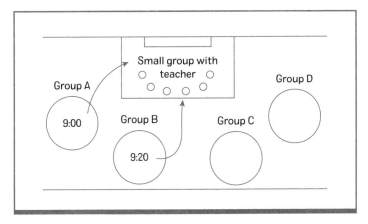

Note: If students are not meeting with the teacher, they are reading independently.

Reasons Why You Might Hold Two Small Groups

- You are able to meet with more than one group because students' reading stamina (their ability to read independently for a longer time) has increased.
- You want to meet with two groups during reading workshop in order to interact with more students across the week.

Pumping up the reading volume: Imagine any grade level and any time of the year. Students are reading, reading, reading, and you want to make sure that they pump up their reading volume even more. Meet with small groups, two per reading workshop, to check in, share hot reads, talk about students' book stacks (books they love or "up next" books to read), and share reading logs or calendars—all in service of boosting access, promoting choice, and inspiring reading across the table. Do this same routine across two or three days in a week, and you'll interact with everyone in the class through small groups.

Writing to think, thinking to write: Consider all of the ways students make their thinking visible. For this example, we will use Reader's Notebooks as our tool for knowing what kids are thinking related to the texts they are reading. We don't want to interrupt kids' reading volume, so having them hold their thinking when it makes sense to them is key. This is all about writing to think and thinking to write. Imagine kids in Group A all reading the same text. Kids in Groups B, C, and D could be reading the same text as Group A, or they could be reading different texts. That's up to you. The point is that you are going to meet with two groups during one workshop. Here's the biggest helpful hint: Set a timer. Gather the kids, set your timer for 20 minutes, and go! During the small group, you can have students read a portion of the text together and make meaning. You can have them pick a page or lift a line that is speaking to or confusing them and explain why. You can have students share some ideas they've written in their notebooks. When 20 minutes are up, call over the next group and then repeat. After two days (or three depending on the size of your class), you will have met with everyone. During Week 2, you can repeat this small group routine or move on to new groupings.

> When 20 minutes are up, call over the next group and then repeat.

Understanding theme: Let's imagine you are helping kids in the intermediate grades understand theme. You pull a favorite text, such as *The Night Gardener* by the Fan Brothers (Fan & Fan, 2016), and take time to read this book aloud. Although this could be a great read-aloud for the whole class, you decide that reading it within close proximity to kids is very important because the illustrations need to be viewed within a hand's reach. You read the book together, discussing theme and creating an anchor chart with each small group that you meet with across the days. You know that it is going to take you two days for every student to experience this learning opportunity, so you'll be ready for a whole group anchor chart share-out (possibly as your minilesson) on the third day.

Reading and writing op-eds: Let's imagine middle school students unpacking how op-eds are written in hopes of using these models from their reading to write one of their own. Students might be reading op-eds during independent reading, or they might be reading a novel of their choice. (We emphasize independent reading time in this middle school example because we notice in classrooms we support that it is often sparse, yet so very important to students' literacy narrative.) Regardless of students' independent reading materials, the teacher hosts small groups focused on an op-ed of choice. This could be about a community issue from a local newspaper, or it could be from *The New York Times* (amazing archives can be found at "Op-Ed at 40," 2010). During *Week 1*, all students enjoy the same article with a small group, and the teacher shoots for meeting with two groups each day.

Week 2: Try something different by meeting with two small groups each day, but each group reads a different op-ed. If the groups create anchor charts noting big ideas and takeaways, you can cross-pollinate ideas and possibly build excitement for students reading op-eds on their own.

Week 3: Try something even more different by meeting with two small groups each day, but the students in each group begin to curate their own op-eds that they will offer up to the small group. See Chapter Seven for more on curating.

ALL STUDENTS READING THE SAME TEXT/BOOK

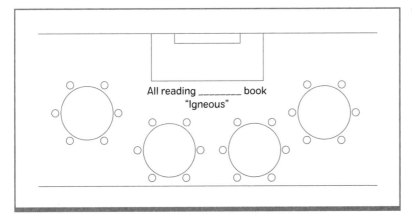

Small Group Example: Igneous Rock Study

Reasons Why You Might Hold
Small Group Meetings at the Same Time

- You want every group to read the same text at the same time, and you plan to float between groups.
- You've set up protocols with students for ways to work together in small groups when you are not present (see Chapter Two, page 47, for more on protocols).
- You are working on an integrated unit, and there is content-related material students will learn about by reading.

Jotting and talking about plot in picture books: You notice that describing the plot is tricky for many of your students. To further their understanding, you create small groups to lift students' experience and knowledge so that they can describe the main events in a story accurately and with confidence. You realize that if they can jot and talk about plot in picture books, they can then work to transfer that skill in longer texts, such as novels, during independent reading. You set up the following schedule, where students will read *the same picture book each day* and hold their thinking on a small group anchor chart that they can share with others at the end of the week.

Monday: You decide to extend Monday's workshop minilesson for shared reading where you will read aloud *White Water* by Michael S. Bandy and Eric Stein (2011), with illustrations by Shadra Strickland, and discuss the plot of the story. You will create a class anchor chart explaining the main details of the story as a model for group work the rest of the week. If any time remains, students will read independently.

Tuesday: *Also an Octopus* by Maggie Tokuda-Hall and Benji Davies (2016)

Wednesday: *Jack's Worry* by Sam Zuppardi (2016)

Thursday: *Across the Alley* by Richard Michelson, with illustrations by E. B. Lewis (2006)

Friday: *A Bike Like Sergio's* by Maribeth Boelts, with illustrations by Noah Z. Jones (2016)

Making meaning of narrative nonfiction: You've been working a lot on the function and format of fiction and nonfiction. Now you'd like your students to appreciate and make meaning of narrative nonfiction. Just as in the previous example, you curate a stack of books that you think your kids will enjoy and that will mix fact (nonfiction) with story plot (fiction). To hold their thinking, students in each small group will co-create a two-column chart listing both respective to the categories just described as they read each book. Here's how the week goes:

Monday: You decide to extend Monday's workshop minilesson for shared reading where you will read aloud *Trombone Shorty* by Troy Andrews (2015) and discuss interesting facts and the plot of the story. You will create a class two-column chart to model what small groups will be doing the rest of the week. If any time remains, students will read independently.

Tuesday: *Josephine* by Patricia Hruby Powell (2014)

Wednesday: *Clara and Davie* by Patricia Polacco (2014)

Thursday: *Balloons Over Broadway* by Melissa Sweet (2011)

Friday: *Fearless Flyer: Ruth Law and Her Flying Machine* by Heather Lang (2016)

STUDENTS READING DIFFERENT TEXTS/BOOKS ON THE SAME TOPIC

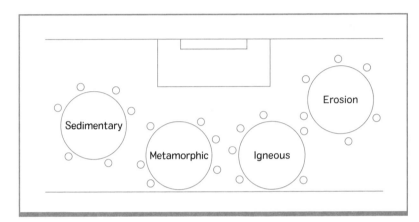

Small Group Example: Four Different Rock Study Groups

Reasons Why You Might Hold Small Group Meetings at the Same Time and Read Different Texts

- You decide each small group will read different texts each time they meet, but by the end of the week, the whole class (all small groups) will have read the same texts.
- You decide each small group will read some texts that are the same and some texts that are different, depending on the unit of study or students' interests.
- You decide that sometimes you will select the texts that students read and other times the small groups will select or a combination of both.
- You select texts based on content integration (science, social studies, math, health, etc.) and/or reading and writing content.
- You determine the duration for each small group (length can be the same or different) depending on teacher insights about differentiating instruction for students.

Example pertaining to literacy: Let's imagine a book club where everyone in the small group is reading the same book or books by the same author. Groups could meet each day to read, discuss, share thinking, and make meaning together.

The teacher can determine when to join in and meet with groups based on students' request or teacher insights from listening in (see Chapter Five for more on joining in and listening in). Creating a schedule for how often groups will meet across the week can be determined by students and/or the teacher, prioritizing time for both independent reading and small group work. Refer to Chapter Three for more on scheduling small group learning.

> Creating a schedule for how often groups will meet across the week can be determined by students and/or the teacher.

Example pertaining to integrated content: You've been working on an integrated unit focused on Earth materials where students are reading and writing across the social studies curriculum. Your small group work can be designed in multiple ways, but the constant in this example is groups meeting at the same time.

During Week 1, each small group could

- Read the same text each day (Monday = igneous rocks; Tuesday = sedimentary rocks, etc.)
- Read different texts by rotating to a different "text station" each day (by the end of the rotation, everyone will have read each text)

During Week 2, small group membership could stay the same or change. You could also

- Include some hands-on experiences where kids are reading about Earth materials, as well as identifying and classifying rocks and minerals

During Week 3, small group membership could stay the same or change. You could also

- Add different types of resources for students to explore and build their background knowledge and to gather information that will help them answer the unit's essential questions. (Students could read texts such as poems, narrative nonfiction picture books about Earth, video clips, and infographics. For more on resource curation, see Chapter Seven.)

During Week 4, small group membership could turn its focus to research or inquiry based on students' interests. You could

- Set aside time for small groups to meet and ask students to create a schedule for when they will meet together to read, discuss, hold thinking, and create
- Use the small group schedule to determine which groups you will meet with, when, and for how long

Use your kidwatching skills (refer to Chapter Four) and students' work (refer to Chapter Six) to figure out how you plan to pivot in and out of flexible, responsive groups (refer to Chapter Five) and to determine what resources to curate for and with students (refer to Chapter Seven) to lift their learning across this unit of study.

Barry's Planning Process for Hosting Two Groups

Let's look now at how Barry taps into the planning strategies and decision-making factors we just outlined. To make his work easier, he used a small group planning template to plan one day (see the example below, and a full-size version in the Appendix on page 291). Barry is going to walk us through his thought process for hosting two groups on a Tuesday in early September. His goal was threefold: to have students share great reads, to get to know his students' tastes as readers, and to have them practice a student-led protocol:

> First, I jotted down my basic goal for grouping: What can I find out about their summer reading experiences to help me better understand their reading habits and preferences? With that in mind, I deliberated between having five small groups meeting at the same time and dividing the class into four small groups and holding a couple of small group sessions in one workshop time. Both groupings have their strengths, but in order to get to know my students' reading preferences, I had to sit at the table, listen, and take notes on each and every student.
>
> Getting students ready for the small groups seemed like a tidy minilesson. Simple and direct—I would have students make a *list of their summer reading titles*, then Turn and Talk with a thought partner to help jar their memories.
>
> Early on in the year, I like to present protocols or construct them with the kids. We had already created an independent reading chart together, so I decided to make the protocol ahead of time. For me, making these protocols begins by imagining how small groups will operate without me there. I penciled out two jobs common in small groups, *facilitator* and *timer*, and added "A facilitator welcomes and invites people to share." To help groups get beyond just repeating their book lists, I figured I had to make some "nudging" prompts: *What makes you say that? Is there anything else you'd like to add?* This went on the "to do" list.

A timer's job is to keep each student's sharing time to a limit of two minutes. With the two roles clearly defined, I knew I wanted all the kids to share the jobs, so I made a *protocol chart* of the steps for conducting this small group meeting. (See the Small Group Planning Template in the Appendix.)

This may seem like a lot of planning, but I find a well-structured small group protocol supports conversations throughout the year. And in this case, these small groups would be repeated four times over the course of two days with the possibility of follow-up meetings. You can see how coaching kids up front to take leadership roles prepares them for smoothly running student-created small groups later on.

Scheduling our summer reading groups was pretty simple. We were only meeting once.

> A well-structured small group protocol supports conversations throughout the year.

But I reminded myself to make the groups ahead of time, to put the names on large sticky notes, and to place the sticky notes on the whiteboard under the weekly schedule. This would curb the "When do I meet with you?" question that can come up dozens of times when the protocol isn't clear.

I also made a note to have just a little time during the "workshop wrap-up" to *invite one or more students to share a title* they hear about in the small group and are excited to read.

Small Group Planning Template

Group: Summer Reading

Texts: Students' individual summer reading lists

Focus/Purpose: Learn and practice student-led small group protocol

	What do students need next? (current small group or new small group)	What will students do in small group?	How will students hold their thinking as they make meaning? Will they share out? • Student created • Teacher created
Planning	Student-led small group protocol chart (timer, facilitator)	Review and apply student-led small group protocol; talk about summer reading habits and books; connect to school-year reading habits and behaviors	Share their summer reading lists; create personal and group lists: • What were great summer reads? • What books might I read this year? • What do avid readers do? (list of habits)

	What do students need next? (current small group or new small group)	**What will students do in small group?**	**How will students hold their thinking as they make meaning? Will they share out?** • Student created • Teacher created
Small Group Workshop	**Minilesson** What will I show, model, and talk about with students to lift the work at the table?	**Work Time** What will students do?	**Debrief** How will we wrap up or share out?
	Everyone makes a list of books completed and things read during the summer.	Heterogeneous Groupings Group A 10–14 minutes Timer: 2 minutes per student Group of 5 Introduce student-led small group protocol. 1. Everyone will have a chance at both jobs. 2. Jobs move one to the left after each student sharing. 3. The facilitator welcomes and invites the person to the left to share a summer read, asks if anyone has any questions, and prompts, "What makes you say that? Is there anything else you'd like to add?" 4. The facilitator puts two minutes on a timer and lets the speaker know when he or she has 30 seconds left, then asks the student to wrap up his or her idea in one or two sentences. Students have Reader's Notebooks headed Summer Reading List." Future reading ideas: • At the end of the meeting, ask for one person to share. • Ask one person to stay and teach the next group the student-led protocol.	Ask one or two students to share their summer reading list and a book they heard about that they want to read this year.

In Barry's example, the chief thing we want you to appreciate is how much Barry invests in being super clear with protocols and super clear with his students that he expects them to know what to do—without his having to remind them. His goal is to push his students to productively work on their own in groups fast. In this next example, we want to appreciate the way Julie plans using the workshop model as a backdrop for kids having the time they deserve to do literacy work.

Across this week's plan, there is a quick kickoff that gets everyone oriented to the work of the day by sharing reading updates and survey results. It's the beginning of the year and the goal is to get students reading, so the focus turns quickly to a 10-minute (or less) whole group minilesson and then students head straight into the heart of workshop—the small group work time. This is the natural time for kids to read independently and for the teacher host or co-host and give way for small group learning to take place. This is how we combat the challenge we refer to in Chapter One. School days are not getting any longer and curriculum isn't being compressed, so we have to maximize our time to let kids do what they need to become stronger and savvier independent readers and thinkers. During the work time, there is an added space outlined (see the following example) that gives a place to jot what groups will meet and on which day. More importantly, you'll notice that not all days have been preplanned (see Monday, Thursday, and Friday), which gives space to host in-the-moment small groups based on students' wants and needs.

Weekly Planning Calendar: Lessons and Learning

My Reading and Writing Life Unit

Week 1 Lesson Plans

What does this mean?	Monday	Tuesday	Wednesday	Thursday	Friday
Kickoff/Opening (5 minutes) How will you launch the day? Will it be a quick "good morning, a knowledge check, a quick share-out with a peer, or another activity?	What are some of our favorite books? Thought partners introduced Partner sticky notes—students share	Quick reading calendar updates—show to thought partner	Quick reading calendar updates—show to thought partner	Quick reading calendar updates—show to thought partner Student literacy survey with thought partner	What does your thought partner's reading calendar reveal about him or her as a reader?

What does this mean?	Monday	Tuesday	Wednesday	Thursday	Friday
Minilesson (10 minutes) What will you teach? • Management • Content	Make an anchor chart for independent reading	Discuss how to work with thought partners and groups of four Create an anchor chart: "What makes a small group work well?"	Review "What makes a small group work well?"	Review independent reading chart Set independent reading behavior goal record in notebook	Teacher demonstration: Who? What? Quick write summary written response with read-aloud book Refugee
Work Time (40 minutes) What will students be doing? What will they be reading, writing, creating, making, and discussing to get stronger and smarter about the skills, strategies, and content related to the unit?	Book selection (if needed) and independent reading	Announce summer reads Small group schedule Independent reading	Announce summer reads Small group schedule Independent reading	Finish student literacy survey Independent reading	Independent reading Quick write: Who and what response in Reader's Notebook Knowledge check: Number of words written and insights
Small Group Learning Opportunities What groups will meet? What group(s) will you join? What will be the focus?	Small group selected to organize personal Reader's Notebooks and reading calendars	Small group: Summer reading conversations Work on protocol for small group timer and facilitator Create chart Heterogeneous: 4 groups (10 minutes) Group A Group B	Small group: Summer reading conversations Work on protocol for small group timer and facilitator Review chart Heterogeneous: 4 groups (10 minutes) Group C Group D	Review surveys Pull small group to gain more insights into reading habits and interests Go over "What makes a small group work well?" chart Kidwatch	Review surveys Pull small group to gain more insights into reading habits and interests Kidwatch or pull another group if needed
Share-Out/ Debrief (5 minutes) How and what will students share out/debrief?	Assess independent reading Set up Reader's Notebooks	Assess independent reading Encourage book shout-outs	Assess independent reading Discuss: What can we work on and get even better at during independent reading? (record)	Assess independent reading Have small groups share out key parts learned from survey	Assess independent reading Discuss: What worked this week during reading workshop?

Note: See the blank full-size version on page 296 of the Appendix. To learn more about how unit planning supports weekly and daily planning, see Chapter Eight.

JUMP IN—AND LEAVE PERFECTION AT THE DOOR

When Julie is supporting teachers, she often notices that despite going through the steps outlined earlier, teachers often short-circuit with worry about pulling off "perfect" small groups with a perfectly engaged rest-of-the-class. Teachers have commented, "The small groups don't go well for me when something is off balance," and "Every time I host a small group, someone who is supposed to be in the group is absent." Teachers too often think that everything has to be aligned to host a small group. For example, there needs to be enough time, students' behaviors need to be on mark for the day, no one in the intended small group is absent, and so on. The truth is, none of that matters. Everything does not have to be perfect to host a small group. The key is to jump in.

Student-Driven Planning

In popular culture and business, we often read about the need to push in versus push out, or the importance of *intaking*. For example, a marketer is always email blasting, getting content out, but really any organization, whether school or church or chocolate shop, is healthier when it finds out what its audience wants *now*. So, in this section, we shift to a bunch of strategies for handing over responsibilities to students for devising and sustaining groups. We will look at *self-assessments* that seed student-curated groups, we will look at the power of having a *bank of at-the-ready questions* to help students sustain productive discussion and help you lean in efficiently, and then we will share examples of co-hosted groups and student-facilitated groups in a section on *putting it into practice*.

SELF-ASSESSMENT MINDSETS AND TOOLS

Mary Howard (2017) reminds us that kidwatching is a mighty tool for differentiation, but simple, ongoing student self-assessment is mightier still. One tool we use to invite students to declare their interests and passions is the Interest and Reading Survey we showed you in Chapter Two on page 39. We demonstrated how knowing kids helps you curate texts specifically for them. Another tool we use is an index card. It's low-tech, but kids' responses teach us so much! What follows are two different types of prompts and student responses. In the first example, the teacher—whether she is a part of the group or not—expects students to spend a few minutes before group time ends jotting down their thinking on an index card. It's not unusual for teachers to have a pile of index cards on each table, in their back pocket, or in a basket on the bookshelf for students to grab at any moment. Any size and color will do, and lines versus no lines yield different results, especially if kids know they can show their thinking through sentences, bullet points, words, or pictures. *You've got to ask kids what you want or need to know.* Be specific, but keep the questions relatively open-ended because you'll get a really good sense of what kids are learning and thinking about. *You'll also learn what they want and need.* The goal of this first student reflection is to figure out what students are thinking about based on that day's small group learning. Asking kids positions them for self-advocacy and greater independence over their own learning. Here's an example:

> You've got to ask kids what you want or need to know. Be specific, but keep the questions relatively open-ended because you'll get a really good sense of what kids are learning and thinking about. You'll also learn what they want and need.

> I walk away thinking about the deeper friendship between Joseph and Jack. How they had each others back despite each others past. I also think about how if only Josephs dad had a second chance, a chance to change.

Side 1: The student responds to the prompt "Based on today's small group, what are you still thinking about?"

> ~~I would want~~ If I had a chance to meet again with this group I'd want to talk about the little details that stood out to us and about if Josephs dad really loved his son, and what would've happened if Joseph lived.

Side 2: The student responds to the prompt "If you had a chance to meet again with this group, what would you like to talk about?"

In the next example, the goal is to zoom in on students' eye-opening or mind-opening experiences from their interactions in small groups. If you ask, "What was your big aha?" kids might share nuggets from the text they were reading. Sometimes, though, kids share ahas about classmates' interpretations or connections they make to other texts or experiences. Because you'll ask kids to put their name or initials on the index cards before you collect them, you'll be able to look through or sort student responses, often giving you insight into what individual or small groups of kids are thinking about or need. You can use this information to group or regroup students. Keeping these index cards in student portfolios or having kids tape some (but not all) responses in a notebook gives you and students a look into how ideas and thinking change across time. When you keep students' index cards as evidence of their learning (formative assessment, discussed in Chapter Six), you send them a message that what they have to say matters. There is something magical about an empty index card. If you talk to kids about how there is no "wrong answer" because you are trying to crack open their head so you can crawl into their ideas and understandings, the card becomes a safe space for students to open up and convey their thinking. If you use this as a regular strategy (give it a try two or three times a week), you'll be surprised at how much students will teach you.

Side 1 asks kids about their big aha from small group learning, and Side 2 gives students a chance to advocate for what they want or need next.

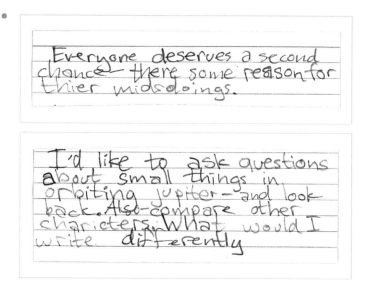

Example Sentence Starters and Questions for Index Card Exit Tickets

- Based on today's small group, I/we want/need . . .
- Based on today's small group, what are you still thinking about?
- If you had a chance to meet again with this group, what would you like to talk about?
- What I hope to read next is . . .

- My big aha in small group today was . . .
- What I want/need next is . . .
- What I am wondering is . . .
- What got cleared up today was . . .
- What is still confusing me or tripping me up in my understanding is . . .
- What I need next is . . .
- I wonder . . .
- I think . . .
- An image or blurb that comes to my mind after today's experience is . . .
- I/we really need 10 to 15 minutes tomorrow to _____ because I/we need to _____.
- How did today's small group go? Is there anything you'd do the same or different?
- What are one or two things you learned?
- What are one or two things that are confusing you?

QUESTIONS THAT HELP READERS SELF-MANAGE

If our goal is for students to become independent readers, writers, thinkers, doers, and creators, then we have to let go and let them practice doing just that. That means giving them the time, space, and know-how to co-host a small group with you and independently host a small group with students as facilitators. Different from a book club or literature circle with assigned roles, this is about giving students the autonomy to determine a few things for themselves as a group. Here are a few questions we've found help our students play "good cop" with each other as they plan their group experiences:

- Out of the choices of texts we have, what will we read?
- Will we read together, in pairs, or independently?
- How much will we read?
- What will we do while we read? Will we hold our thinking and share that out? Will we create something? What's our purpose for reading, in addition to making meaning?
- When will we get back together?
- What will be our focus when we come back together?

> This is about giving students the autonomy to determine a few things for themselves as a group.

QUESTIONS THAT REVEAL STUDENTS' PASSIONS

If we want to teach into students' passions and group kids based on commonalities, we have to find out what makes their motors run. Of course, kidwatching and listening in to small groups helps us learn that type of information. We can also just ask them. Here are a few questions that you can use:

- What skills come naturally to you? How could you use those skills to do something good for your classroom or community?
- What's something that, when you get really involved in it, makes you lose track of time?
- What gets your blood boiling? What's something in your school or community that you'd like to fix?
- Describe a time (moment, activity, accomplishment, etc.) that made you feel really good or confident. What were you doing, and why did it bring you joy?
- If you had the whole day free, what are three things you'd really enjoy doing?

QUESTIONS THAT BOTH YOU AND STUDENTS CAN USE AS DISCUSSION TOPICS

Reading and enjoying it is a process. No two readers do it in the same way. The possible topics for small group discussion are as vast as authors, readers, and themes. We trust you and your students to figure that out! Here, though, we focus on some questions we think are critical for leaning in and for student discussions about process. They can seed conferences; they can be the *reason* particular students gather; they can be written about in Reader's Notebooks. In all these ways, they promote student autonomy in small groups because they require learners to self-regulate, monitor, and reflect.

Questions About Texts

- How much did you know about the subject before you began reading this text(s)?
- How did you hold your thinking about what you were reading?
- Have your ideas changed about this topic? How?
- How are you stronger and smarter as a reader because of this work?
- What resources did you use while reading to help lift your own learning?
- What texts do you want to read again? What texts or types of texts do you want to read next?

Questions About Reading Process

- When you got "tripped up" in your reading, what did you do to clear up confusion?

- How do you feel about your reading or your process as you read this text(s)?
- What connections to the text did you make? Why were those connections important or significant?
- What was especially satisfying to you about either the process or the finished product?

Questions About Small Group Learning

- How did you and your small group approach the text(s) that you read?
- How did working in a small group help you lift your own reading muscles?
- Did you and the members of your small group think in similar or different ways?
- How did you and the members of your small group support one another?
- If you were working with this same small group again, what's one thing you'd like to change? What's one thing you'd do the same?
- What do you need next from your small group? How can the members of your small group help you, and how can you help them, in the future?

Questions About Self-Reflection

- What is one thing you'd like to improve?
- What is one goal that you'd like to set for yourself for the next few weeks?
- What texts would you like to read next, and why?
- What's one thing you want me to know before we begin our small group work in our next unit of study?

Putting It Into Practice: Examples From Our Classrooms

Okay, so what does it really look like in a classroom when you begin to allow students to meet on their own? You don't have to press the accelerator from 0 to 60 right away! Here are some scenarios to show you how to start slow.

CO-HOST GROUPS EXAMPLES

- After their small group read an article about the controversial new dog park in town, a few students explained that they just didn't understand what the article was saying. So you asked these students to hang back with you, while the other kids went off to independent work time. This small pop-up group worked through the text a second time together. What this small subset of students needed was to draw a map and outline all of the places being referenced in the article because some of the details were tripping them up.

- Students fill out an exit ticket, and several kids write that they are tired of their current book and that they want to abandon it. In response to that feedback, you invite anyone in the class who is feeling that way to join you to talk through it and make a plan for determining reasons and strategies to stick with the book or abandon it and move on.

- There is a current event on the news, and students are itching to discuss it. Since this may not be relevant or of interest to everyone in the class, you co-host a small group for anyone who is interested in talking about, reading, processing, or even writing about the news.

STUDENTS-ONLY GROUPS EXAMPLES

- After a shared reading with the whole class, if some students want to spend more time debriefing, let them do it! Sometimes kids don't need to talk about their comprehension strategies. Sometimes they need to talk about what a text meant to them.

- During an end-of-workshop share-out, students in a small group explained that they had been reading about the upcoming Olympics. Because that piqued the interest of a few other students, the Olympics small group members invited them to join them for the first few minutes of independent reading so that they could peruse the articles and resources in their group's bucket. Providing this opportunity can inspire reading about new topics and increase reading volume.

- Students were "lifting a line" or "quoting a quote" to signal big takeaways in the author's message. There was a buzz from a few students who disagreed, which resulted in a new student-led small group forming to further their position and/or learn from others.

MANAGEMENT TIPS

As we have shown, effective planning is a combination of planning ahead and daily planning and pivoting. Hosting, co-hosting, and no-hosting each day may seem tough to pull off, but if you look at your calendar each week and each day, remember this: The only critical things you need to figure out are *when groups will meet; what groups you, the teacher, will join; and what groups will meet without you.*

Photo by Christian Ford

To Get to What You See Here, **Try This**

1. Figure out a system that doesn't require you (the teacher) to be in charge of initiating or activating the students meeting in groups with others as needed.

2. Create a system so that students can sign up to co-lead a share-out, a student-led small group, or a mid-workshop help session (such as writing names on the whiteboard or a clip system).

3. Assign a team captain to help manage the sign-up system or create a shared agreement with students about how to accomplish this with efficiency and independence.

One Last Thing

Planning is our way of charting the course. It helps us create intentional plans that support what students should know, understand, and be able to do. Creating those plans, with students' curiosities, passions, habits, and needs in mind, gives us action-ready ways to create dynamic, small group learning opportunities for our students. Switching up small groups regularly gives us the ability to support learners as they come to understand important ideas and the know-how of whether or not they have achieved the desired results. So, let's get to it. Plan and set sail!

Conclusion

It's About Joy. Period.

Gratitude keeps us humble!

Photos by Christian Ford

Proximity. It's an interesting thing for teachers and students alike. Small group learning gives us the proximity we need to *listen in* so that we can listen to students as they discuss and think together about the texts they are reading. Small group learning also gives us the time and space to *join in* those conversations where we might ask questions, suggest ideas, explore wonderings, and help lift the learning at the table. All of these experiences provide *educational intel* about students' knowledge, skills, and understandings so that we may support students' individual curiosities, passions, habits, and needs.

The five teacher moves we've talked about in this book work together to support students' reading independence through small group learning experiences.

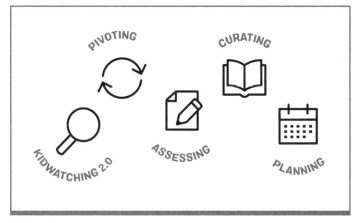

iStock.com/artvea

We *kidwatch* so that we are well informed about our students' curiosities, passions, habits, and needs (see Chapter Four). Responsive teaching is all about meeting the needs of individual students. Responding requires that we *pivot*, changing up groups regularly and in response to what we know kids need collectively and individually (see Chapter Five). When we think of assessment as a knowledge check—a time and a place to check kids' knowledge and understandings—we can *assess* with the attention of responding to what we learn (see Chapter Six). Growing students' reading muscles is no easy task. It's complicated work, especially for students who find reading to be more of a job than a joy. One way to combat that feeling is to *curate* texts for kids that feel like they were picked just for them (see Chapter Seven). The goal is to choose texts for kids that they will not want to put down. In turn, we want to teach kids to curate texts for their own reading diets while also finding texts for others because curation is for everyone! Being in tune with our students helps us *plan* with more intentionality and gives us the fuel we need to couple curricular demands with students' wants and needs (see Chapter Eight). Unit planning, which includes weekly and daily plans, is hard work. *Reflecting*, along the way, will help you figure out what worked and what you need to do next with and for your students. Give yourself the gift of scheduling quick reflection time—just five minutes right after reading workshop and at the beginning of your planning time or at the end of the day. Reflection is our tool for growth because it helps us look back in order to plan forward.

As we wrap up this book, we encourage you to put all five of these teacher moves into action, but remember you don't have to do them all at once. The moves work together, creating a support system for small group learning, but you can dip into each move individually and try it out, reflecting along the way, letting students and their work guide you. You don't have to take it on all at once. Pick one launch idea from Chapter Two, or find an exciting and relevant text related to a current event in kids' lives and kick off some shared reading. Turn that shared reading into a small group experience as we show in Chapter Nine. Regardless of where you begin, we encourage you to use our five moves and make them your own—to continue to inspire curiosity and joy by working closely with students.

If creating and working with small groups was easy, more teachers would employ them. They are messy because they begin and end with relationships. They require us to speak more, to listen more, and to shoulder more responsibility for our own learning. The joy is in knowing we have all worked hard and pushed ourselves a bit more because of a greater sense of belonging and need to participate.

Research studies have shown that if you want to live a happy and fulfilling life, you must be curious about the world around you. Question, ponder, explore. Do that while hanging with people, and joy often follows. Establish and grow relationships. This book is about creating and working in small groups because it brings out curiosity and joy. *Exquisite things happen when we are inquisitive together.* We hope you find joy while sitting across from your curious kids. We hope you are curious while sitting across from joyful kids. Let kids lean on you to solve challenges. Let kids lean on one another too. And let yourself lean on kids to uncover what they know, are able to do, and need next to solve the challenges inherent in becoming independent learners.

Appendix

*Ready-to-Copy Teacher and
Student Reflection/Planning Pages*

 Available for download at **resources.corwin.com/wrighthoonan**

How Much Time Are Readers Actually Working?

Analyze the amount of time you have for reading workshop. Fill in the pie chart to represent what percentage of time you are teaching and students are working.

Now estimate the amount of time during the day that you are talking and students are talking. Consider the "60/40 Rule"—students should be talking 60% of the time, and teachers 40%. Think about how small group discussions might help you maintain this golden ratio.

Listening In

What do I see? What do I hear?	Why does it matter to student learning?	Wonderings

What do I see? What do I hear?	Why does it matter to student learning?	What could/should I do to nudge, teach, and inspire this group now?	Other wonderings for future teaching/ small group learning

What questions do I have?	What did I learn?	What could/should I do to nudge, teach, and inspire this group now?	Other wonderings for future teaching/ small group learning

What kinds of things do you enjoy doing after school and on the weekends?

What trips or experiences have been the most memorable for you?

What pets do you enjoy?

If you could spend time learning more about something, what topics would you curiously pursue?

What book(s) have you read aloud that you remember with fondness?

What two or three titles stand out when you think about books you have completed?

Which reading categories or genres have you found enjoyable?

How would you describe your daily reading habit? Circle any topics/genres below that interest you.

History	Sports	Art
Animals	Adventure	Teen	Romance
Mystery	War Stories	Poetry	Biographies	Humor
Science Fiction	Horror	Dystopian
Graphic Novels	Fantasy	Science

Thought Partner Planning Grid for Younger Students

Choosing the right book/text *or* broadening my choices (ideas that expand my ideas about texts and push me to read new things)	Figuring out how to solve new/ unknown words (using strategies that help unpack new words)	Tracking my thinking over time (how I write/talk about reading)	Making connections (how I connect thinking across texts)	Strategic reading (how I use reading strategies to build reading muscles)
Making my thinking and learning visible (how I • Use rubrics • Use checklists • Show what I know through the work I create • Do knowledge checks • End demonstrations)	Getting organized (how I get ready for reading/writing experiences)	Working in a whole group partnership (how my partner supports me during whole group experiences)	Fluency building (how my partner models for me/helps me think about the way my reading sounds)	Strategic writing (how I use writing strategies to build writing muscles)
Word Study Sleuth (helps me investigate and understand how words work)	Grammar Guru (helps me use proper grammar)	Conventions Guru (helps me use conventions that convey what I'm trying to say)	Technology Thought Partner (pushes me in building my technology skills)	Other

Choosing books/ texts *or* broadening my choices (ideas that expand my ideas about texts and push me to read new things)	Figuring out how to solve new/unknown ideas, themes, and concepts (making connections to past learning and/or talking to others to unpack new/unknown ideas)	Tracking my thinking over time (how I write/talk about reading)	Making connections (how I connect thinking across texts, genres, authors, concepts, and themes)	Strategic reading (how I use reading strategies to build reading muscles)
Making my thinking and learning visible (how I • Use rubrics • Use checklists • Show what I know through the work I create • Do knowledge checks • End demonstrations)	**Staying organized** (how I stay organized around reading/writing experiences)	**Working in a whole group partnership** (how my partner supports me during whole group experiences)	**Working in a writing mode partnership** (how my partner models for me/helps me think about what mode of writing could convey my thinking)	**Strategic writing** (how I use writing strategies to build writing muscles)
Word Study Sleuth (helps me investigate and understand how new/unknown words work)	**Grammar Guru** (helps me use proper grammar)	**Conventions Guru** (helps me use conventions that convey what I'm trying to say)	**Technology Thought Partner** (pushes me in building my technology skills)	**Other**

1. Get started quickly by sitting with your thought partner.

2. Pause and reflect on the question being posed.

3. Attend to the question by turning and talking or turning and listening.

4. Share talking time.

5. Listen to remember what has been shared.

Here's another way to get small group learning off the ground. You can use this plan at the beginning of the year, or you can start at any point in the year.

Day 1 (Whole Group Focus)

Time: 10 minutes

What to Focus On:

Teach: Tell your students that the word *text* can mean a lot of things.

Show: Provide a few examples (books, newspaper articles, text messages, etc.).

Anchor: Co-create an anchor chart of ideas titled "What Is a Text?" while students brainstorm different examples of texts. Review or create an anchor chart called "Different Ideas for Holding Your Thinking" focused on different ways kids can make their thinking visible in their Reader's Notebooks.

Assess: Survey students by giving a quick formative assessment to determine student reading/learning interests. Hand them an index card and ask them to write a top 10 list of the things they like to read (topics, genres, authors, etc.).

Materials: Examples of different types of texts, chart paper, student interest survey

Teacher Homework/Action: (approximately 15–20 minutes) Look at student survey results. Group students together (groups of two or three or four to six) based on results. Find one short text that each group could read tomorrow.

Day 1 (Small Groups During Independent Work Time)

Time: 25 minutes

What to Focus On:

Say: "Let's get together in the smallest small group there is. Find a partner or a trio. Grab a text or two from the choices on top of the bookshelf. Your small group can read the same text or a different one. Decide if you will read together or alone."

Explain: "Make sure you have your Reader's Notebook handy. While you read, or after you finish the selection, hold your thinking. If you need a boost, look at our anchor chart 'Different Ideas for Holding Your Thinking.'"

Materials: Text(s), students' Reader's Notebooks

Day 2 (Whole Group Focus)

Time: 15 minutes

What to Focus On:

Share: Share some examples of survey results with students. For example, say, "I'm so excited because five kiddos are interested in nature-related topics and three kids want to learn more about Judy Blume and her books."

Teach: Explain that you broke the class into small groups based on the interest surveys. Some groups have four, five, or six students, while others have two or three. Explain that for the next week or so, the students will be meeting with their small group.

Say/Talk About: "You will each have a two-pocket folder to store your texts individually. Your group will also have a bucket or bin to store all of your folders and any texts that there is only one copy of. You can then share that one copy with the whole small group. Let's talk about the different ways your group might work." You could

- Read the same text together, aloud, and hold your thinking in your Reader's Notebook
- Read the same text together, independently; discuss what you read; and hold your thinking in your Reader's Notebook

Anchor: Co-create an anchor chart while students brainstorm different examples of how they could go about their reading in the small group.

Get Organized: Give groups time to find a meeting spot, gather supplies, and make decisions about today's small group reading routine.

Materials: Two-pocket folders, bucket/bin, texts, Reader's Notebooks

Day 2 (Small Groups During Independent Work Time)

Time: 25 minutes

What to Focus On:

Decide: Choose two groups to join today.

Pay Attention To: Small group volume meter. Help students make adjustments as needed.

Attend to Small Groups and Note-Take:

- Who is doing the talking?
- How did students decide to approach the work?
- What do you see or hear? What are you wondering?
- What texts could this group read next?

Materials: Two-pocket folders, bucket/bin, texts, Reader's Notebooks

Teacher Homework/Action: (approximately 15–20 minutes) Find one or two texts that the members of each group could add to their two-pocket folders.

Day 3 (Whole Group)

Time: 7 minutes

What to Focus On:

Say/Talk About: "How did yesterday's small group go? What worked? What was clunky?"

Teach: Teach into and address some of the reflections shared by students.

Explain: "Today's small group routine is the same as yesterday's. When you meet, decide if your group wants to make any adjustments to how you will go about your work today. Once you make some decisions, dig in and get to work."

Materials: Two-pocket folders, bucket/bin, texts, Reader's Notebooks

Day 3 (Small Groups During Independent Work Time)

Time: 30–40 minutes

What to Focus On:

Decide: Choose two or three groups to join today.

Attend to Small Groups and Note-Take:

- Who is doing the talking?
- How did they decide to approach the work?
- What do you see or hear? What are you wondering?
- What texts could this group read next?

Materials: Two-pocket folders, bucket/bin, texts, Reader's Notebooks

Day 3 (Small Group or Reading Workshop Debrief)

Time: 5–10 minutes

What to Focus On:

Share Out: Choose one or more of the following prompts to stir up conversation:

- What did your group look, sound, and feel like the past two days? How did you approach the work?
- What did your group learn from your text(s) that is worth sharing?
- How did your group members hold their thinking about what they read?
- Do you know of any texts at home or here at school that would be a good addition to your small group's bucket? If so, please bring them for our small group work tomorrow.

Materials: Two-pocket folders, bucket/bin, texts, Reader's Notebooks

Student Homework/Action: Look for one text (short or long) that could be added to your group's bucket of texts.

Teacher Homework/Action: (approximately 15–20 minutes) Find one or two short texts that the members of each group could add to their two-pocket folders, *or* longer texts (individual copies of picture books, chapter books, anthologies, etc.) that could be added to the small group's bucket.

Day 4 (Whole Group)

Time: 10 minutes

What to Focus On:

Teach/Say: "You are going to share out what you brought to add to your text set." Show the text to the group and read the title and author. "Remember, you didn't have to read this for homework, so you don't have to share what the text is about. If anyone in your group wants a copy of the text for his or her folder, please use a sticky note and tell me how many copies you need."

Share Out: Small group members sit near one another and share out, using a sticky note to mark any copies that are needed.

Explain/Say: "Today's small group routine is the same as yesterday's. After 15 minutes, I'm going to hit the chime, and I'd like for you to stop and share out. I'll explain more when we come back together. Dig in and happy reading."

Materials: Two-pocket folders, bucket/bin, texts, Reader's Notebooks, sticky notes

Day 4 (Small Groups During Independent Work Time)

Time: 35 minutes

What to Focus On:

Decide: Choose two or three groups to join today.

Attend to Small Groups and Note-Take:

- Who is doing the talking?
- How did they decide to approach the work?
- What do you see or hear? What are you wondering?
- What texts could this group read next?
- How are students holding their thinking? Are there examples from students' work that you should share with the whole group during the debrief?

Materials: Two-pocket folders, bucket/bin, texts, Reader's Notebooks, sticky notes

Turn In: Say, "Mark one or two pages where you've held your thinking where you'd like me to take a peek. Use a sticky note to mark the place(s) in your Reader's Notebook. Feel free to write me a note if you want me to know anything specific."

Day 4 (Debrief)

Time: 10 minutes

What to Focus On:

Share: Put two or three student examples of *holding your thinking* under the document camera. As you display the students' work, ask them to join you. *Share the mic* with each student (that's when the teacher and student share the "stage" to explain or show an idea or some type of thinking), display the text that was read, and support the student as he or she explains how thinking was held.

Ask/Share: If other students have examples they'd like to share, invite them to join you. If time doesn't permit, you can begin tomorrow's whole group by continuing the debrief.

Materials: Two-pocket folders, bucket/bin, texts, Reader's Notebooks, sticky notes

Teacher Homework/Action: (approximately 10–20 minutes) Look across Readers' Notebooks. Find one or two short texts that the members of each group could add to their two-pocket folders *or* longer texts (individual copies of picture books, chapter books, anthologies, etc.) that could be added to the small group's bucket.

Day 5 (Whole Group)

Time: 5 minutes

What to Focus On:

Say: "Today your group is going to make some decisions about how your small group will work for the next week. Your end goal is to determine how often your group will meet next week and what the focus will be when you meet. Some questions to guide you are

- How many days will you meet during independent work time?
- On the days you are meeting, how much time will you meet? The whole work time or just a portion? If just a portion, will you meet at the beginning or at the end?
- What will your group read, discuss, or share during each of your small group sessions?
  o Will you read together?
  o Will you read individually?

- o Will you read the same text(s)?
- o Will you read different texts?
- Who will be the captain or team leader of your group?"

Explain: Hand students a blank calendar and explain that they will meet to talk through their small group meeting calendar and determine if they are going to meet together in a small group today or read independently. Remember, some students are choosing to read other texts for independent reading while some students are continuing to read the texts from their small group. Either is a good choice.

Materials: Two-pocket folders, bucket/bin, texts, Reader's Notebooks, sticky notes, small group planning calendar

Turn In: Completed small group meeting calendar for your team.

Day 5 (Small Groups)

Time: 30 minutes

What to Focus On:

Decide: Choose two or three groups to join today.

Attend to Small Groups and Note-Take:

- How are they using the planning calendar?
- How did they decide to approach the work?
- What do you see or hear? What are you wondering?
- Did the group use the remaining time to read the small group text set or read independently?

Materials: Two-pocket folders, bucket/bin, texts, Reader's Notebooks, sticky notes, small group planning calendar

Teacher Homework/Action: (approximately 10–20 minutes) Look across the small group planning grid. Determine which groups you will meet with next week based on needs. Create your schedule based on small group planning grids: When are they meeting? How often and for how long? Some other considerations for meeting with groups include

- The small group plan is unfinished, or the group may need to revise the plan.
- The small group is meeting all week, all of the time. Meet with these students to determine how independent reading will play into their work since that is also a priority.
- The small group is in need of more or different texts, and you need the group members to help determine the next direction so that you can curate new texts with their interests and ideas in mind.

Day 6 (Whole Group)

Time: 5 minutes

What to Focus On:

Say: "This is the day you launch your small group plan. As a group, revisit your plan and get to work!"

Materials: Two-pocket folders, bucket/bin, texts, Reader's Notebooks, sticky notes, small group planning calendar

Day 6 (Small Groups/Independent Work Time)

Time: 40 minutes

What to Focus On:

Decide: Choose two or three groups to join today.

Attend to Small Groups and Note-Take:

- Are they following their plan?
- Who is doing the talking?
- How did they decide to approach the work?
- What do you see or hear? What are you wondering?
- What texts could this group read next?
- How are students holding their thinking? Are there examples from students' work that you should share with the whole group during the debrief?

Materials: Two-pocket folders, bucket/bin, texts, Reader's Notebooks, sticky notes, small group planning calendar

Day 7–10 (Whole Group)

Time: 5–10 minutes

What to Focus On:

Consider: If there are management suggestions that you need to share, take time to do that before launching into small group work (e.g., ways to work together, productive conversations, and sharing ideas).

Materials: Two-pocket folders, bucket/bin, texts, Reader's Notebooks, sticky notes, small group planning calendar

Day 7–10 (Small Groups)

Time: 35–40 minutes

What to Focus On:

Decide: Choose two or three groups to join today.

Attend to Small Groups and Note-Take:

- Are they following their plan?
- Who is doing the talking?
- How did they decide to approach the work?
- What do you see or hear? What are you wondering?
- Is there a text that you want the group to read together with you?
  - What will you need to teach into?
  - Where will kids get tripped up (vocabulary, background knowledge, making meaning, etc.)?
  - What do you want to show or model for them?
  - What new skills, strategies, knowledge, or understandings do you want to focus on?
- What texts could this group read next?
- How are students holding their thinking? Are there examples from students' work that you should share with the whole group during the debrief?

Materials: Two-pocket folders, bucket/bin, texts, Reader's Notebooks, sticky notes, small group planning calendar

Day 7–10 (Debrief)

Time: 10 minutes

What to Focus On:

Consider: The debrief time can be related to students' independent reading or small group work. As you meet with groups, study students, and attend/respond to the learning in the room, determine whether students will debrief

- As a whole group
- In their current small groups
- In mixed small groupings in order to cross-germinate ideas across groups
- In pairs or trios

Materials: Two-pocket folders, bucket/bin, texts, Reader's Notebooks, sticky notes, small group planning calendar

Teacher Homework/Action: (approximately 10–20 minutes) Look across Readers' Notebooks. Find one or two short texts that the members of each group could add to their two-pocket folders, *or* longer texts (individual copies of picture books, chapter books, anthologies, etc.) that could be added to the small group's bucket. Look to see how students are holding their thinking. Are there examples from students' work that you should share with the whole group during the debrief?

Day 11 (Whole Group)

Time: 15 minutes

What to Focus On:

Teach: Tell your students that there are lots of ways to "show what we have learned or what we know" and that part of our job is to figure out what we can make, create, or design to show our reading muscles.

Show: Provide a few examples (a series of notebook entries tied together, a reflection journal of big ahas, a top 10 list of important knowledge and understandings related to the texts, a reflection of how thinking has changed over time and across texts, etc.). Explain that these are examples of work products that the students can create to demonstrate their understanding.

Anchor: Co-create an anchor chart of ideas titled "How Can We Show What We Know?" and ask students to contribute ideas to the chart.

Explain: During work time this week, there are several options. Note that by the end of the week students will each turn in at least one work product that demonstrates their understandings of the small group texts read the past two weeks:

- Continue to read small group texts as a group or independently
- Work on work products as a group or independently
- Read independently (small group texts or independent reading choice)

Materials: Two-pocket folders, bucket/bin, texts, Reader's Notebooks, sticky notes, small group planning calendar, anchor chart "How Can We Show What We Know?"

Day 11–14 (Small Groups)

Time: 30 minutes

What to Focus On:

Decide: Choose two or three groups to join today.

Attend to Small Groups and Note-Take:

- How are the group or individual students using their time?
- How did they decide to approach the work?
- What do you see or hear? What are you wondering?
- Is there a text that you want the group to read together with you?
    - What will you need to teach into?
    - Where will kids get tripped up (vocabulary, background knowledge, making meaning, etc.)?

- o What do you want to show or model for them?
- o What new skills, strategies, knowledge, or understandings do you want to focus on?

- Are any new interests or inquiries coming to the surface that could fuel curating texts for future use?
- How are students using their thinking in their Reader's Notebooks to make, create, or design a work product to show their reading muscles or demonstrate understanding of the texts they read?
- Are there examples of students' work products that you should share with the whole group during the debrief?

Materials: Two-pocket folders, bucket/bin, texts, Reader's Notebooks, sticky notes, small group planning calendar

Day 11–14 (Debrief)

Time: 5 minutes

What to Focus On:

Consider: Give opportunities for students to share out:

- How are you using your work time this week?
- How are you using your thinking in your Reader's Notebook to make, create, or design a work product to show what you know or demonstrate understanding of the texts you read?

Materials: Two-pocket folders, bucket/bin, texts, Reader's Notebooks, sticky notes, small group planning calendar

Day 15 (Whole Group Gallery Walk)

Time: 40 minutes

What to Focus On:

Explain: Explain to students that a Gallery Walk is a time where they can display their work at their table and invite others (today it's our classmates) to take a look at the work they have created. This is a judgment-free time about celebrating success, not a time to provide feedback.

Gallery Walk: Students will showcase their work product(s), even if they are still in draft form, to their classmates by displaying their work in the "classroom gallery."

Invite: Ask students to enjoy roaming through the classroom gallery and looking at Reader's Notebooks, two-pocket folders, and buckets/bins.

Materials: Two-pocket folders, bucket/bin, texts, Reader's Notebooks

Day 15 (Debrief)

Time: 10 minutes

What to Focus On:

Share Out: Students can share out noticings and big takeaways from the Gallery Walk.

Materials: Two-pocket folders, bucket/bin, texts, Reader's Notebooks, sticky notes, small group planning calendar

Teacher Homework/Action: (approximately 10–20 minutes) Listen carefully to students as they share out and look for patterns or insights related to

- New/repeat texts you could put in front of students
- Opportunities related to new small group configurations
- Students' insights about what they need next

Kidwatching Notes:
Observations Lead to Small Group Invitations

What do you see/hear?	Why does it matter to student learning?

Name	What do we know about the student as a reader/writer? (asset-based evidence)	What would we like to know more about?	What are some possible literacy invitations for the student?	What does the student need that he or she is not getting or may not be able to get independently?	What are some small group opportunities that might benefit the student?

Who	Noticings	Wonderings

Note Catcher

Take a moment to think about a student in your life and fill out the following note catcher.

Who is this student?	What do you want to know?
What do you know about this student?	
What are his or her assets?	
What are the student's curiosities, passions, habits, and needs?	

Reflecting on Learning Targets

What are the students up to? Write each student's name in a box and take notes on what you see or hear in relation to the learning target—or learning targets:

Exit Tickets

I used to think _____.

Then I read/discussed/studied/inquired about _____.

Now I think _____.

I'm still wondering _____.

✂ ....

I already know _____.

Then I read _____.

Now I know _____.

I'm wondering _____.

✂ ....

Topic/Idea

I already know about _____.

I'm wondering _____.

After reading _____, I learned _____.

Now I'm wondering _____.

✂ ....

I really want to learn more about _____.

I already know _____.

My next steps in learning more are _____.

Planning for Flexible Groups

Grouping	Details				
Small Group 1	Who	What	When	Where	How
Small Group 2	Who	What	When	Where	How
Small Group 3	Who	What	When	Where	How
Small Group 4	Who	What	When	Where	How

What do you see/what do you notice? Describe the student work.

What are the implications for a focus for instruction? What do students need next?		
Whole Group	**Small Group**	**One-to-One**

	Students	What will you do next with/for these students?
Who was thinking deeply?		
Who needs more strategies, examples, or time?		
Who is not showing evidence of the learning targets?		

Students	What will you do next with/for these students?
Who can teach others?	
Who is on the right track?	
Who is not quite there, yet?	

Small Group Planning Template

Group:

Texts:

Focus/Purpose:

	What do students need next? (current small group or new small group)	**What will students do in small group?**	**How will students hold their thinking as they make meaning? Will they share out?** • Student created • Teacher created
Planning			
Small Group Workshop	**Minilesson** What will I show, model, and talk about with students to lift the work at the table?	**Work Time** What will students read, write, talk about, create, design, or do?	**Debrief** How will we wrap up/share out?

A Little Bit About . . .

| A little bit about_____ |

Do you have a favorite pop star, YouTuber, singer, band, movie, or author? Tell me any/all that you want me to know.

If school let out a few hours early and your only job was to have fun for four hours, what would you do?

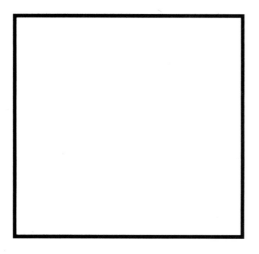

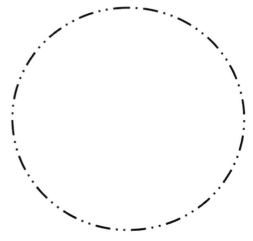

How would you describe how/where you learn best?

What do you want me to know that I haven't asked you?

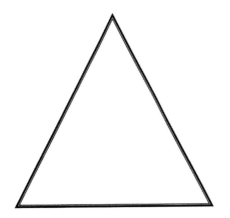

Tell Us Your Thoughts . . .

Name: _____

	Love it! 5	4	Kind of 3	2	Not really 1
Building things					
Coloring, designing, making creations					
Watching/playing online games					
Being outside					
Diving right into something without a set of directions					
Picking your own groups to work with at school					
Working with 3 people versus 6					
Reading short versus long texts (books, poems, articles, etc.)					
Fruit instead of candy					
Staying up late even if it means I'll be tired the next day					

Unit Planning Template

Unit Title:	
Created By:	

Define *What* and *Why*: Big Ideas Behind the Unit	Determine Student Work Products: Assessments *for* and *of* Learning (Demonstration of Understanding)
	What will students produce?
Curate Key Resources/Mentor Texts	
What will students consume?	
Small Group Learning Opportunities	**Other Important Information**

Outline Essential Questions	
Use the Standards	**Write Learning Targets**
	Long-Term Targets
	Short-Term Targets

Unit Planning Calendar

Unit: _____

Things we are wrestling with this week	Monday	Tuesday	Wednesday	Thursday	Friday

Week: _____

What does this mean?	Monday	Tuesday	Wednesday	Thursday	Friday
Kickoff/Opening How will you launch the day? Will it be a quick "good morning," a knowledge check, a quick share-out with a peer, or another activity?					
Minilesson What will you teach? • Management • Content					
Work Time What will students be doing? What will they be reading, writing, creating, making, and discussing to get stronger and smarter about the skills, strategies, and content related to the unit?					
Small Group Learning Opportunities What groups will meet? What group(s) will you join? What will be the focus?					
Share-Out/ Debrief How and what will students share out/debrief?					

References and Further Reading

Alcott, L. M. (1868). *Little women*. Boston, MA: Roberts Brothers.

Allington, R. L. (2001). *What really matters for struggling readers: Designing research-based programs*. Boston, MA: Allyn & Bacon.

Allington, R. L. (2002, June). What I've learned about effective reading instruction from a decade of studying exemplary elementary classroom teachers. *The Phi Delta Kappan, 83*(10), 740–747.

Allington, R. L. (2014, October). How reading volume affects both reading fluency and reading achievement. *International Electronic Journal of Elementary Education, 7*(1), 13–26.

Allington, R. L., & Gabriel, R. E. (2012, March). Every child, every day. *Educational Leadership, 69*(6), 10–15.

Andrews, T. (2015). *Trombone Shorty*. New York, NY: Abrams.

Assessment for Learning. (n.d.). Success criteria and rubrics. *Education Services Australia*. Retrieved from http://www.assessmentforlearning.edu.au/professional_learning/success_criteria_and_rubrics/success_criteria_landing_page.html

Atkin, J. M., Black, P., & Coffey, J. (2001). *Classroom assessment and the National Science Education Standards*. Washington, DC: National Academies Press.

Bagdasarian, A. (2002). *First French kiss and other traumas*. New York, NY: Farrar, Straus and Giroux.

Bandy, M. S., & Stein, E. (2011). *White water*. Somerville, MA: Candlewick Press.

Barron, T. A. (2007). *The hero's trail: True stories of young people to inspire courage, compassion, and hope* (Newly rev. and updated ed.). New York, NY: Puffin Books.

Bayrock, F. (2009). *Bubble homes and fish farts*. Watertown, MA: Charlesbridge.

Bear, D. R., Invernizzi, M., Johnston, F. R., & Templeton, S. (2012). *Words their way: Word study in action*. Glenview, IL: Pearson Learning.

Benjamin, A. (2015). *The thing about jellyfish*. Boston, MA: Little, Brown.

Bennett, S. (2007). *That workshop book: New systems and structures for classrooms that read, write, and think*. Portsmouth, NH: Heinemann.

Berger, R., Rugen, L., Woodfin, L., & EL Education. (2014). *Leaders of their own learning: Transforming schools through student-engaged assessment*. Hoboken, NJ: Jossey-Bass.

Berghoff, B., Egawa, K. A., Harste, J. C., & Hoonan, B. T. (2000). *Beyond reading and writing: Inquiry, curriculum, and multiple ways of knowing* (Whole Language Umbrella Series). Urbana, IL: National Council of Teachers of English.

Berra, Y. (n.d.). Quotes. *Goodreads*. Retrieved from https://www.goodreads.com/quotes/23616-if-you-don-t-know-where-you-are-going-you-ll-end

Bildner, P. (2004). *Twenty-one elephants*. New York, NY: Simon & Schuster.

Blauman, L. (2011). *The inside guide to the reading-writing classroom, grades 3–6: Strategies for extraordinary teaching*. Portsmouth, NH: Heinemann.

Boelts, M., & Jones, N. Z. (2016). *A bike like Sergio's*. Somerville, MA: Candlewick Press.

Bottner, B., & Kruglik, G. (2004). *Wallace's lists*. New York, NY: HarperColllins.

Boushey, G., & Moser, J. (2014). *The Daily 5: Fostering literacy independence in the elementary grades*. Portland, ME: Stenhouse.

Brown, S. T. (2005). *Oliver's must-do list*. Honesdale, PA: Boyds Mill Press.

Burkins, J. M., & Croft, M. M. (2010). *Preventing misguided reading: New strategies for guided reading teachers*. Newark, DE: International Reading Association.

Burkins, J., & Yaris, K. (2016). *Who's doing the work? How to say less so readers can do more*. Portland, ME: Stenhouse.

Calkins, L., & Ehrenworth, M. (2016, June). Growing extraordinary writers: Leadership decisions to raise the level of writing across a school and a district. *The Reading Teacher, 70*(1), 7–18.

Chappuis, J., Chappuis, S., Stiggins, R. J., & Arter, J. A. (2014). *Classroom assessment for student learning*. Boston, MA: Pearson.

Chernow, R. (2004). *Alexander Hamilton*. New York, NY: Penguin.

Clark, M. (2012, August 22). A pancake brings corn and berries together. *The New York Times*, p. D2.

Clarke, S. (2006). *Unlocking formative assessment: Practical strategies for enhancing pupils' learning in the primary classroom*. London, England: Hodder Murray.

Clay, M. (1993). *Observation survey of early literacy achievement*. Portsmouth, NH: Heinemann.

Clay, M. (1994). *Reading recovery: A guidebook for teachers in training*. Portsmouth, NH: Heinemann.

Collins, S. (2010). *The hunger games*. New York, NY: Scholastic.

Council of Chief State School Officers & National Governors Association. (2010). *Common Core State Standards for English language arts and literacy in history/social studies, science, and technical subjects*. Retrieved from http://www.corestandards.org/wp-content/uploads/ELA_Standards1.pdf

Covey, S. R. (2013). *The 7 habits of highly effective people: Powerful lessons in personal change*. New York, NY: Simon & Schuster.

Daniels, H. (2017). *The curious classroom: 10 structures for teaching with student-directed inquiry*. Portsmouth, NH: Heinemann.

Dewey, J. (1913). *Interest and effort in education*. Boston, MA: Houghton Mifflin.

Doubet, K. J., & Hockett, J. A. (2015). *Differentiation in middle and high school: Strategies to engage all learners*. Alexandria, VA: ASCD.

Duckworth, A. (2016). *Grit: The power of passion and perseverance*. New York, NY: Scribner.

Duhigg, C. (2017). *Smarter faster better*. New York, NY: Random House Books.

Duke, N. K. (2001). *Building comprehension through explicit teaching of comprehension strategies*. Presentation to the Second Annual MRA/CIERA Conference.

Duke, N. K. (2001, September 22). Building comprehension through explicit teaching of comprehension strategies. *Michigan State University*. Retrieved from http://www.ciera.org/library/presos/2001/2001MRACIERA/nduke/01cmndk.pdf

Durkin, D. (2004). *Teaching them to read* (6th ed.). Boston, MA: Pearson.

Dweck, C. S. (2007a). *Mindset: The new psychology of success*. New York, NY: Ballantine Books.

Dweck, C. S. (2007b). The perils and promises of praise. *Educational Leadership*, *65*(2), 34–39.

Dweck, C. (2014). The power of believing that you can improve. *TED Talk*. Retrieved from ted.com/talks/carol_dweck_the_power_of_believing_that_you_can_improve

Dweck, C. (2015, September 22). Carol Dweck revisits the "growth mindset." *Education Week*. Retrieved from https://www.edweek.org/ew/articles/2015/09/23/carol-dweck-revisits-the-growth-mindset.html

Eagan, C., & Bates, A. (2017). *The story of Barbie and the woman who created her*. New York, NY: Random House.

Education Services Australia. (2017). *Assessment for learning*. Retrieved from http://www.assessmentforlearning.edu.au/professional_learning/success_criteria_and_rubrics/success_criteria_landing_page.html

Ehrenworth, M. (2017, February). Why argue? *Educational Leadership*, *74*(5), 33–40.

Esquith, R. (2007). *Teach like your hair's on fire: The methods and madness inside room 56*. New York, NY: Viking.

Fan, T., & Fan, E. (2016). *The night gardener*. New York, NY: Simon & Schuster.

Fanelli, S. (2001). *My map book (rise and shine)*. New York, NY: HarperCollins.

Finger, B. (2015). *13 bridges children should know*. Munich, Germany: Prestel.

Fisher, D., Frey, N., & Hattie, J. (2016). *Visible learning for literacy, grades K–12: Implementing the practices that work best to accelerate student learning*. Thousand Oaks, CA: Corwin.

Fisher, D., Frey, N., & Hattie, J. (2017). *Teaching literacy in the visible learning classroom: K–5 classroom companion to visible learning for literacy*. Thousand Oaks, CA: Corwin.

Fletcher, R. (2003). *A writer's notebook: Unlocking the writer within you*. New York, NY: HarperCollins.

Fountas, I. C., & Pinnell, G. S. (1996). *Guided reading: Good first teaching for all children*. Portsmouth, NH: Heinemann.

Fountas, I. C., & Pinnell, G. S. (2001). *Guiding readers and writers: Teaching comprehension, genre, and content literacy*. Portsmouth, NH: Heinemann.

Fountas, I. C., & Pinnell, G. S. (2006). *Teaching for comprehending and fluency: Thinking, talking, and writing about reading, K–8*. Portsmouth, NH: Heinemann.

Fountas, I. C., & Pinnell, G. S. (2016a). *Guided reading responsive teaching across the grades* (2nd ed.). Portsmouth, NH: Heinemann.

Fountas, I. C., & Pinnell, G. S. (2016b, September 29). A level is a teacher's tool, NOT a child's label [Blog post]. Retrieved from http://blog.fountasandpinnell.com/post/a-level-is-a-teacher-s-tool-not-a-child-s-label

Fountas, I. C., & Pinnell, G. S. (2017). *Guided reading: Responsive teaching across the grades* (2nd ed.). Portsmouth, NH: Heinemann.

Fox, M. (1989). *Wilfrid Gordon McDonald Partridge*. La Jolla, CA: Kane/Miller.

Gladwell, M. (2013). *Blink: The power of thinking without thinking*. New York, NY: Back Bay Books.

Glover, M., & Keene, E. O. (2015). *The teacher you want to be: Essays about children, learning and teaching*. Portsmouth, NH: Heinemann.

Godwin, K. E., Almeda, M. V., Seltman, H., Kai, S., Skerbetz, M. D., Baker, R. S., & Fisher, A. V. (2016). Off-task behavior in elementary school children. *Learning and Instruction, 44,* 128–143.

Goldberg, G. (2016). *Mindsets and moves: Strategies that help readers take charge, grades 1–8.* Thousand Oaks, CA: Corwin.

Goldberg, G., & Houser, R. (2017). *What do I teach readers tomorrow? Nonfiction, grades 3–8: Your moment-to-moment decision-making guide.* Thousand Oaks, CA: Corwin.

Goodman, K., Fries, P., & Strauss, S. (2016). *Reading, the grand illusion: How and why people make sense of print.* New York, NY: Routledge.

Goodman, Y. M. (2003). *Valuing language study: Inquiry into language for elementary and middle schools.* Urbana, IL: National Council of Teachers of English.

Goodman, Y., & Owocki, G. (2002). *Kidwatching: Documenting children's literacy development.* Portsmouth, NH: Heinemann.

Graves, D. H. (1983). *Writing: Teachers and children at work.* Portsmouth, NH: Heinemann.

Graves, D. H. (1985, Fall). All children can write. *Learning Disabilities Focus, 1*(1), 36–43.

Grimwade, G., & Suh, J. (2014). The most beautiful goals [Infographic]. In G. Cook (Ed.), *The best American infographics 2014* (pp. 58–59). Wilmington, MA: Mariner Books.

Guthrie, J. T., Wigfield, A., & Humenick, N. M. (2006, March/April). Influences of stimulating tasks on reading motivation and comprehension. *The Journal of Educational Research, 99*(4), 232–245.

Harvey, S., & Daniels, H. (2015). *Comprehension and collaboration: Inquiry circles for curiosity, engagement, and understanding* (Rev. ed.). Portsmouth, NH: Heinemann.

Harvey, S., & Daniels, H. (2017). *Strategies that work: Teaching comprehension for understanding and engagement* (3rd ed.). Portsmouth, NH: Heinemann.

Harwayne, S. (1999). *Going public: Priorities and practice at the Manhattan New School.* Portsmouth, NH: Heinemann.

Hattie, J. (2008). *Visible learning: A synthesis of over 800 meta-analyses relating to achievement.* New York, NY: Routledge.

Hattie, J. (2012). *Visible learning for teachers: Maximizing impact on learning.* New York, NY: Routledge.

Hill, B. C., Johnson, N. J., & Noe, K. L. (1995). *Literature circles and response.* Norwood, MA: Christopher-Gordon.

Howard, M. (2009). *RTI from all sides: What every teacher needs to know.* Portsmouth, NH: Heinemann.

Howard, M. (2017, August 17). Tweet @DrMaryHoward.

Hruby Powell, P. (2014). *Josephine: The dazzling life of Josephine Baker.* San Francisco, CA: Chronicle Books.

Hurley, M. (2011). *The world's most amazing bridges* (Landmark Top Tens). Oxford, England: Raintree.

Johmann, C., & Rieth, E. (1999). *Bridges: Amazing structures to design, build and test* (Kaleidoscope Kids). Charlotte, VT: Williamson.

Johnston, P. H. (2004). *Choice words: How our language affects children's learning.* Portland, ME: Stenhouse.

Johnston, P. H. (2012). *Opening minds: Using language to change lives*. Portland, ME: Stenhouse.

Jones Prince, A. (2005). *Twenty-one elephants and still standing*. Boston, MA: Houghton Mifflin.

Keene, E., & Zimmermann, S. (1997). *Mosaic of thought*. Portsmouth, NH: Heinemann.

Korman, G. (2017). *Masterminds*. New York, NY: Balzer & Bray.

Krashen, S. D. (1993). *The power of reading: Insights from research*. Santa Barbara, CA: Libraries Unlimited.

Krashen, S. D. (2011). *Free voluntary reading*. Santa Barbara, CA: Libraries Unlimited.

Lang, H. (2016). *Fearless flyer: Ruth Law and her flying machine*. Honesdale, PA: Calkins Creek.

Latham, D., & Vaughn, J. (2012). *Bridges and tunnels: Investigate feats of engineering with 25 projects* (Build It Yourself). White River Junction, VT: Nomad Press.

Lyon, G. E. (1993). Where I'm from [Poem]. Retrieved from http://www.georgeellalyon.com/where.html

McTighe, J., & Wiggins, G. (2013). *Essential questions*. Alexandria, VA: ASCD.

Michelson, R. (2006). *Across the alley*. New York, NY: Putnam.

Micucci, C. (2009). *The life and times of corn*. New York, NY: Houghton Mifflin Harcourt.

Miller, D. (2002). *Reading with meaning: Teaching comprehension in the primary grades* (2nd ed.). Portland, ME: Stenhouse.

Miller, D. (2011). Not so gradual release: Teaching comprehension in the primary grades. In H. Daniels (Ed.), *Comprehension going forward: Where we are and what's next* (pp. 46–57). Portsmouth, NH: Heinemann.

Miller, D. (2015). I've got research. Yes I do. I've got research. How about you? [Blog post]. Retrieved from https://bookwhisperer.com/2015/02/08/ive-got-research-yes-i-do-ive-got-research-how-about-you/

Miller, D., & Anderson, J. (2011). *The book whisperer: Awakening the inner reader in every child*. New York, NY: Scholastic.

Mills, H., & Jennings, L. (2011, May). Talking about talk: Reclaiming the value and power of literature circles. *The Reading Teacher, 64*(8), 590–598. doi:10.1598/rt.64.8

Mills, H., & O'Keefe, T. (2011, May). Inquiry into assessment strategies: From kidwatching to responsive teaching. *Talking Points, 22*(2), 2–8.

Mills, H., & O'Keefe, T. (2015). How Reggio ruined me for anything less than inquiry-driven learning. In M. Glover & E. O. Keene (Eds.), *The teacher you want to be* (pp. 30–49). Portsmouth, NH: Heinemann.

Morrison, T. (1977). *Song of Solomon*. New York, NY: Knopf.

Morrison, T. (2011). *Song of Solomon*. London, England: Vintage.

Mulligan, T., & Landrigan, C. (2018). *It's all about the books: How to create bookrooms and classroom libraries that inspire readers*. Portsmouth, NH: Heinemann.

New Jersey Institute of Technology. (2018). High tech bridges of the future [Infographic]. Retrieved from https://graduatedegrees.online.njit.edu/resources/msce/msce-infographics/high-tech-bridges-of-the-future/

Newkirk, T. (2012). *The art of slow reading: Six time-honored practices for engagement*. Portsmouth, NH: Heinemann.

Oh, E. (Ed.). (2017). *Flying lessons and other stories*. New York, NY: Crown.

Op-ed at 40. (2010). *The New York Times.* Retrieved from http://archive.nytimes.com/www
.nytimes.com/interactive/2010/09/25/opinion/opedat40.html

Overdeck, L. (2017). *How many guinea pigs can fit on a plane? Answers to your most clever
math questions.* New York, NY: Feiwel & Friends.

Owocki, G., & Goodman, Y. (2002). *Kidwatching: Documenting children's literacy development.* Portsmouth, NH: Heinemann.

Palacio, R. J. (2012). *Wonder.* New York, NY: Knopf/Doubleday.

Paratore, J. R., & Robertson, D. R. (2013). *Talk that teaches using strategic Talk to help students
achieve the Common Core.* New York, NY: Guilford.

Parrott, K. (2017, October 12). Fountas and Pinnell say librarians should guide readers by
interest, not level. *School Library Journal.* Retrieved from http://www.slj.com/2017/10/
literacy/fountas-pinnell-say-librarians-guide-readers-interest-not-level/#_

Pfister, M. (2011). *Questions, questions.* New York, NY: NorthSouth Books.

Pinnell, G. S., & Fountas, I. C. (2011). *The continuum of literacy learning, grades preK–8:
A guide to teaching.* Portsmouth, NH: Heinemann.

Polacco, P. (2014). *Clara and Davie.* New York, NY: Scholastic Press.

Pollan, M. (2009). *The Omnivore's dilemma: Young readers edition.* New York, NY: Dial Press.

Prince, A. J. (2005). *Twenty-one elephants and still standing.* Boston, MA: Houghton Mifflin
Harcourt.

Radencich, M. C., & McKay, L. J. (1995). *Flexible grouping for literacy in the elementary grades.*
Boston, MA: Allyn & Bacon.

Ratliff, T. (2009). *You wouldn't want to work on the Brooklyn Bridge!: An enormous project that
seemed impossible.* New York, NY: Franklin Watts.

Richardson, J. (2016). *The next step forward in guided reading.* New York, NY: Scholastic.

Robb, L. (2008). *Differentiating reading instruction: How to teach reading to meet the needs of
each student.* New York, NY: Scholastic.

Robb, L. (2012). *Smart writing: Practical units for teaching middle school writers.* Portsmouth,
NH: Heinemann.

Robinson, K., & Aronica, L. (2015). *Creative schools: The grassroots revolution that's transforming education.* New York, NY: Penguin Books.

Routman, R. (2014). *Read, write, lead: Breakthrough strategies for schoolwide literacy success.*
Alexandria, VA: ASCD.

Russell, R. R. (2009). *Dork diaries 1: Tales from a not-so-fabulous life.* New York, NY: Simon
& Schuster.

Santman, D. (2005). *Shades of meaning: Comprehension and interpretation in middle school.*
Portsmouth, NH: Heinemann.

Schatz, K. (2015). *Rad American women A–Z: Rebels, trailblazers, and visionaries who shaped
our history . . . and our future!* San Francisco, CA: City Lights.

Schlosser, E., & Wilson, C. (2007). *Chew on this: Everything you don't want to know about fast
food.* New York, NY: Houghton Mifflin.

Schotter, R. (1999). *Nothing ever happens on 90th street.* New York, NY: Scholastic.

Schotter, R. (2006). *The boy who loved words.* New York, NY: Scholastic.

Scieszka, J. (2005). Watch your brothers. In J. Scieska (Ed.), *Knucklehead* (pp. 35–36). New York, NY: Penguin Group.

Serravallo, J. (2010). *Teaching reading in small groups: Differentiated instruction for building strategic, independent readers.* Portsmouth, NH: Heinemann.

Serravallo, J. (2014). *The literacy teacher's playbook, grades 3–6: Four steps for turning assessment data into goal-directed instruction.* Portsmouth, NH: Heinemann.

Serravallo, J. (2015). *The reading strategies book: Your everything guide to developing skilled readers.* Portsmouth, NH: Heinemann.

Shakespeare, W. (2000). *Henry V.* Herts, England: Wordsworth Editions.

Short, K. G., Harste, J. C., & Burke, C. L. (1996). *Creating classrooms for authors and inquirers.* Portsmouth, NH: Heinemann.

Shreaves, R. (2012, September 25). Big bad corn [Infographic]. *Mother Nature Network.* Retrieved from https://www.mnn.com/food/healthy-eating/blogs/infographic-big-bad-corn

Sibberson, F., & Szymusiak, K. (2003). *Still learning to read: Teaching students in grades 3–6.* Portland, ME: Stenhouse.

Smith, F. (2006). *Reading without nonsense.* New York, NY: Teachers College Press.

Smith, M. W., Wilhelm, J., & Fredrickson, J. (2012). *Oh, yeah?!: Putting argument to work both in school and out (exceeding the Common Core State Standards).* Portsmouth, NH: Heinemann.

Spinelli, E. (2008). *The best story.* New York, NY: Dial Books.

Spinelli, J. (2000). *Stargirl.* New York, NY: Knopf Doubleday.

Stanny, B. (2012, June 19). A fascinating new concept: How "thought partners" add value to your business. *Forbes.* Retrieved from https://www.forbes.com/sites/barbarastanny/2012/06/19/a-fascinating-new-concept-how-thought-partners-add-value-to-your-business/

Stine, M., & Who HQ. (2016). *Where is the Brooklyn Bridge?* New York, NY: Penguin Books.

Sullo, B. (2009). *The motivated student: Unlocking the enthusiasm for learning.* Alexandria, VA: ASCD.

Sweeney, D. (2011). *Student-centered coaching: A guide for K–8 coaches and principals.* Thousand Oaks, CA: Corwin.

Sweet, M. (2011). *Balloons over Broadway.* Boston, MA: HMH Books for Young Readers.

Telgemeier, R. (2010). *Smile.* New York, NY: Graphix-Scholastic.

Tokuda-Hall, M., & Davies, B. (2016). *Also an octopus.* Somerville, MA: Candlewick Press.

Tomlinson, C. A. (2003). *Fulfilling the promise of the differentiated classroom: Strategies and tools for responsive teaching.* Alexandria, VA: ASCD.

Tomlinson, C. A., Moon, T., & Imbeau, M. B. (2015). *White paper: Assessment and student success in a differentiated classroom.* Alexandria, VA: ASCD.

Tovani, C. (2011). *So what do they really know? Assessment that informs teaching and learning.* Portland, ME: Stenhouse.

Transportation for America. (2017). The fix we're in for: The condition of U.S. bridges [Infographic]. Retrieved from http://t4america.org/maps-tools/bridges/infographic

Vygotsky, L. S. (1962). *Thought and language* (E. Hanfmann & G. Vakar, eds. & trans.). Cambridge, MA: MIT Press.

Vygotsky, L. S. (1978). *Mind in society: The development of higher psychological processes* (M. Cole, V. John-Steiner, S. Scribner, & E. Souberman, Eds. & Trans.). Cambridge, MA: Harvard University Press. (Original work published 1934)

Walther, M. (2018). *The ramped-up read aloud: What to notice as you turn the page.* Thousand Oaks, CA: Corwin.

Weimer, M. (2012, October). Teaching metacognition to improve student learning [Blog post]. *Faulty Focus.* Retrieved from https://www.facultyfocus.com/articles/teaching-professor-blog/teaching-metacognition-to-improve-student-learning/

Wheatley, M. J. (2002, April). It's an interconnected world. *Shambhala Sun.* Retrieved from http://margaretwheatley.com/articles/interconnected.html

Wiggins, G. P., & McTighe, J. (2005). *Understanding by Design* (2nd ed.). Alexandria, VA: ASCD.

Wiggins, G. P., & McTighe, J. (2011). *The Understanding by Design guide to creating high-quality units.* Alexandria, VA: ASCD.

Wilhelm, J., & Smith, M. W. (2014). *Reading unbound: Why kids need to read what they want—and why we should let them.* New York, NY: Scholastic.

Wiliam, D. (2011). *Embedded formative assessment: Strategies for classroom assessment that drives student engagement and learning* (2nd ed.). Bloomington, IN: Solution Tree Press.

Woodson, J. (2012). *Each kindness.* New York, NY: Penguin Books.

Yates, K. (2015a). *Simple starts: Making the move to a reader-centered classroom.* Portsmouth, NH: Heinemann.

Yates, K. (2015b, October 10). Small group instruction: More than a level and kidney table. *Simply Inspired Teaching.* Retrieved from http://simplyinspiredteaching.com/2015/10/10/small-group-instruction-more-than-a-level-and-kidney-table/

Zuppardi, S. (2016). *Jack's worry.* Somerville, MA: Candlewick Press.

Index

Tripped up, getting, xxxvii, 124, 195, 256
Troubleshooting, 143–146
Turn and Talk, xxxvii, 50

UbD. *See* Understanding by Design
Underlines, 157
Understanding by Design (UbD),
    210–211, 222–223
Unit planning
    assessments, 217, 226–227
    beliefs about, 211–212
    big ideas, 217, 220–221, 234
    curating resources, 225
    daily and weekly plans, 234–238
    dynamic, 225, 230
    essential questions, 222–223
    example, 227–229
    learning targets, 153, 223–225
    process, 217–219
    reflection in, 229–230
    small group opportunities,
        123–124, 215–216
    standards and, 211, 221–222, 224–225
    steps, 219–227
    student work products, 157–158,
        225–227
    templates, 217–219, 294, 295
    timing, 217
    yearlong plans, 210, 215–216
    See also Planning

Values, "we value" statements, 65–67
Voluminous reading, xxxii–xxxiii, 26

Weekly planning
    calendar, 234, 236–238, 296
    collecting student work, 166–167
    examples, 236–238, 250–251
    small group opportunities, 235,
        239–247, 258–259
    steps, 234–236
    See also Planning
"We value" statements, 65–67
Wheatley, Margaret J., 7
Whole groups
    minilessons, 13
    planning, 235
    reliance on, 12–14
    small groups within, 49–51,
        75–80
    using, 15
Wiggins, Grant P., 210–211, 222–223
William, Dylan, 92
Women in history small groups, 205
Workshop. *See* Reading workshop
Work time, xxxvii, 13, 14,
    70–71, 266
Writing. *See* Exit slips/tickets; Reader's
    Notebooks
Writing about reading small groups,
    128–139

About the Authors

Photo by Rachel Langosch

Julie Wright is a teacher, instructional coach, and educational consultant with over 25 years of experience in rural, suburban, and urban education settings. She holds National Board Certification as well as a BS in education, a master's in language arts and reading, a reading endorsement, and extensive school leadership postgraduate work, including a preK–Grade 9 principal license from The Ohio State University. She has served as an adjunct faculty member at Ashland University and University of Wisconsin, teaching graduate courses focused on curriculum, instruction, and assessment and instructional coaching, respectively. Julie gets her inspiration from her husband, David, and their three children, Sydney, Noah, and Max.

Photo by Christian Ford

Barry Hoonan teaches fifth and sixth grade at Odyssey Multiage Program on Bainbridge Island, Washington. He works with teachers both in the United States and internationally, including appointments as a three-time Fulbright Teaching Exchange teacher in the United Kingdom, a teaching fellow at Harlem Village Academy in New York City, and (next year) a teacher-consultant at the American School of Brasilia. Barry is a co-author of *Beyond Reading and Writing: Inquiry, Curriculum, and Multiple Ways of Knowing* (NCTE, 2000), and is a recipient of NCTE's Edward Hoey Award and of the Bonnie Campbell Hill Washington State Literacy Award.

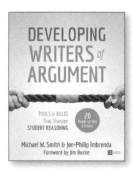

PATTY McGEE

Put down the red pen, pick up this book, and learn to say the right thing at the right time to develop fearless, original, and intentional writers—in any content area.

NANCY AKHAVAN

Practical and engaging, this book gives you a clear framework for "working the minds" of your students, helping them forge their own paths to becoming better readers and writers.

DAVE STUART JR.

How'd you like to streamline your practice so you're teaching smarter, not harder—and kids are learning, doing, and flourishing in ELA and content-area classrooms? This book shows the way.

GRAVITY GOLDBERG AND RENEE HOUSER

Discover how to move your readers forward with in-class, actionable formative assessment. Your readers are showing you what they need next—lean in, listen, look, and assess.

GRETCHEN BERNABEI

This kid-friendly cache of 101 lessons and practice pages helps your students internalize the conventions of correctness once and for all.

DOUGLAS FISHER, NANCY FREY, RUSSELL J. QUAGLIA, DOMINIQUE SMITH, AND LISA L. LANDE

Learn how focusing on relationships, clarity, and challenge can put you in control of managing your classroom's success, one motivated student at a time.

CORWIN Literacy

N188E2

A SAGE Publishing Company

CORWIN HAS ONE MISSION: to enhance education through intentional professional learning.

We build long-term relationships with our authors, educators, clients, and associations who partner with us to develop and continuously improve the best evidence-based practices that establish and support lifelong learning.